AUDIOFUTURISM

Audiofuturism

SCIENCE FICTION RADIO DRAMA AND THE BLACK FANTASTIC IMAGINATION

andré m. carrington

FORDHAM UNIVERSITY PRESS NEW YORK 2026

Fordham University Press also publishes its books in a variety of electronic formats. Some content that appears in print may not be available in electronic books.

Visit us online at www.fordhampress.com.

For EU safety / GPSR concerns: Mare Nostrum Group B.V., Mauritskade 21D, 1091 GC Amsterdam, The Netherlands, gpsr@mare-nostrum.co.uk

Library of Congress Cataloging-in-Publication Data available online at https://catalog.loc.gov.

Printed in the United States of America
28 27 26 5 4 3 2 1
First edition

In loving memory of Andre Alexander Lancaster, 1979–2018.
He saw the future.

Contents

AUDIOFUTURISM

Introduction

Jim Crow and the Golden Age

When I came across this figure in Henry Sampson's history of African Americans in radio and television, I felt I had uncovered the cipher to a seemingly inexplicable pattern that determines how critics talk about the relationship between race, medium, and genre. Around fifteen years ago, I downloaded an audio recording of a radio play based on a novella by Samuel Delany: *The Star-Pit*. I knew I would write about it as an example of science fiction by a Black author in a medium that I had never studied before. But I didn't want to discuss it in isolation, and I couldn't situate it as part of anything like a "tradition" specific to Black authors or audiences in the genre. Figure 1, which draws on statistics compiled by Christopher Sterling and John Kitross in *Stay Tuned*, their canonical history of broadcast media, demonstrates that no such tradition exists.

> While programming on the networks was nearly evenly distributed between music, variety, drama, and other types, Negro programming was dominated by music. In the 1930s and early 1940s Negro music was broadcast live from a radio station or from a remote location, in contrast to the 1950s when it was almost all recorded. Negro amateur shows, quiz shows, news, and sports were heard to a lesser extent, and drama accounted for less than 4 percent of all programming.[1]

When DJs on local stations carved out a programming niche for Black audiences in those early years, they found that playing recorded music could be a cost-effective way to inculcate listening habits that kept their particular segment of the public coming back to their stations and their advertisers' businesses.[2] They cemented the association between popular music and Black culture in

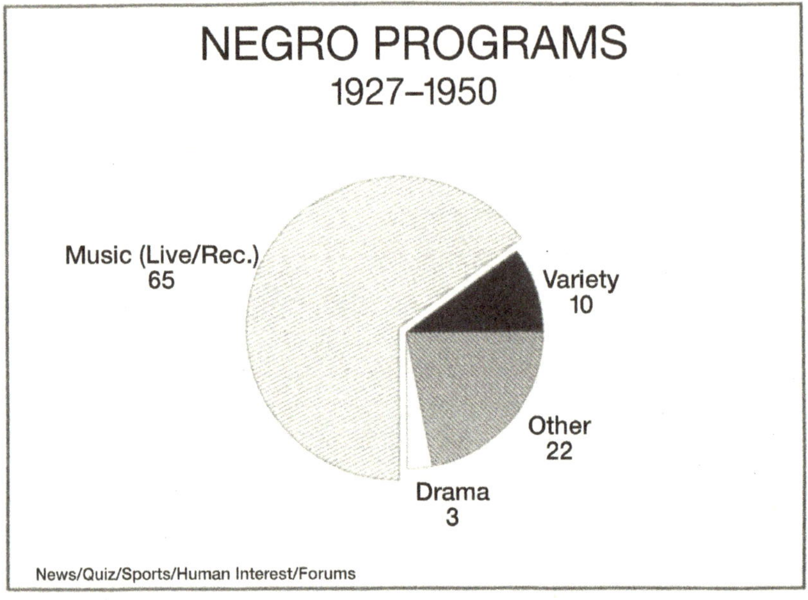

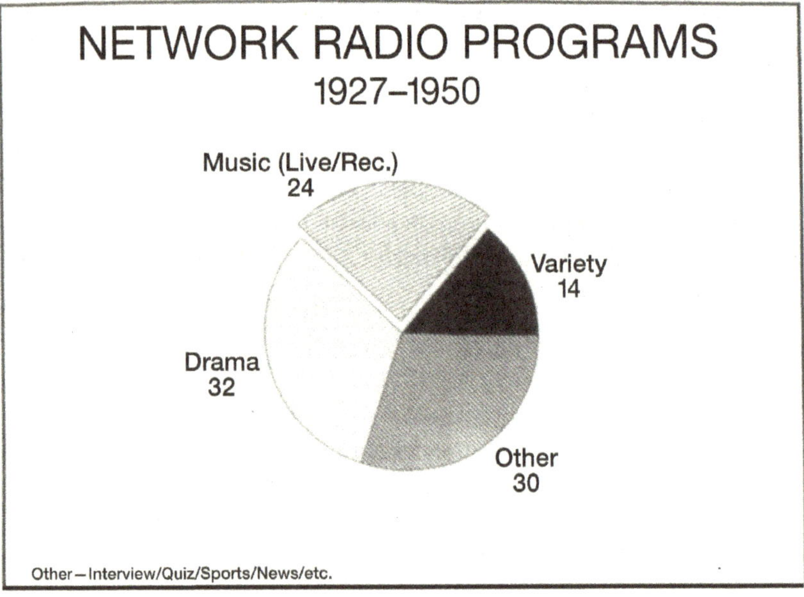

Figure 1: Radio programming, 1927–1950. Stations broadcasting to Black audiences featured far more music and very little drama compared to programming on national radio networks. *Source*: Henry Sampson, *Swingin' on the Ether Waves* (Scarecrow, 2005), 1:4.

the shadow of national networks catering to households on the privileged side of the color line. Alongside the pilots, clergymen, schoolteachers, homemakers, and vaudevillians, the networks brought figures from the pages of pulp magazines and comics into the fold to sell soap and cigarettes. They would negotiate industry-wide agreements to make recorded music a fixture across the airwaves,[3] but they would never enroll Black storytellers in their fantastic enterprise on quite the same scale.

Drama is an indispensable part of the history of radio, and there is a bountiful archive of science fiction radio plays encompassing everything from *The War of the Worlds* to *The Hitchhiker's Guide to the Galaxy* to contemporary podcasts. Scholars of old-time radio and science fiction[4] know the names in this tradition and where to find them: *Buck Rogers. Superman. Dimension X. X Minus One. Exploring Tomorrow. The Weird Circle. Suspense. Hour 25. MindWebs.* Throughout the twentieth century, radio brought the unlimited possibilities of speculative fiction to the public through dramatizations made for listening. Across the Atlantic, BBC audiences could hear SF at many different points in the broadcast schedule, from *Saturday Night Theatre* to the proliferating formats that showcased *Journey Into Space* and *Doctor Who.* The history of science fiction had set the stage for Delany's radio play, in some respects, but why did it seem to stand alone? I knew that works by Black authors would be uncommon among the sources of science fiction radio plays, but I had no idea that this absence would be so defining for the art form itself. In order to tell the story of the radio plays in this book, I had to set aside the histories of science fiction and American radio that would explain their place in a tradition—if they belonged to any. The tradition of science fiction radio drama is quintessentially modern and American—no better and no worse than any other area of the cultural landscape—in its dedication to African Americans' absence. In the no-place reserved for them by their absence from a tradition, adaptations of Black speculative texts achieved something that science fiction had never made possible despite its influential presence on the radio. They had become something else at the intersection of radio and African American literature. I named what they do *Audiofuturism,* because it sounds like the promise of something yet to come.

Reorienting the study of American literature and culture to hold Blackness at its center has been a unifying intellectual endeavor for scholars who come before me. I began to consider an academic career in American Studies after reading Mary Helen Washington's field-defining 1997 presidential address to the American Studies Association, "Disturbing the Peace: What Happens to American Studies If You Put African American Studies at the Center?" in college.[5] The provocation remains generative, today. A host of astute critics have refined work that centers Blackness in the study of speculative fiction in recent years, including Ekow Eshun, Rhonda Frederick, Sandra Grayson, Isiah Lavender, DeWitt Kilgore, Diana Mafe, Adilifu Nama, Sami Schalk, Darieck Scott, Ebony Thomas, Rebecca Wanzo, and Deborah Whaley. They teach us how fiction, film, television, comics, visual art, and fan cultures alternately perpetuate and disrupt overdetermined relationships between race and the fantastic genres. Radio drama comprises an unwritten chapter in this saga.

Audiofuturism is a performative construction: It names a phenomenon that has never been cohesive enough to self-consciously name itself. The authors and audiences who realized Black speculative texts in the form of radio drama in the twentieth century and their contemporary successors do not express a need to see themselves as part of the same lineage. In the interest of learning from Black speculation in a new way, however, I set out to find a new set of critical coordinates. When it comes to African American literature, radio drama is every bit as viable as a modality for reiterating the aesthetic and social experience of reading as it has proven to be for science fiction, fantasy, utopia, and horror by other authors. Adaptations of this nature range across time and venue, and the critical apparatus appropriate to them is scattered across different fields. Comprehending the relationship between Blackness and the speculative in this art form requires thinking about race, medium, and genre simultaneously. We begin to break the hold that disciplinary conventions impose on our analysis when we question how each of these analytical categories circumscribes our ability to deploy the others.

Audiofuturism investigates unexplored corners of speculative fiction to address questions at the meeting point of Black culture, literary adaptation, and sound studies. Scholarship in each of these areas has prepared us to learn from the works I analyze in this book. The radio plays themselves and their predecessor texts are each compelling in their own right, but only in the scope of a concerted effort to consider them together can they illuminate broader tendencies of the cultural landscape. In this Introduction, I begin to outline the nature of the gap that persists across the relevant disciplines where radio adaptations of Black speculative texts are concerned.

The chapters of this book focus on dramatizations for broadcast in slightly different audio formats of works by four Black writers: Roi Ottley, Samuel R. Delany, Octavia E. Butler, and Toni Morrison. The appellation "speculative fiction" suits them all to the extent that the umbrella term is more than the sum of its parts. I will not belabor the definitions of various genres, except to emphasize that each author's work exemplifies criteria that have established the basis for including particular forms of writing under a more general rubric of speculative aesthetics. The applicable subcategories in question are: for Ottley's nonfiction, utopia; for Delany's novella, science fiction; for Butler's novel, fantasy; and for Morrison's, horror. The audio form also links these works together in a peculiar sense, whereas the implicit reference to sound in the use of the term "radio" has shifted over time and space. The technology is conducive to live and recorded sound, designed for ephemeral communications as well as repetition, inclusive of musical and nonverbal content as well as speech. Along with a vast range of musical genres, news, and talk programming, drama represents one niche within a much wider array of uses for the medium. Every radio play and, by extension, every possible convergence between Blackness and speculation in the art form has the potential to serve as an object lesson for students of storytelling and performance.

The overlapping histories of radio and science fiction unfold on the same terrain as the history of struggles over race and racism. It has always troubled me, therefore, to hear terms like "the Golden Age of radio" and "the Golden Age of science fiction" invoked to describe eras that are defined, in my view, by the systematic oppression of people of African descent. To cite a prophetic source on this dilemma: "Where does the Negro stand today in entertainment? He stands on one leg, with the other tied behind him by Jim Crow."[6] This sentiment was one of many assessments Langston Hughes provided for Black opportunities in the arts during the first half of the twentieth century. Despite his participation in efforts to advance Black cultural and political interests through the mass media, his attitude regarding the balance of power in the culture industries remained consistent throughout decades of developments in print, stage, screen, and radio. In 1943, reluctantly obliging a request to develop radio programs on race themes for the New York–based Writers' War Board, he wrote, "Personally, I DO NOT LIKE RADIO, and I feel that it is almost as far from being a free medium of expression for Negro writers as Hitler's airplanes are for the Jews."[7] Even as they labored against the tides of tokenism, subordination, stereotype, and outright exclusion, Hughes and his contemporaries witnessed the mainstream of the American artistic and intellectual establishment edifying itself as if Black people had played no meaningful role in its existence. We were overlooked in its histories, sidelined in its debates, passed over for its rewards, and counted out of its future. As long as Black youth could be Jim Crowed out of schools, second-class citizens Jim Crowed out of suffrage and civil society, and workers Jim Crowed out of jobs and benefits, artists would be likewise Jim Crowed out of opportunities to challenge the presumption of racial hierarchy with their imaginative visions.

Audiofuturism gets specific in the chapters that follow, and the itinerary of this book as a whole is my invention rather than an attempt to reveal an overarching, self-evident tendency in cultural production and critique. Superb histories of radio in Black America come from scholars like William Barlow, Henry Sampson, and Barbara Savage.[8] By focusing on efforts to secure a portion of the airwaves for Black voices and listeners, their accounts laid the groundwork for critical contributions by Jennifer Stoever and Alex Weheliye, to whom I owe my sense of what Blackness and radio have meant to each other. My approach to speculative fiction as a field where considerations of race are not just relevant but vital is similarly indebted to the groundbreaking interventions performed by race-conscious scholars of the genre, only some of whom I have referenced here. As I will discuss, academic writing has only recently begun to grasp the scope of Black speculative practice in the arts. The balance of this introductory essay assesses how this book intervenes in conversations between scholars and publics concerned with African American literature, literary adaptation, and sound studies, before outlining the subjects of each chapter.

Black Speculation

In recent years, Black speculative fiction has become a recognizable subject of scholarship in its own right. What differentiates this area from a subfield of science fiction studies is its steadfast relationship to African American literature. Understanding contemporary studies of Black speculation, Afrofuturism, and the Black fantastic in literature and the arts requires a solid foundation in knowledge of Black culture and its social contexts. In some cases, this extends to subjects entirely separate, and considered mutually exclusive from, the areas of knowledge that inform the language of science fiction. Readers of Black speculative fiction will find themselves at sea without some exposure to the lessons in religious studies, anthropology, and history that figure prominently in Black intellectual traditions. While it will come as no surprise to readers steeped in African American history to see references to specific syncretic religious practices connected to West Africa or the Caribbean invoked in contemporary urban fantasy writing or in historical fiction to revisit situations that have been fundamentally transformed by the civil rights struggles of the twentieth century such as interstate travel or overt employment discrimination, these themes will disorient readers unfamiliar with the circumstances of Black life in the Americas. When Black authors write speculative fiction, they write from "within the circle," as Frederick Douglass phrased it. It's not only our repertoire of terms but our criteria for learning what is meaningful and why that places us into a shared tradition. So, while the authors in this study were working at the same moments and in the same markets as their white counterparts, they also lived, like Black authors today, in a parallel reality differentiated by the color line.[9] Their relationship to the history of science fiction and fantasy writing is not necessarily characterized by marginality or deviance but by the abundant presence of signs from a world largely unexplored by their white counterparts. For that reason, I find it useful to frame the historical backdrop against which the story of *Audiofuturism* unfolds through the juxtaposition of historical moments that overlap: Jim Crow and the Golden Age.

The Golden Age of science fiction, which is largely coterminous with the era of old-time radio, is a useful myth. The decades that saw institutions for disseminating science fiction flourish, roughly the late 1930s through the early 1950s, are well documented in histories of the genre.[10] The incidents of this era exert a profound influence on writers who lived through them as readers: not one author who purports to treat science fiction as a tradition can fully extricate themselves from the romance of Edgar Rice Burroughs's Mars, the impact of John Campbell as editor of *Astounding*, or the extensive output of the writers who broke out of magazines to bring novels like *Foundation* and *The Space Merchants* into the popular imagination. Fantasy is nowhere legible without the momentum of Robert Howard's Conan and the conventions introduced by Tolkien's Middle Earth. Lost to this tradition, however, is any accountability for the status of Pauline Hopkins, George Schuyler, and Zora Neale Hurston as outliers. It is not simply the prejudice of editors and critics during their lifetime or thereafter that accounts for the exclusion of these writers, irrespective of their works' fantastic elements, from the status of forerunners to science fiction's Golden Age. Rather, the concerns in their writing with African American and Diasporic communities and historical processes specific to them—colonialism, segregation, and demands for enfranchisement as equal members of the human race in legal terms and in civil society—offset their contributions to American fiction from the space occupied by science fiction.

While the historical developments that created a favorable environment for mass print culture and radio coincided with racial segregation in the United States, it is only when chronicling the work of Black authors that Jim Crow can be identified as the cause behind what they wrote, where it was published, and who read it. How curious would it be, for example, if we began or ended an account of Orson Welles's adaptation of H. G. Wells's *War of the Worlds* for radio not with the distribution of Wells's fiction to both sides of the Atlantic in magazines, nor with the legacy of the Federal Writers' Project and the Mercury Theatre on the Air, but with the fictive solidarity of white employers who discriminated against Black people, favoring their white peers whenever possible? What level of abstraction is necessary to chalk up the brand popularity of Superman and Ray Bradbury on the radio to the fact that they never had to compete for attention with Hopkins's race women and Schuyler's mad scientists? The Golden Age was just that if and only if the readers remembering it are white. Jim Crow is the structural explanation for the scarcity of Black writers among the venues where science fiction made its mark in twentieth-century mass culture, and in turn, it is the rationale for their placement in another world situated at its margins. Naturally, Hopkins could publish stories along with columns in the *Colored American*, Schuyler could write his entertaining fare under a pseudonym for the *Pittsburgh Courier*, while Hurston's explorations of the occult reached readers of folk tales rather than *Weird Tales*. The demands to which all of these publications rose and acquiesced were as surely racial as they were aesthetic and economic. The media ecology of the era, wherein one set of venues in print culture was understood to respond principally to racialized conditions while others only occasionally and regretfully acknowledged the existence of an entrenched system of racial hierarchy, established the market in which the Golden Age of science fiction took place.

As a thought experiment: Using the Book of the Month Club as an index of how race and genre function in mass market literature, it would be natural to observe how the genre question and the race question unfold separately. The club's selection of works by Richard Wright and Frank Yerby brought Black writers to Americans' bedsides, and criticism on these authors attests to the significance of broad-based distribution as a factor in their works' influence on mainstream perceptions of African American literature.[11] Meanwhile, the role of science fiction in this milieu emerges in relation to books by Theodore Sturgeon and Philip K. Dick, which differentiate themselves from "mere genre" fare through their recognition by the arbiters of "serious" literature.[12] Distributing a science fiction novel by a Black author, like Samuel Delany's *The Einstein Intersection*, might have provided the club with a useful way to rehearse what happens when mainstream tastemakers weigh genre distinctions and racial representation together, but science fiction publishers had already obliged, and the honor of determining its meaning fell to their judges, instead.[13] The point of this counterfactual is to reiterate that Black speculation emerges out of a relationship to the literary history of science fiction that is vexed, at best, and it is pointedly out of sync with its Golden Age. When making sense of how works by Black authors made it onto the radio airwaves, it is much more useful, therefore, to consider the long shadow cast by Jim Crow.

Shifting the frame from the Golden Age to Jim Crow is a useful heuristic for analyzing how Black speculative fiction eludes critiques of mass culture in the twentieth century. Whereas the Golden Age of science fiction is a meaningful arena to observe alternatives to mimetic realism in popular media, the choice to embrace or resist realist representation has always been distinctly tied to racialized differences in perception and persuasion for Black artists.[14] Contemporary scholarship is newly attentive to the place of fantastic and speculative modes in Black writing, thanks, in part, to a long history of reckoning with realism on different terms. The late Richard Iton's *In Search of the Black Fantastic* aimed to transform how we saw politics as such through the lens of Black culture. It altered the horizons of Black cultural criticism: Iton looks inward, to the affective and conceptual dimensions of what Black intellectuals and their audiences had in mind when they enunciated their motives in art, as well as outward, to aspirations that couldn't be mapped onto conventional social movement agendas. Though it includes "fantastic" in its title, his text has as much in common with Elizabeth Alexander's *The Black Interior* as Robin Kelley's *Freedom Dreams*. Iton's reconsideration helped pave the way for Margo Natalie Crawford's *Black Post-Blackness* and Rhonda Frederick's *Evidence of Things Not Seen*, two studies that look past the discernible obstacles of antiblackness to instead emphasize the utopian, heterodox, and affective investments of Black writers' work. These critics delineate a tradition that links Octavia E. Butler and Nalo Hopkinson to Amiri Baraka and Toni Cade Bambara not simply on the basis of identitarian affinities but out of consideration for the aesthetic strategies through which each author augmented the worldviews of their respective publics. Insofar as these authors mobilized some of the same devices that canonical SF writers used within the conventions of the genre, their work enriches our account of the affordances of speculative fiction. Appropriately, contemporary scholarship on Black speculation commemorates the work of Martin Delany, Sun Ra, and Alma Thomas more often than it revisits the oeuvres of Robert Heinlein, Anne McCaffrey, and J. G. Ballard.[15]

As Isiah Lavender writes in *Afrofuturism Rising*, "It seems natural to ponder whether afrofuturism is merely a 'colored wave' within SF history, analogous to aesthetic movements such as the New Wave or cyberpunk. However, by symbolically thinking of afrofuturism as its own pocket universe . . . we see and read the wavelengths radiating from this distant universe as its gravity expands."[16] To capture only some of this critical ambition for *Audiofuturism*, I hope this book contributes to speculative fiction, literary adaptation, and sound studies by centering Blackness and expanding the circle. It disidentifies with the history of science fiction to place the Black fantastic imagination in all its vitality at the center of a legacy shared between speculative fiction and radio drama.

Literary Adaptation

Radio adaptations of Black speculative texts represent the convergence of cultural traditions that thrived in the twentieth century and continue to inspire creativity in the twenty-first. While the rise of podcasting is the most obvious sequel to the Golden Age when old-time radio rose to prominence, the subjects of this book have a peculiar relationship to "radio" even before we qualify the application of that term to different audio media. The works I examine in the chapters that follow originated in print forms. In the information age, content is king, but scholarship in media history and literary adaptation alike demonstrates that mediums matter in addition to the contents they convey. I use the term "adaptation" throughout this study to keep multiple objects in focus at all times. Every radio play or dramatization relies on its precursor text as a source of meanings to reproduce or transform. As I hope to illustrate, however, an adaptation's capacity to deviate from its source is as integral to its significance as its capacity to recapitulate those features it derives from precedents. Particularly when they transpose stories across media, adaptations initiate processes of meaning making that imbue new works with their own unique significance. If *Audiofuturism* participates in the transition from one school of thought to another in the study of adaptation, it is because the book diverges from characteristic patterns in a field typified by analyses of film renditions of literary texts.

Even though texts and authors firmly situated within the boundaries of literature are the point of departure for the radio plays examined in this book, and even though the texts in question were written in the twentieth century, *Audiofuturism* brings contemporary critical considerations to bear on the series of adaptations it investigates. In the past, for many audience members and critics, a concern with how faithfully or effectively films realize the value of storytelling that takes place in books has dominated adaptation studies. Toward the end of the twentieth century, as poststructuralist and transnational approaches gained ground in literary and film studies, numerous critics professed a consensus desire to move away from "fidelity" as a problem to afford priority.[17] Gerard Genette's theory of paratextuality provided a language to situate texts alongside one another while bracketing their relations of primacy and subordination, as epitexts, and he articulated the significance of differentiation within printed works, marking covers, indices, captions, et cetera as peritexts.[18] These developments fueled investigations of media adaptations, including film and television as well as video games.[19] Linda Hutcheon and Julie Sanders authored influential works that questioned how and why adaptations signal their relationships to the texts that inform them directly and implicitly, which further emphasized the horizontal relationship between different art forms—print, visual, and audio—in everyday life. The economic and technological environment that contemporary media critics describe as "convergence culture," according to Johannes Fehrle, "further destabilizes received notions of anteriority, authorship, and reception by opening the object of inquiry to texts that differ from older ones that were less physically mutable."[20] Displacing literature and film from their presumptive centrality in adaptation studies helps loosen the hold of any single set of disciplinary conventions or medium-specific limitations on the kind of questions the field can pursue. This flexibility is particularly useful in the present, but it has retrospective implications, as well. Although many of the patterns observed in television adaptations of written texts originated earlier in radio, for example, and even as radio drama took shape alongside adaptations for the stage, audio media has never occupied a place in adaptation studies proportional to its presence or influence on the media landscape.

Simone Murray's *The Adaptation Industry* is a succinct representation of the "new" adaptation studies most pertinent to this book. Taking the field to task for its preoccupation with a false dichotomy between the cultural esteem of literary works and the political-economic significance of film marketability, Murray frames contemporary adaptation as a "cultural economy." She perceptively treats adaptation as an engine facilitating existing relationships among its constituent cultural institutions: publishing and film production. Through this approach, she is motivated to outline how an "encompassing adaptation industry both constrains and—crucially—*enables* adaptations in little-analysed ways. In particular, this study posits cultural and commercial concerns not as mutually antithetical or self-cancelling, but as complexly interrelated."[21] Although Murray's research highlights the dynamic interaction of contemporaneous actors responsible for adaptations, "authors; agents; publishers, writers' and film festival directors; literary prize-judging committees; screenwriters; and producers and distributors," she also orients her intervention toward the history of the book.[22] Although she distances her account from reader-response criticism in some respects, Murray acknowledges that audiences play a decisive role in sustaining the economic environment in which the adaptation industry thrives. We assess the reception of adaptations in economic as well as interpretive terms to gauge their role in maintaining the relevance of longstanding classics and polishing overlooked gems of literature from prior eras. Applying an industry-centric (or at the very least, industry-conscious) approach to adaptations for radio, by treating it as an economic as well as cultural enterprise throughout *Audiofuturism*, is a bid to restore media history's attention to the interdependence of authors, broadcasters, actors, and audiences in the past. For Black authors and their publics, commercial, aesthetic, and political strategies have always been intertwined. And for speculative fiction, regarding adaptation as an industry that has constrained and also *enabled* its production in multiple creative modes defies any presumption that the market limits work in the genre to formulaic pablum.

John Rieder's *Science Fiction and the Mass Cultural Genre System* models the history of science fiction in print in the fashion most compatible with the account of adaptation offered in *Audiofuturism*. It comprises a materialist history of SF driven by "systemic transformations" in the manner of composing, reproducing, and packaging narrative texts; distributing them to readers; and sustaining the expectations that proved reliable for keeping readers engaged in the consumption of genre fiction in the formats available on the market at a given time and place.[23] Rieder refers to this circuit of production and consumption as a mode of "publicity," insofar as it propagates the features that characterize the genre by instantiating them in concrete form.[24] A similar system organized the publicity of other print genres, such as the western, the comic book superhero, and the romance. Radio drama midwifed these genres throughout its Golden Age, publicizing each of them through adaptation. As the mass cultural system inaugurated by pulp magazines evolved to accommodate paperback novels and later variegated into high- and lowbrow niche periodicals, radio, television, and film spectacles, and eventually, multimedia franchises with high production value and avant-garde literary forays, adaptation took on an undeniably salient role in publicizing it—making it recognizable across media. Rieder stresses that academic genre classifications, whether descriptive or prescriptive, are quite different from those that prevail among practitioners in other cultural institutions. In his words, "the work done by the mass cultural genre system, a form of intellectual activity that emerges spontaneously within advanced capitalist relations and is therefore organic to it" differs from "the work done by the traditional genre system located and maintained in the schools."[25] Like Murray's intervention in adaptation studies, Rieder's periodization of science fiction invites inquiry into different structural influences on the shape of storytelling at any given time. While neither critic addresses the role of radio directly, both of them treat visual media as a set of venues whose openness to technical innovation and susceptibility to capture by market forces prove consequential for artists, audiences, and critics alike.

As Rieder writes in regard to Frederic Jameson's analysis of the ideology of form, the heterogeneity within any text, however carefully it positions itself in relation to a generic tradition, "carries within it the long history of cultural change and social struggle underlying the narrative choices available at any given time and place."[26] This is all the more true for adaptations, which signal their place in a genre through the vestiges of their prior instantiations. Adaptations of Black speculative texts are doubly and triply marked by African American literature's negotiations with the print cultures out of which science fiction emerged as a legible genre tradition, combining "different permutations of the marvelous voyage, the utopia, lost-race adventures, stories of time travel, and the future war," as well as by the racialized history of broadcast media.[27] While we rightfully expect Black speculative texts to invoke their authors' heritage thematically and through the social constituencies they represent, when they are refracted through the crystal prism of radio, they will also drag along seemingly unrelated considerations of verbal expression, format, seriality, commercialism, sound effects, and other qualities through which the medium and its industry devised a certain repertoire to associate itself with the Golden Age of science fiction—with little to no regard for Jim Crow as its cultural surround. The task of this book is to demystify how radio drama reckons with the baggage otherwise known as the ideology of form to make Black speculation audible on the airwaves, just like Black authors make their relationship to SF legible in writing.

Sound Studies

My choice in this book to analyze works in analog as well as digital audio formats, transmitted via electromagnetic waves, cables, and satellites in orbit, requires additional perspective on the evolution of sonic storytelling. The term "radio" is a metonym for audio media, but twentieth-century broadcasting remains its paradigmatic example. While oral traditions are the most universal form of storytelling through sound, the context for this study is much more specific. A sustained assault on the modern, colonial episteme in the twentieth century, exemplified by Black philosophers like Frantz Fanon and Sylvia Wynter and by feminists like Laura Mulvey and Donna Haraway, has required critics to spell out their investment in sight as the dominant faculty of the human sensorium. Historicizing, geographical, and decolonial critiques have refined the field of visual culture while also making the case for sound studies as an alternative font of knowledge. Foundational contributions to sound studies emerge from the analysis of music and poetics, especially in literature and musicology. In relation to textual forms, however, sound is still naturalized in some ways that necessitate prying it out of its settled place as background noise to the signal of discourse to examine how, like the visual, it functions in social and institutional processes. Here, I consider radio drama as a specific variety of sound publicized through radio, with its attendant conventions shaping and shaped by its conditions of production and reception. Those conditions include: Whose stories are radio programs telling? What formats play on various local stations, and which broadcasts are remembered as part of a Golden Age? How do different segments of the audience discern when they are being addressed, and what role does listening play in their everyday life? What opportunities do new formats open up, and for whom? The storied history of science fiction radio drama offers tantalizing responses to these questions. The objective of this book is to set the agenda for answering them in a way that makes it impossible to silence the Black fantastic imagination.

Jennifer Lynn Stoever, in *The Sonic Color Line,* insists that "listening operates as an organ of racial discernment, categorization, and resistance in the shadow of vision's alleged cultural dominance."[28] Worldmaking practices enacted through sound are encoded in the African Diasporic, Indigenous, and multilingual oral traditions that inform American English. Technologies for reproducing, recording, preserving, and modulating sound, from musical instruments to textual representations of speech to noise ordinances, attest to the imbrication of sound in the communal arrangements that rose and fell with settler colonialism and industrialization. While Stoever leads the pack among critics like Josh Kun, Jonathan Sterne, and Gustavus Stadler who scrutinize the social significance of actual sound in everyday life, her work is an especially meaningful precedent for *Audiofuturism* because of its consistent attention to African American writers' deployments of sound. Every moment in Black and American literature is shot through with the differential power of what Stoever calls the "sonic color line" and the "listening ear," the twin structures through which race organizes "textual representations of listening and the auditory imaginary."[29] From Fred Moten's reverberations on Aunt Hester's scream to Julie Beth Napolin's theory of "narrative acoustics" as conditions of possibility for place making and subject formation, sound studies redounds with evidence for the specifically sonic terms in which race matters in literature.[30]

The intersection of sound studies and African American literature leads away from literary adaptation. Instead, critics like Louis Chude-Sokei, Carter Mathes, Matthew Morrison, Henry Ivry, and others follow the cues of a Black intellectual tradition that places music at the forefront of its radical creativity. The anecdatum that opens this Introduction suggests that Black artists and intellectuals have made their mark on the listening public principally through music. Genealogies of Afrofuturism or the Black fantastic, where many of Black culture's homegrown alternatives to science fiction and fantasy writing reside, are utterly saturated with musical performance. Cutting-edge scholarship on Afrofuturism and sound studies finds, axiomatically, that Black music is capable of answering even the most provocative questions:

> Which recent sound practices and sonic materialities correspond with the thought figures of Afrofuturism? Which discursive and performative strategies within and around sonic materialities render these Afrofuturist? Which specific sound practices and sonic materialities are put

> in relation to these discourses? What are the semantic, aesthetic, and political effects of these constellations?[31]

So how could this book call itself *Audiofuturism* without being about Black music?

My rationale for emphasizing narrative rather than music as an object of Black sound studies comes, in part, from my confidence that the scholars just mentioned have ensured that the field will continue covering that inarguably necessary ground. Erik Steinskog displays the benefits of continuing to emphasize music in *Afrofuturism and Black Sound Studies* by drawing on Alexander Weheliye, Tavia Nyong'o, and Paul Gilroy to rehearse "an argument about the sonic as the principal modality of articulation [which] contributes to marking a major difference between the Western and Afro-diasporic understandings of modernity."[32] While distancing his interlocutors from claims to any "essentialist difference between Europe and Africa, as based in the eyes versus the ear, in vision versus sound, in literature versus music," Steinskog intensifies the exploration of Blackness, technology, and sound within music.[33] Using Kodwo Eshun's formulation "sonic fictions" to underscore the continual dialogue between music, storytelling, and other modes of creativity in Black culture, he gestures to a growing Afrofuturist canon inspired by experiments further afield: "There are still changes to come for what Afrofuturism—or sonic fiction—is or how it sounds when the artists, composers, and musicians do not inscribe themselves in the discourse of Afrofuturism."[34] A Black sound studies steeped in music should welcome recent interventions such as *Janelle Monáe's Queer Afrofuturism* by Dan Hassler-Forest, *Black Utopias* by Jayna Brown, and the essays in *Boogie Down Predictions: Hip-Hop, Time, and Afrofuturism*. The musical touchstones of Afrofuturism prove indispensable to the advancement of film, comics, and performance studies, as well as literature. Music is demonstrably integral to any rapprochement between Black culture and science fiction studies—to the point that John Corbett and Greg Tate referred to popular music genres *as* "black science fiction."[35] The comparative impertinence of another sonic art form—radio drama—to the edification of Black sound studies contributes to the impression that the significance of audio adaptations in science fiction studies has nothing to do with race.

Two of the most recognizable works of science fiction in the English language are radio plays: the aforementioned *War of the Worlds* and *The Hitchhiker's Guide to the Galaxy*. These works, both literary adaptations, furnish considerable lessons for sound studies. Writing for science fiction scholars, Karen Hellekson reiterates a warning about the "ocularcentric bias" of modern cultural criticism when describing radio and podcasts as part of an understudied tradition.[36] This norm could be suspended in relation to SF, however, because early in its history as a mass medium, SF in "radio presented long-form series as well as short half-hour or hour-long stories, often adaptations, and acted synergistically with other media, notably print and comics."[37] Radio was a pillar of the mass cultural genre system Rieder describes, and it is no wonder the contemporary resurgence of audio in the era of digital streaming features original and adapted SF podcasts. Rather than attempting to relate the historical development of radio when expert studies by the likes of Susan Douglas and Tom McEnaney have already accomplished that task,[38] I will instead return to Sampson's infographic from the outset. Although it does not appear to tell us about genre conventions in explicit terms, Sampson's account informs the reader that Black people were performing a wide variety of technological, intellectual, political, and commercial feats through the use of radio in its Golden Age. Because we were systematically segregated out of the ranks of certain magazine and newspaper editors and publishers, literary agents, print advertisers, actors, producers, technicians, and other positions in the adaptation industry responsible for articulating science fiction's relationship with radio, Black people were never the protagonists of any narratives about radio drama's history with the genre. Until now.

Whether it is updating an English scientific romance for American city dwellers or turning a time travel expedition into the accompaniment for a long drive, science fiction radio drama—in adaptation, at least—invokes both literary and broadcast traditions. Even productions that originate in audio formats rely on recognizable codes sedimented into the art form by preexisting works. We can hear this operation when Hellekson writes, "We can be in a spaceship's huge, empty cargo hold or claustrophobically stuffed in a spacesuit. Voices are altered to sound thrillingly alien. Music cues us emotionally, telling us how to feel. We learn to associate certain sound effects with specific events, like a shimmering sound indicating teleportation."[39] Sometimes, *Audiofuturism* is about the metaphysical stakes of using sound to simulate the seemingly impossible stimuli portrayed in speculative fiction—the feel of acceleration beyond the speed of light, the choice to pursue a vocation that's never existed in history, the language spoken by the dead. More often, however, it is about how dramatizations of Black speculative texts alter the soundscape of radio by bringing the cultural and intellectual prerogatives of the literature they adapt to new publics. My analyses of adaptations in this book articulate a new understanding of Blackness in popular media by identifying connections between Black cultural politics and the tradition of science fiction dramatizations in the audio medium—a tradition that has otherwise rendered itself indifferent to radio's racial discourse.

The tradition that Gustavus Stadler associates with American Studies in an essay titled "Whiteness and Sound Studies" seeks to interrupt an incipient lapse into colorblindness that would withdraw sound studies to a degree of abstraction that would separate it from the history of particular art forms.[40] The inexhaustible salience of race in popular music serves as a constant reminder that sound studies can never truly extricate itself from Blackness. Whereas certain varieties of music characterize critical thinking about race in the field, many contributors to sound studies situate their work across a disciplinary divide from practitioners of ethnomusicology, performance studies, media history, and more grounded disciplines. Marie Thompson elaborates on the significance of these tendencies in "Whiteness and the Ontological Turn in Sound Studies": "Where music is thought to obscure material being of sound by virtue of its cultural, representational and meaningful content; experimental music and sound art is understood to interrogate the affective, non-representational and non-discursive dimensions of the sonic."[41] Thompson assesses how "recent figurations of the ontological in sound studies are co-constituted with a 'modest' white aurality. This works to distinguish and amplify what is heard as 'sound-itself' (which is metonymically associated with 'abstract' noise, hums and drones), while muffling sound's relationship to the social world; and holds apart sound art's abstract materiality from lived sociality."[42] A simplistic bifurcation of sound studies into a pure "sound itself," on the one hand, and a miscegenated "sound in context," however, runs the risk of conflating Black sound with loudness.[43]

Relegating the Black fantastic imagination to sonic modalities that are recognizably "expressive, dramatic, or loud" is the kind of category error that Kevin Quashie militates against in *The Sovereignty of Quiet*.[44] While we might not always say the same for Afrofuturist music, I would argue that dramatizations of Black speculative texts belong to the manifestations of Black being that Quashie describes as "quiet." Listeners scarcely expect to encounter the sounds of racialized resistance in radio drama, but as I discuss throughout this book, the sounds of Black narratives are not always those we might expect. Historians of science fiction would balk at the notion that every radio play needs a theremin or a rocket engine to belong within the genre. By utilizing sounds appropriate to the stories they tell, dramatizations of Black speculative texts complicate the tradition of science fiction radio drama without necessarily disrupting it. The difference these productions make for the art form becomes audible precisely because they are carefully modulated, rather than categorically "loud."

Identifying the specific institutional practices and conventions through which racial discourse operates is important because it allows us to contest racism in concrete ways. For instance, the axiom that race is a primarily visual phenomenon creates a strong headwind for arguments like Stoever's and my own that racism influences our sense of hearing. Therefore, by analyzing a specific genre tradition with a meaningful presence in the everyday life of generations of modern subjects, I seek to further the argument that real and imagined meanings of Blackness are embedded into our habits of reading and listening in concrete terms. Radio, like any other medium, can take its listeners' relationship to Blackness for granted, it can cater to our racialized dispositions, and it can challenge our perceptions in subtle or quite provocative ways. In any format, featuring Black voices or rendering them silent is only the beginning of the process by which Blackness becomes meaningful to radio; just as much is at stake when we consider what they have to say.

To stay attuned to the sociogenic nature of sound, *Audiofuturism* learns from critics who situate radio within the historical circumstances that make it meaningful. This study is guided by objectives that have advanced since scholars began reckoning with the potential of radio drama as an art form. Its alignment of sound studies with other disciplines underscores their shared traditions. In 1924, the classical Hungarian film theorist Béla Balázs wrote, optimistically, "Radio drama will become an art of its own and, like film, struggle upward through kitsch, coarse triviality, and stupidity to high poetic potential."[45] The potential that early critics cite for the medium hardly requires the isolation of sound from its culturally specific contexts. For Rudolph Arnheim, writing in the 1930s, "If wireless [radio] claims the whole attention of the theorist of art . . . it is a no less enthralling phenomenon for the sociologist."[46] The media historian Shawn VanCour advises that "Arnheim's definitive account of the medium . . . moved beyond strictly aesthetic matters to take up many decidedly extratextual issues, [such as] the effects of policy regulations, industry structure, and audience demographics on preferred forms of program content, and the impact of domestic reception conditions on the experience of radio artworks."[47] Even as they remained skeptical toward the intellectual value of the new mass media in relation to conventional art forms, scholars recognized that situating radio adaptations in relation to their textual and theatrical precedents would help students "develop the concept of literature as a genetic process: the new always evolving from the old and being constantly shaped both in content and in technique by external and internal forces."[48] The author of the latter, writing for the journal of the National Council of Teachers of English, in 1950, proposed:

> After analyzing radio drama for the effect of the medium on the form and the content of the play, we can now go back to a study of a Shakespeare play, the product of a great mind, yet at the same time the product of the specific requirements of the stage and the audience at the time. . . . And then could we not go on ahead to look at the motion picture as an art form that has developed as a result of the peculiar nature of the camera and the tremendous audience fixed on the screen, and then on again to television to speculate on what form television drama will take as a result of its own compulsions and laws? And would not such a study be an acknowledgment that drama is not separate and disparate but a broad stream branching into many tributaries, all of which offer rich reward to the explorer?[49]

Although we are accustomed to treating cultural texts as part of a larger tradition within the academic profession, part of the joy of teaching with popular adaptations is that they often represent students' first encounters with certain authors and their work. It can be refreshing to set aside the stories that a genre or a medium tells itself about its history in order to rediscover its possibilities.

The Spectrum

Think of your itinerary through this book like you are scanning the radio dial. Each chapter represents a different frequency: adjacent to the others in the same range but distinct enough from them to be tuned separately without interference. They did not originate in order, but they are arranged that way now. The four chapters of this book are arranged chronologically with respect to their subject matter. While the Introduction has laid out intellectual concerns that are useful to bear in mind before reading any given chapter, they do not necessarily need to be read in succession. The order corresponds to the original publication dates of the texts at the center of each chapter, but adaptation opens up a range of possibilities for reconsidering the historicity of literature and media. Some works were adapted for radio almost immediately after their publication, while in other cases, many years passed before the audio production. Each chapter addresses some specific technological, economic, and policy developments shaping the distribution and interpretation of radio drama in different times and places. As these material conditions shift across the sites of *Audiofuturism*, so do the contours of readership and listening audiences for the works under examination. I cite readers, listeners, and critics on the meanings of the works I address, but I have not made a systematic account of the reception of radio adaptations of Black speculative texts a priority in this book. My analysis is most cohesive within the respective chapters. I treat each adaptation as both an instance of creative work in the speculative mode within a distinct art form as well as a demonstration of the ideological objectives and cultural value of a particular work of speculative writing. This method of dual interpretation coalesces across chapters through repetition. Although I do not argue that *Audiofuturism* already exists in the form of a tradition, I am leveraging the juxtaposition of all these texts and their adaptations to inspire other critics to revisit our preconceived notions about genre traditions and media history. We might also retroactively inscribe a different set of precedents for future developments in sound studies through our attention to overlooked milestones in sonic fiction.

The first chapter begins where Jim Crow and the Golden Age left off. Chapter 1, "Race, Reverie, and Utopia: *New World A-Coming*" focuses on a World War II–era radio series, *New World A-Coming*, based on a bestselling nonfiction book by the Black newspaper veteran Roi Ottley. It revisits a moment known for Popular Front activism by communists and other left cultural politics. Ottley's book emerged out of New Deal efforts to employ writers and researchers. It reached a crossover audience seeking insight into the heritage and demands of the newly urbanized Black masses. During the war, the radio series brought Ottley's slice-of-life perspective on Black America—a phrase that was more aspirational than vocative at the time—into the service of the Double Victory campaign championed by the Black press. The show, one of few precedents for Richard Durham's groundbreaking *Destination Freedom* program, came to WMCA in New York with support from an interracial, interfaith coalition. With guest stars from Broadway and a theme song by Duke Ellington, the show dramatized the struggle against Jim Crow as part of the fight for a future beyond fascism. This chapter draws on recordings and scripts from the series, biographies, Black (and national) newspapers, and records from the National Negro Congress. It outlines the role of radio drama and the war effort in the broader saga of Black freedom that Ottley called "A Passage to Utopia."

Chapter 2 focuses on the radio adaptation of Samuel Delany's *The Star-Pit*. The bohemian subculture in which Delany was living, writing, and making music in the 1960s placed him in the company of radio and theater professionals who eagerly accepted the challenge of dramatizing his science fiction heterotopia from the pages of *Worlds of Tomorrow*. Alongside those artists, Delany voiced the play's narrator and protagonist, a hard-drinking Black spaceship mechanic living on the far edge of the galaxy. In the 1967 production, silence, experimental music, and sound effects communicate nonverbal aspects of the futuristic storyworld, where polyamorous marriages and psychedelic drugs are the norm. I find the figurative device of catachresis integral to the story's portrayal of new, imagined varieties of human difference, and the sounds used in the play realize this speculative intervention. These features of the story and its adaptation place it in vibrant dialogue with literary queer studies. Sources for this chapter include the Pacifica Radio Archives, Delany's published memoirs and journals, and critical writings by fellow science fiction scholars.

Touchstones of African American literature play a pivotal role in Chapter 3. "The Audible Epigraph in Octavia E. Butler's *Kindred*" studies a dramatization of Butler's 1979 novel, which combines the neo–slave narrative with time travel. With the exception of references to oral histories collected by the Federal Writers Project (WPA Slave Narratives) and published autobiographies by enslaved women, my research for this chapter was largely undertaken at the Huntington Library, where Butler bequeathed her archive. In 2001, two teachers who were students of history brought *Kindred* to the new medium of "internet radio" for the website of the newly launched Sci-Fi Channel. *Kindred* depicts a contemporary African American writer transported to the plantation where her ancestors were enslaved. To situate the production in the antebellum era, its directors incorporated quotations from Black women's slave narratives—read by notable actors—into the play at interstitial moments. Behind the scenes, the adaptation realized part of Butler's lifelong struggle to make a living as an author by negotiating the rights to her intellectual property. *Kindred* was an attestation to Butler's class consciousness and her self-conscious positioning as a Black woman writer who was virtually singular in the field of science fiction. The audio version of the narrative, starring Alfre Woodard as the heroine, represents a snapshot of the adaptation industry in a moment of technological and cultural change.

The final chapter, "Haunting and Futurity in the *Woman's Hour*," assesses the 2016 BBC radio adaptation of Toni Morrison's *Beloved*. The adaptation, written by the Jamaica-born playwright Patricia Cumper, tasks a Black British cast with conveying the novel's intense psychological and supernatural tableau. The community of formerly enslaved subjects in the novel displays the limits of human resilience. Morrison crafts a story of loving bonds frayed by trauma and repaired through connection, and the adaptation makes ample use of the oral tradition represented in the novel. This production, made for the digital age, inherits conventions from generations of British radio while contributing to the influence of Black British theater and world literature on the listening public. National difference and colonial history haunt this adaptation, but Morrison's presence on the BBC airwaves as a public intellectual functions to demystify the work's historical setting. Rather than sharpening contrasts between the geographic frames of reference invoked by the adaptation, my analysis highlights how both the radio play and the novel rely on sound as a means for constructing narrative. My efforts to situate this rendition of *Beloved* in the context of scholarship on radio history, narratology, performance, and Black speculative writing were predicated on privileged access to scripts from Patricia Cumper and recordings from the BBC archives.

Taken together, the radio plays I discuss in this book chart an unexpected constellation for Black speculation in popular media. My analyses are guided by constant attention to African American literary innovation and excitement about the challenges it poses for adaptation. As the growing academic investment in the critical benefits of speculative practices attests, the creative traditions of science fiction and fantasy have offered invaluable resources for envisioning and embodying ways of life that surpass realist representation. Each chapter of *Audiofuturism* highlights how Black authors and those responsible for adapting their work deploy novel techniques for imagining possible relationships to the real conditions facing their respective publics—notwithstanding disparate relationships to the recognized conventions of speculative fiction. Adaptations of Black speculative texts enrich an art form that has been instrumental to the genre traditions that prevail across literature and popular media. Listening to the Black fantastic has transformative value for science fiction, literary adaptation, and sound studies.

1

Race, Reverie, and Utopia

New World A-Coming

New World A-Coming was a bestselling book by the Black journalist Roi Ottley that inspired a radio series by the same title. The radio show, directed by playwright Mitchell Grayson with actor Canada Lee as its star, premiered on New York's WMCA in 1944.[1] *New World*'s adaptation for radio became a pivotal development in the broader process of negotiating the relationship of Black artists and audiences to American mass culture. Its aim was repositioning African Americans for a central role in the global future of the United States after our entry into World War II, and its means for doing so was the interpretation of our heritage and everyday life in the context of interracial cooperation toward liberal democracy. It was a unique intervention in the Golden Age of mass media that demonstrated how performance over the airwaves could bring minoritarian aspirations to the world stage.

Before and during the war, the rise of authoritarianism in Europe and the threat posed to the established imperialist world order by Japan vindicated mass culture criticism's concern with propaganda. Decades after W. E. B. Du Bois contended that "all art is propaganda and ever must be, despite the wailing of the purists," Walter Benjamin decried fascists in Italy aestheticizing politics and called for the politicization of aesthetics.[2] Looking toward the future, avant-garde and popular artists resisted dogma and insinuated themselves into mass consciousness.[3] As Jennifer Wilks and Carole Boyce Davies have written, Black women throughout the Diaspora challenged conventional ideologies of class, nation, gender, and sexuality espoused by race men.[4] Recording and translation made folklore, literature, and performance available to new locales. The Book of the Month club, which had sold *Gone with the Wind* to its subscribers, brought Richard Wright's shocking critique of the status quo in *Native*

Son to the middle class. Culture was a battleground. For Black authors and artists like those who contributed to the bold experiment in culture that *New World A-Coming* represents, radio drama was a means to reveal the utopian ideals harbored by those who needed hope the most.

While not directly supported by the Office of War Information or other government initiatives, *New World A-Coming* was a public influence operation with stakeholders in different cultural institutions of its era. Each half-hour episode of the series amplified attention to an issue of particular interest to Black Americans by connecting it with the national priorities of the war effort: unity, industry, victory, and peacetime prosperity. Accordingly, I would situate the subject of this chapter in a long tradition of artistic endeavors that combat derogatory and exploitative uses of culture through *counterpublicity*: showcasing desirable alternatives to dominant, controlling imagery while also addressing a "minor" or parallel public sphere where ideas and possibilities circulate differently.[5] On the radio, *New World A-Coming* articulated its namesake text's revelatory effort to cultivate Black self-regard as an essential element of an egalitarian future.

Ottley's Outlook

New World A-Coming was the brainchild of Vincent Lushington "Roi" Ottley, an ambitious writer born to emigrants from the Caribbean and who would build his reputation in Harlem's effort to recover from the Great Depression.[6] His background afforded some privilege: He was educated on a track scholarship at the scarcely integrated St. Bonaventure University in upstate New York, and he was a lifelong friend and ally to the iconic politician Adam Clayton Powell Jr.[7] In the 1930s, Ottley became a columnist for the *Amsterdam Star-News*, one of the pillars of the Black press.[8] There, he joined some of the first Black journalists' efforts to unionize, garnering national attention from labor and civil rights leaders. His minor celebrity afforded him a leading role in Federal Writers' Project activities in Harlem, which formed a pivotal and controversial chapter in his career.[9] At the time he published *New World*, Ottley was working for the CIO, the more progressive national coalition of labor unions.[10] According to some contemporaries, including Ralph Ellison and John Hope Franklin, as well as later scholars, Ottley had claimed a great deal of research material collected by his colleagues and used it, without credit, to write his first two books.[11] The most credible detractors at the time were FWP veterans who had worked on an incomplete manuscript, "Negroes of New York," under Ottley's supervision. A defense of Ottley by Edward Perry notes that Ottley had cited the manuscript in his bibliography and identifies some famous contributors: "Claude McKay, J. A. Rogers, Dorothy West, Bruce Nugent, Carlton Moss, Ralph Ellison, Alvin Moses, Sadie Hall, John Clarke, and Bennie Butler."[12]

Houghton Mifflin published *New World A-Coming* in its "Life in America" series in 1943. It included twenty-three chapters on topics ranging from Black migration to the North to the ethnic diversity of Harlem, the meaning of Joe Louis, conspiracy theories regarding Black Nazi sympathizers, the place of Jewish people in Black communities, and the life and times of Ottley's friend and future congressman, Powell. Notwithstanding the objections just discussed, the book's reception by the Black press was overwhelmingly favorable nationwide.[13] Reviews in the *New York Times*, *Philadelphia Inquirer*, and *Detroit Free Press* brought it to the attention of white readers and critics.[14] The book was not only serialized in the *Amsterdam News*, but it also enjoyed the crossover appeal to get condensed for inclusion in the Christmas 1943 issue of *Coronet*, a photo-heavy monthly from the publisher of *Esquire*.[15]

The model of success that Ottley initiated with *New World A-Coming*—where success entailed communicating knowledge about Black life that was valuable to those white folks willing to listen—would prove uniquely suitable for radio. In recognition of its contribution to understanding race and racism, *New World* won the Anisfield-Wolf Prize in 1944, preceded by Hurston's *Dust Tracks on a Road* and followed by Myrdal's *An American Dilemma*.[16] Along with Ralph Ellison and James Baldwin, Ottley was among the last beneficiaries of a fellowship from the Julius Rosenwald fund, which played a key role advancing the careers of his generation of writers and artists.[17] In 1944, the Rosenwald fellowship sponsored Ottley's travel to Europe, where he would be credentialed as the first Black war correspondent for a national publication, *Liberty*. As its slogan declared, *Liberty* was "a weekly for everybody." Before Ottley, its past bylines included Leon Trotsky, Cornelius Vanderbilt, President Roosevelt, and Bob Hope. Its masthead opened doors that remained closed to the Black press. A 1945 tribute to Negro war correspondents honored writers from the *Courier*, the *Norfolk Journal and Guide*, the Baltimore *Afro-American*, and the National Negro Publishers Association. The profile of Ottley appeared with the following qualification: "Roi Ottley, although not representing the Negro press, has been accredited as a war correspondent and has reported from many fronts on the participation of the Negro troops."[18] His career held out the promise of double victory during the war: the pursuit of racial equality working hand in hand with the defeat of fascism. The subtitle of *New World A-Coming, Inside Black America*, portrayed the internal resources of Black communities as assets to a pluralistic society rather than peculiarities that could be brushed aside in deference to white priorities. While the recognition that

Figure 2: Photograph of Roi Ottley, c. 1940, associated with the promotion of his book *New World A-Coming*. *Source*: Schomburg Center for Research in Black Culture, Photographs and Prints Division, New York Public Library.

Ottley secured from gatekeepers afforded him access to white audiences, the message that *New World A-Coming* carried to the airwaves came from homegrown institutions like the Black press.

Ottley's book's explanation of the place of the mass media in Black life offers a window into the way *New World A-Coming* would use radio, a site in culture that had been the source of problems, as a venue for solutions. Addressing misconceptions born of white ignorance and racial prejudice was one side of the equation. The other end was demonstrating how the removal of those impediments to Black people's full potential would help achieve national goals.

Ottley's chapter about the Black press situated Black and white news coverage related to the war within a general account of the relationship between them. His analysis began by accounting for a serious misunderstanding: The white public believed that Black reporters' focus on their communities' own suffering under Jim Crow reflected an overall dissatisfaction with the country itself. The headlines he gathered from the aftermath of Pearl Harbor establish the basis on which doubts about Black patriotism persisted: "U.S. Forces Britain to Jim Crow Troops," in the *Amsterdam News*; "Fiendish Mob of Texas Whites Lynch Innocent Negro Accused of Attack," in the *Courier*; and "Negro Preachers Put Out of Senate at Gunpoint" (most likely from Adam Clayton Powell's *People's Voice*).[19] Ottley conceded that "blatant advertising of racial inequalities in the United States by Negro newspapers is of undoubted propaganda value to the Axis."[20] His observation that the Black press was out of step with the federal government's priorities was further underscored by the observation that "Archibald MacLeish, as director of the Office of Facts and Figures [precursor to the OWI], called an informal conference of Negro editors and attempted to persuade them to lay off the rough racial stuff."[21]

Ottley aimed to disabuse readers of the notion that attention to lynching and other injustices undermined the nation's reputation as a beacon for democracy by shifting their perspective on the media landscape as a whole. He pointed out that "in one sense, Negro newspapers are the Negro affairs supplements of the white dailies. . . . Negro papers print considerable news and features which can find no place in the white press."[22] Additionally, he wrote, "nearly every Negro who reads a white daily also subscribes to at least one Negro newspaper." This was practical, since the preponderance of the papers in question were published weekly.[23] Ottley would have his readers treat Black papers as a "supplement" in the vital sense; that is, the work performed by Negro press was necessary to keep the public sufficiently informed because the mainstream news was deficient with respect to race. As an acknowledgment of this reality, he said, "The Negro press has made a bid for a white public. Any success in this endeavor is proudly hailed. When Henry Ford, the auto mobile manufacturer, bought a year's subscription to the *Courier*, his check was reproduced with this head: 'FORD SUBSCRIBES . . . HERE'S THE PROOF.'"[24] When white audiences took Negro concerns seriously, the benefits accrued to all parties involved.

In the radio series, Ottley's approach to Black journalism would furnish material for an episode titled "The Story Behind the News in the Negro Press." This show, for which Ottley wrote the script, aired on April 23, 1944. It explained the reasons why Black papers drew attention to topics disfavored in the white press. It opened with the lede from a Black newspaper that quoted Gandhi disparaging British and American policy: "The white Allies have no moral cause for which they are fighting so long as they are carrying this double sin: the sin of India's subjection and the subjection of Negroes, says Gandhi, the Indian leader." Ominous music signals an understanding that his accusation about the Allies' morality, and the papers' choice to disseminate it, is a harsh judgment. To illustrate the episode's title, the narrator suggests, "Let's step into the office of a Negro paper and listen while the editorial writers discuss the reasons for quoting Gandhi." The ensuing vignette rehearses an imaginary conversation between two Black newspaper men:

> JOHN: The Negro's condition is no longer simply a domestic one. It has international overtones. The color problem today is a large element in the strategy of totally defeating the Axis.
>
> BILL: How about starting the editorial this way? The condition of the Black man in the United States has become the barometer of democracy to the Colored leaders of the world and suggests to them, should certain fascist leaders in America have their way, the "thought" of democracy which may dominate the new world a-coming.
>
> JOHN: That's right! And that's good. The fact is that conflicts between the races are inevitable, unless there's cooperation and desire by whites to see that freedom is the desire and right of all people.

The danger, in their view, was that an inadequate notion of democracy would pass itself off for the real thing around the world. Even if they won the war, the Allies couldn't win the peace for their ideals with such half-measures. Instead, characters representing the Black press—consistent with Ottley's book and with other episodes in the series—impressed upon the audience that the only path to enduring victory was improvement in race relations. This understanding encompassed struggles against imperialism, to the extent that the Allies ascribed racial inferiority to their colonial subjects in India, Malaysia, and Java.

Subsequent segments of the episode dealt with developments in education, labor, and civil rights, including the treatment of Negro soldiers, on which the Black press had reported faithfully despite little understanding from a general public who relied on white sources. It culminated in a declaration of principle that was substantively the same as the one that appeared in the pages of *New World A-Coming*:

> The editorial line of the Negro press today expresses the urgent need of extending democracy to the American Negro and the profoundly positive effect it would have in galvanizing Negroes into action, as

> well as the reassuring effect it would have upon the colored peoples elsewhere in the world. Viewed on its broadest plane, this is in fact a crusade for democracy. . . . The negro press believes that America can best lead the world away from racial and national antagonism when it accords to every man regardless of race color or creed his human and legal rights.

In his book, Ottley had identified this agenda by name and provided further details. It was called Double Victory:

> launched in the spring of 1942 by the *Courier*, to which nearly every Negro newspaper and pulpit has lent support. The program includes the purchase of war bonds and stamps, contributions to blood banks, participation in civilian defense, and conservation of waste materials; educational equality; and equal opportunity in war industry, as well as a fight against all forms of discrimination based on race, color, creed or class, the poll tax, and political disfranchisement.[25]

The radio series would endorse the same actions and pursue its strategy through similar rhetorical means.

In the radio series based on *New World A-Coming*, contributors inspired by Ottley's book—sometimes acting out scripts he had written—consistently associated democracy with desegregation, and they ascribed anti-American, pro-Japanese, pro-Nazi implications to measures that might limit Negro involvement in the war effort. Insisting on the resemblance between antidemocratic, fascist ideology and Jim Crow helped insulate the series' powerful accounts of pervasive American racism from criticism with respect to its overall attitude about the righteousness of the Allied cause in the war. After the success of *New World* in print and on the air, Ottley would go on to write for the *Pittsburgh Courier* and *PM*, a stylish, leftist daily that eschewed advertising.[26] He published several more books, including some reflecting his overseas experiences on assignment for *Liberty* and the *Courier*. At the close of his life, when he was only fifty years old, he was based in Chicago, where he wrote for the *Defender* and contributed a regular column to the white mainstream *Tribune*.[27] Beyond the indelible impact of its original author, however, the radio series encouraged and educated its audience through collective, participatory techniques.

Double Victory

For *New World A-Coming* to continue its look inside Black America on the radio, it would have to reproduce the book's credibility. The public intellectual

J. A. Rogers had praised it in the *Courier* for "the best reporting of the present racial situation in America," and Ben Burns of the *Chicago Defender* called it "a comprehensive, apt and at the same time entertaining book concerning the resolute black men of this decade who are fighting a really historic battle on the race front."[28] Burns testifies to the authenticity of Ottley's insider perspective, noting that, within the book's pages, "much may not be new to the Negro man in the street." Rogers balances his accolades with consideration for what the book omits; he suggests that Black radicals like Hubert Harrison and Cyril Briggs deserved a place in the retinue of Negro intellectuals it had invoked. He also commends Ottley for showing restraint, noting that he "wisely makes no prediction of the sort of New World that is coming." According to Hamilton Butler in the *Detroit Free Press*, white readers could trust the author, since he "is himself a Negro, a Harlem newspaper man."[29] Butler credited Ottley's profession with demystifying the agenda of the colored masses who had "flocked to Detroit and other northern cities in search of higher wages and the right to vote," observing, "An outspoken Negro press is carrying the torch." The white reading public who encountered *New World* in *Coronet* could rest assured, "Ottley writes of 'Black America' with singular knowledge of Negro racial problems."[30]

First-person accounts formed one dimension of the radio program's invaluable contribution to motivating the public. The other essential element was staging interracial collaboration. To that effect, it was significant that the series came to WMCA through the efforts of a newly assembled philanthropic association, "the Citywide Citizens' Committee on Harlem." Led by Adam Clayton Powell Sr. and leaders from the Ethical Culture Society, the Urban League, and an ecumenical range of other organizations, the committee's heterogeneous imprimatur identified Harlem as part of an all-inclusive city, rather than isolating the Black community. The producer and director for the episodes was Mitchell Grayson, who had directed radio productions on WNYC and WOR, including works by Norman Corwin.[31] Grayson maintained similar political commitments throughout his stage and radio career, directing later radio programs on civil rights and the dangers of the atomic bomb after *New World*.[32] As the series' primary announcer and the narrator in most of its dramatizations, rather than its sole protagonist, Canada Lee's voice represented the drive for national unity as well as the particular subject of "the segregations, discriminations and humiliations the Negro has endured for centuries," as the *Courier* described the show. A diverse range of performers known to varying degrees by different segments of the public realized the scenarios portrayed in the series.

New World A-Coming was distinctive for its independence—which was necessary at a time when the burgeoning radio networks and sponsors were unlikely to devote resources to airing controversial subject matter—as well as its format. Independent stations like WMCA were few and far between before and during the war; this would change in the postwar era. But there was a qualitative difference in the programming addressed to Black listeners and the majority of network broadcasts. As Henry Sampson indicates in his history of Black broadcasting, in the era from 1927 to 1950, music was overrepresented among programming for a Negro audience, accounting for two-thirds of the broadcast schedule, with drama making up only 4 percent.[33] Meanwhile, radio drama in its Golden Age comprised a third of the content of network broadcasts, while music played for less than a quarter of the time. Dramatic presentations on race were not unprecedented, but they were not regular, either. CBS once produced a program by Columbia Workshop's William Robson, titled "An Open Letter on Race Hatred," depicting the violence that had erupted on the streets of Detroit in the summer of 1943, when white Michiganders refused to open up housing or work alongside newly arrived Black residents.[34] Part of that broadcast was simulating the eager German and Japanese reception of news about racial violence in the United States, which served as a wake-up call to white Americans to stop providing fuel for the enemies of democracy. In a listening environment where this was such an exceptional gesture for a radio network to make, a weekly half-hour dramatic program written primarily by and about members of the Black community effectively transported the audience to another world.

After introducing the program and the Citywide Citizens' Committee to the listeners, the first *New World* episode established its complementary modes of enunciation. Virtually every broadcast included scripted enactments of representative scenarios from Black American life and an inspirational rallying point addressed directly to the listening audience. The dramatic component in the premiere began with an incident in which a Negro soldier attempts to enter a hotel in Virginia where he has been contracted to play the piano for a concert selling war bonds.[35] When he calls for the bellhop, he is greeted with suspicion and quickly ejected from the premises on the order of a white sergeant, who tells him, "Don't you know you don't belong here?" and "Well, you're still in Virginia!" The sound effects suggest the soldier is handled roughly as he is kicked out. At the conclusion of the vignette, Canada Lee asserts ominously, "Japan would have liked to have had that story. As a matter of fact, Japan has used stories like that in the past—they shout them to the world by shortwave!" Just as Robson's "Open Letter" had done on CBS, this framing unambiguously casts reports of ongoing racial discrimination in the United States as fodder for Axis propaganda.

The local significance of the episode resides in its appeal to the Black public's struggle for equality in their own country. But when it is inserted into a narrative of international rivalry, the greater threat of Japan using true stories from the homefront to demoralize American soldiers escalates Jim Crow to a problem of global proportions. The conflict between democratic ideals and discriminatory practices appears on the world stage as a contest between the desirable liberal democratic order and an imperialist nightmare. The treatment of these incidents on the broadcast juxtaposes the possibility of aberrant, irrational encounters with discrimination, on the one hand, with a fatalistic warning, on the other: Any diversion from the war effort in the interest of maintaining domestic mores would prolong the suffering of all soldiers, all Americans, and all people exposed to the Nazi and Japanese threat. As Lee puts it, "Very often, Negroes become discouraged. And today, the Negro's attitude is especially important if we're to have a total population waging a total war."

To articulate the show's perspectives in other terms, Lee introduces a member of the Citywide Citizens' Committee, the activist and photographer Dorothy Norman:

> NORMAN: Our committee, whose members act as individuals rather than as representatives of other organizations, is an interracial interfaith group working for racial justice in greater New York. . . . Ultimately, our aim is to help create a living democracy in which all sections of the population will share in the rights as well as the responsibilities of citizenship. All those who listen are part of this program, for we will all reap the benefits of the new world that we must build only as we take responsibility for creating it.

Norman specifies that her utopian vision includes "better housing, education, health, employment, security, [and] civil rights," and she also declares that it includes everyone. Furthermore, their goals are concrete, rather than purely idealistic: "These must not only be dreams. If we believe in democracy, we must believe in making them available for all, without regard to race, creed, or color." The episode follows with one of the only appearances on the air by Ottley himself:

> OTTLEY: The most important task before the American people today is winning the war. And winning the peace. We present these shows in the hope that they will prove to be effective contributions toward establishing better race relations so that all people will unite and

> work toward winning the war. And eventually the peace. . . . Today people have their eyes lifted to the hills, hoping for that better world to come. Mr. Lee is about to tell us a final incident which when I heard it certainly gave me a lift, for it seemed to point the way.

The language of "winning the peace" gained uptake as Black observers grew concerned that the Allies might win in Europe with their countries' racial attitudes still intact.[36] In February 1945, after his stint abroad reporting for *Liberty*, Ottley recommended promoting the slogan "win the peace" as a way to remind Americans and Europeans that democracy had yet to cross the color line. He wrote, "With the exception of the French, not a single statesman has within the realm of his thinking any reference to the Atlantic Charter as it should affect colonials." Americans and Britons were poised to lead the world into the future, but fresh from witnessing Negro soldiers "heaving and toting materials and doing the porter work of this war almost exclusively," he wrote, "Our racial patterns bewilder the Europeans." "Win the peace" expressed the belief that the conduct of the war, and not just its outcome, would set the stage for the future of race relations.

In addition to using representations of Negro patriotism to persuade metropolitan white audiences that their new neighbors were assets to the war effort, the task of adapting the book for radio was itself an argument for racial unity. The research behind *New World A-Coming* was collaborative in nature, but the individual authorship to which Ottley laid claim gave its storytelling the appearance of cohesion and unity in purpose. While some episodes of the radio program echoed Ottley's presentation of chapters in the book, they all played out in a polyvocal fashion. A collective mode of presentation that could peer inside Negro life in America while also displaying the significance of what happens to Black America for the wider public suited the show's message. This meant opportunities for Black performers in a radio format where their roles were otherwise limited, which, in turn, signaled shared investment from WMCA and the civic organizations behind the show to their art and its message. As they would insist when it came to making the ramp-up of wartime industry an opportunity for Black workers, the purveyors of *New World* on the radio shaped the Black presence on the airwaves into a reminder not to squander the nation's valuable talent.

Two particular episodes of the series illustrate how the war effort could usher in a new world through labor relations. The racialized, gendered status quo created the false impression that wartime mobilization and improvements in Black communities' standards of living were disparate, even opposing interests. Despite the urgent demand for workers to perform the jobs for which deployed, wounded, and dying white men were unavailable, Jim Crow relegated Negro soldiers to the sidelines and excluded their homefront brethren from the production boom. The opening this contingency provided for white women to undertake paid labor showed how their segment of society would play a different role in the new world to come. The *New World A-Coming* episode on Executive Order 8802 and the Fair Employment Practices Committee, which Grayson adapted from Ottley's chapter on the subject in his book, took up this same task for Black workers. An original script by Ottley on what he termed "The Mammy Legend" would pave the way for further transformations.

On November 5, 1944, the "Executive Order 8802" episode opens with Canada Lee making the case for the audience to take an interest in the topic. He declares the driving questions, "Who's for it?" and "Who's against it?" Statistics can only begin to make the case, and they are the same as those printed in the book: The 1940 census counted over five million Negroes in the workforce, but wartime manufacturing excludes them in large numbers. "In Texas, of 17,435 defense jobs, 9,117 were barred to Negroes, and in Michigan, the figure was 22,042 out of 26,904. Moreover, contrary to the assumption that Negroes are barred only when they seek skilled work, no less than 35,000 out of 83,000 unskilled jobs were declared closed to Negro applicants." The numbers cannot relate the meaning of the story, so testimonials provide the necessary substance. In turns, a series of indignant voices recount lost opportunities across the country. A man accuses those rejecting him of "blocking a total war effort." An unemployed man who had worked as a painter for decades reveals that even though his skills were in great demand, the site to which he had applied hired painters from another state instead. Ruby Dee, then a rising star and activist, plays a woman applying for a job at a sewing factory only to be told "if women like me got defense jobs, there'd be a shortage of maids!" Her predicament will receive a full-length treatment in the "Mammy Legend" episode. A drum roll underscores each speaker's words, and dramatic horns build suspense between testimonials. The discontent resonates from one account into the next. As part of a collective, these characters expose the prevalence of discrimination across the country as a weakness on a national scale. Crucially, they each articulate their exclusion from the war effort in terms that portray "total war" as a new and singular agenda that is placed in peril by persistent discriminatory habits.

The action shifts to New York, in the spring of 1941, where the labor leader A. Philip Randolph visits Walter White at the offices of the NAACP. The scene stages a conversation between the race men about the growing discontent among Black workers. White confesses, "It grieves me so deeply that I'm beginning to think that we've just got to have a Senate investigation of this entire matter and settle this thing once and for all."[37] They take for granted that the president (Roosevelt) is on their side, but Randolph broaches the idea of a mass demonstration to "command respectful attention" from the legislators and their constituents. White advises that such a mobilization would require a great deal of organizing, and Randolph answers, with earnest insistence, "Well, we could charter a special train, hire a caravan of buses—even hitchhike! We'll make it work!"

For audience members unfamiliar with Randolph's reputation as leader of the Brotherhood of Sleeping Car Porters or White's role as executive secretary of the nation's oldest civil rights organization, the backroom conversation portrays them both as passionate yet rational leaders ready to muster all the resources they could demand toward a noble goal. The portrayal is consistent with what informed observers already knew about Randolph and White's influence and their respective inclinations. The former speaks for the strategic power of solidarity and strength in numbers, while the latter—soft-spoken and easily mistaken for a white man—represents a tradition of investigation and social consciousness, coalition building, and philanthropy. Like the testimonials from aggrieved parties across the nation, the two characters symbolize many activists pressing for a political solution to wartime job discrimination.

Immediately after this segment, listeners hear that the chief executive has issued a historic order, with no indication that the promised march aroused anxiety or reactionary measures. The effect is to make both the problem and its solution appear obvious, and the rewards, mutual. As an instrumental version of "Battle Hymn of the Republic" plays in the background, an actor portraying President Roosevelt reads words from the order, dated June 25, 1941. The music links the historical event and the president responsible for it to the framing that Lee provides when he describes 8802 as the "first order directly pertaining to the Negro since Lincoln." Associating wartime progress and its leadership with the new world that was ushered in by the Great Emancipator encourages the audience to perceive their present moment as revolutionary. Like Reconstruction, however, the change is not without its complications. Rather than creating the false impression that the order's establishment of the Fair Employment Practices Committee had actually eliminated racial discrimination, the remainder of the episode illustrates how the titular policy changes made it possible to do something about discrimination in the future.

A scene set in Chicago, for example, depicts a Black steamfitter recounting visiting an office with the question, "This is the place to come isn't it? The President's Fair Employment Committee?" His complaint concerns his being barred from a job that was only hiring union members. Yet the steamfitters union wouldn't admit Negro workers. Taking up his cause, a new character,

Mary Forsyth, played by the Black songstress Muriel Smith of Broadway's *Carmen Jones*, shows up at the union in question to investigate.[38] As the white man to whom she is speaking defends his position with a brusque, "Now look here, ma'am, are you telling me," she interrupts him. She declares, "There's a presidential order. . . . Your union will have to change its policy." Although he hedges, saying he will have to call a meeting of his current members, Forsyth responds, knowingly, "By all means." She explains that the railway mail union had recently voted Negroes into their membership, indicating that he should expect the same.

A similar confrontation takes place between another FEPC investigator and a shipyard manager. This interaction recapitulates a passage from Ottley's book, as the investigator rebuts each of the manager's excuses for refusing to hire Negroes in spite of the executive order. The exchange reflects Ottley's list of "the four major objections raised by white employers and the facts used by the government agencies to refute them."[39] The pretexts claim that Negroes and whites wouldn't work together, that Negroes couldn't perform the work required, that integrating the workforce would diminish production, and that unions wouldn't permit integration. Evidence to the contrary comes from Alabama to Denver and Virginia, and it features blacksmiths, caulkers, machinists, and more. The investigator finally asks, directly, "Would you yourself object to having Negro workers?" When the manager denies it, the investigator cuts through his dissemblance:

> I've been handling a lot of complaints. I don't find many men, union officials or employers, who say that they object to any kind of workers. They say, like you, that other people would object: workers, the public. But I think most Americans are fair minded. I think that you people that are afraid are afraid only of shadows.

This response parallels Ottley's attestation: "An employer who meets union resistance to his attempts to hire Negroes may invoke the full support of the federal government, the President of the United States, and the heads of both major labor groups," the American Federation of Labor and the Congress of Industrial Organizations.[40] Whether or not they admitted it, management and labor alike could only cling to their racial prejudice at the cost of alienation from national leadership as the FEPC began to turn the tide against job discrimination.

The most incisive vignette of the episode involves an FEPC investigator and the head of an aircraft plant, played by the stage and future screen actor Sanford Bickart.[41] The plant administrator states his case:

> I built this aircraft plant from scratch. So today it's one of the largest in the United States. I'm doing more war work than most of my competitors. I need more help. All I did was ask the United States employment service to send me, uh, thirty girls for assembly work.

The speaker's verbal hesitation betrays what he has left out of his request as he relates it to the FEPC, which is the reason the FEPC has paid him a visit. "Yes," the investigator says, exasperatedly, "Thirty white girls." He continues, "Unless you request thirty qualified girls, regardless of color, you're discriminating, and the government won't help you do it." Undeterred, the administrator maintains, "I won't hire Negro girls in my plant. Now if you're so anxious to help the war effort, send me thirty white girls." Music swells to punctuate the confrontation. The otherwise heroic aircraft manufacturer emerges as a villain, in this moment, by placing warfare at risk just to accommodate his own sexual-racial bias. No one could get away with antagonizing the war effort in the moral universe of *New World A-Coming*, and so the story concludes as a tale of contrition. Canada Lee recounts,

> Of course the United States employment service refused to cooperate with this employer, and a short time later, when he was desperately in need of more help, he came around to the FEPC . . . when finally the employer accepted assembly workers without discrimination, he found that qualified Negroes were just as efficient as anyone else he'd employed. Then he said he'd make a public statement.

And in that statement, he would make himself into an example: "I learned the hard way. I'll admit that I made a mistake. I'm hiring all the help I can get now. And all that I ask is that they can do the work. It's the best way in the long run. It's the only American way." Though Bickart's character sounds chastened by the experience, the musical transition away from this scene is an ennobling phrase from "America, the Beautiful." By humbling those who would put their own bigotry above the nation's priorities, this episode of *New World A-Coming* promises that inclusivity will benefit everyone, in the long run.

The June 18, 1944 episode, titled "The Negro Domestic," addressed sexual-racial and labor marginalization in a much more intimate setting. The script for this episode, written by Ottley, was reprinted in a 1945 book, *Radio Drama in Action: Twenty-Five Plays of a Changing World*, along with Robson's "Open Letter," Norman Corwin's "London by Clipper," and Langston Hughes's historical recreation "Booker T. Washington in Atlanta." Of all the *New World* scripts to anthologize, this one clearly made a strong impression that was also consistent with the wartime demand for "public service" broadcasting.[42] Canada

Lee begins the show by announcing, "If there's one thing that irritates Negroes today, it is the Mammy legend often romanticized in song and story."[43] Invoking the subject as a legend and identifying its romanticization as a problem delineates this episode's task: demystification.

The episode fulfills one of the key interventions of bringing Ottley's book to the radio by displacing harmful myths with an up-to-date, inspiring counternarrative situated in the context of the war. First, Lee introduces several unnamed speakers who think fondly of the woman who works in their household as "Mammy." They praise her cooking, her tirelessness, and her devotion, saying, "She thinks more of us than we do of ourselves." They refer to her as "Old Sarah," "Julia," and "a Black diamond," but never with her own surname or honorific such as "Mrs." One man jokes, "Someday they'll need a waffle maker in heaven, and then, we'll lose her!" The speaker's attempted compliment unwittingly betrays a level of spiritual bankruptcy that leads him to fantasize, however jokingly, that even Paradise wouldn't release the Negro from servitude. The facetious line echoes a 1925 poem by Countee Cullen, "For a Lady I Know":

She even thinks that up in heaven
Her class lies late and snores,
While poor black cherubs rise at seven
To do celestial chores.[44]

Lee challenges these shallow paeans to Mammy from white speakers, saying, "While such people exalt Mammy verbally, they often don't seem to understand that she has developed strong feelings about her role as a servant, about her own identity, and particularly about her own race." However, he will not perform this contestation in the third person as the narrator. Instead, he welcomes the main protagonist to the episode, whom he describes as "a Negro domestic in the home of Mr. and Mrs. Frederick Millburn. Her name is Martha Howard."

Not only does she enter the drama with a formal act of naming, a courtesy that no "Mammy" figure was afforded in the previous anecdotes, but her first line is, "Yes, I'm Martha Howard." By answering to her own name and declaring herself the subject of the story that ensues, the character begins undoing the mythology assigned to her by white employers and storytellers and authoring her own account of her occupation, her social position, and her desires. Structuring the drama with a domestic worker at its center upsets the typical "Mammy" legend. It relates the story of a woman known under that byname in the style that earned *New World* credibility from the press, "without the old embellishments of Uncle Tom and the other typed characterizations often utilized by producers to portray the race on the American scene."[45]

Defying misconceptions would form an integral part of *New World*'s contribution to mass media. The columnist Horace Cayton issued a clarion call in a January 1943 edition of the *Courier*, with the subtitle, "We Must Reach the White Mass Through Radio, Press, and Screen."[46] He lamented, under the heading "MOVIES WORST OFFENDER," that "The Negro, except on rare occasions, is presented in print, over the air and on the screen as a buffoon or a semi-dangerous moron . . . every Negro that walks on a movie set has to start 'skinning them back' and showing his teeth." The expression referred to a minstrel performance convention that directed blackface actors to smile from ear to ear, revealing their teeth, gums, and lips to attain the exaggerated mien expected from racist iconography. Cayton's demand for alternatives emphasizes the misrepresentation of the Negro in mass culture as well as the degrading demands it placed on performers at the time. This was the era of the ascendancy of *Amos 'n' Andy*, the minstrel show by white voice actors who brought the blackface idiom to the radio with unparalleled success. An excellent body of scholarship enumerates the catalog of racist archetypes, alternatives, and critiques into which *New World* introduced its anti-Mammy episode. Most importantly, for readers of the present study, is the way the drama dignified the role by affording the character a measure of self-determined agency in ongoing national and world events. This set it apart from contemporary romances like *Gone with the Wind*, which rewarded Hattie McDaniel with an Oscar for portraying author Margaret Mitchell's subordinating rendition of Mammy.

The star of the episode was already a household name for many Black and white listeners: Georgette Harvey. Sanford Bickart, acting as announcer at the start and end of the episode, describes her as a "well-known character actress and star of the stage and radio."[47] Harvey had traveled the world as a vaudeville performer before originating the role of Maria in DuBose Hewyard's *Porgy* and reprising it for the acclaimed Gershwin opera *Porgy and Bess*. She was also a founding member of the American Negro Theatre, the subject of another *New World* episode.[48] As Martha Howard, she is the caretaker to the Millburns' ten-year-old son, Junior. The majority of lines in the play consist of dialogue between her and the child, but her character also speaks in soliloquy to connect to scenes from her life to the audience's present. Stage directions and verbal emphases included in the printed version of the script indicate the pacing and tone of the dialogue.

JUNIOR: [*Off mike*] Martha! [Rattling pans, pots, dishes][*Approaching*] Martha! [*Pause*] Martha, what are you thinkin' about?

MARTHA: Pardon me, Junior, but I was just lost in thought . . .
JUNIOR: About what, Martha?
MARTHA: Oh, I got a letter this morning from my boy Charlie . . .
JUNIOR: [*Excitedly*] Charlie? In the army?
MARTHA: Yes. He's comin' here tonight. He's got a furlough.
JUNIOR: [*All agog*] Where's he been fighting?
MARTHA: Well, now, he hasn't been fighting yet. He's just finishing his basic training—but I guess he'll be goin' overseas 'most any day now . . .
JUNIOR: *Gosh*, I wish I could be a soldier!
MARTHA: Good land, this war'll be over long before that. I hope. [*Reflectively*]. Hmmmm . . . That's one reason why Charlie's in a uniform. So's you won't have to go when you grow up.
JUNIOR: I wish I could see him. Is he an officer?
MARTHA: No, Junior. He's only a private. Same as every other GI Joe.
JUNIOR: Will I be awake when he comes here tonight?
MARTHA: I don't know. Depends on what time his train comes in.
JUNIOR: I'd *like* to see him . . . even if he gets here when I'm sleeping.
MARTHA: We'll have to ask your mother about that. You've got to get up in time for school in the morning.
JUNIOR: I'll ask mother right away. I want to see Charlie.
MARTHA: [*Smiling*] Seems like only yesterday he was no bigger than you—runnin' around in short pants—I can hardly believe he's old enough to be in the army.[49]

From their conversation, the audience can tell that Howard is accustomed to accommodating Junior's inquisitive nature. His admiration for Charlie—whom he already knows by reputation—is palpable and endearing. Significantly, the conversation commences only when Junior comes into proximity with Martha's work. The first sounds he makes as he approaches come from "off mike," situating Martha as the focal point of the audience's acoustic perception as well as the narrative. The conversation commences an interruption to Martha's train of thought, and it advances and digresses according to shifts in the object of her contemplation and emotions. She does not simply inhabit the scene. She sets it.

On the evening of Charlie's arrival, the Millburns are hosting a Mr. and Mrs. Richards for dinner, prepared by Howard, of course. They are all surprised by the visit, and she is elated to see her son. Junior is thrilled to meet a young man who will fly in the Air Corps to fight Nazi and Japanese forces. But the elder Millburns and the Richardses express disbelief at Charlie's impressive accomplishments.

FATHER: So, you're in the Air Corps, eh, Charles?
CHARLIE: Yes, sir. And I've just been accepted for further training at the flying school.
JUNIOR: Boy, that's swell! Isn't it, dad?
FATHER: *[Interrupts]* You mean, ground crew . . . don't you?
CHARLIE: Why, no. As a pilot, sir.
FATHER: Aren't the qualifications pretty stiff?
CHARLIE: Yes, sir. But I just made it. I was lucky that I had completed two years of college before I went into the service. That helped plenty. I'll tell you.
FATHER: Well, er, that's fine . . .
JUNIOR: Mother, one of the boys in our school . . . one of the older boys . . .
MOTHER: Junior, your father's talking. It isn't polite to interrupt.
JUNIOR: I'm sorry. [*Adding quickly*] But, mother, the Air Corps wants lots of boys.
FATHER: [*Patronizingly*] Well, I guess you're learning a whole lot in the army. Negroes are getting opportunities for the first time, I hear.
CHARLIE: Yes, sir.
FATHER: You seem to be doing well, and I hope you'll make the most of your opportunities. I suppose your people have their own training grounds and divisions . . . .
CHARLIE: Well, sir, that's one thing about the army none of us likes. Especially when they say this is a war for democracy! That kind of treatment . . . Negro this and white that . . . doesn't seem fair to us. But I guess that will be all reckoned with in the future.
MOTHER: How do you mean that, Charles?
CHARLIE: Well, Mrs. Millburn, when you're in the army . . . and you fight for something . . . you fight for something that's right. That's the reason why I think we're fighting this war . . . for things that are right. Everybody in a uniform takes a chance on giving up his life. Negro soldiers are not different. We believe we're fighting for something that's right. And we don't think we ought to be separated on any 'count.
MOTHER: I see what you mean, Charles.
CHARLIE: And I think there's some headway being made, too.
MOTHER: Yes, Charles, go on.

CHARLIE: Well, in a few months, if I make the grade, I'll be in a flier's uniform. That's a little headway, I think. There were no Negro fliers in the last war . . .
JUNIOR: Gosh, Charles, I wish I were flying with you!
MRS. RICHARDS: Now, Junior, you know you can't do that.
JUNIOR: Why, Mrs. Richards?
MRS. RICHARDS: Well, it's just not done, that's all.[50]

The range of attitudes on display reflect generational shifts brought on by the war. Charlie's experience provides him with the authority to offer a new definition of democracy that entails integration as a means and an end. Frederick Millburn's incredulity and his wife Millicent's solicitousness show the ignorance and hesitancy of middle-class white Americans as Negroes attained the social mobility they had been denied up to this point. And Mrs. Richards's effort to temper Junior's unflagging enthusiasm shows resistance to his identification with and desire for Charlie as a role model. Charlie could be exemplary and even exceptional, but Junior voices an aspiration to be *like* him as well as *with* him, in social proximity. The adults in the room discipline him for envisioning a form of homosocial bonding that requires Black and white brothers-in-arms to regard each other as peers rather than reinforcing the hierarchical relations they have modeled in their respective households.

Martha Howard recounts putting Junior to bed and overhearing a conversation that, in her words, "gave me a start."

MRS. RICHARDS: [*Fading in, acidly*] Well, my dear, your son certainly seemed interested in your cook's son.
MOTHER: Oh, that's quite natural. All young boys idolize soldiers in uniform.
MRS. RICHARDS: Yes . . . but he doesn't seem to realize that your cook's son is a Negro!
MOTHER: Mrs. Richards, I don't think there's anything to fear in that. Martha is a Negro, but she is also an American woman . . . and the mother of a very intelligent boy who would be a credit to any parent.
MRS. RICHARDS: Well, I wouldn't encourage that kind of relationship in my home.[51]

Martha relates that she was "stunned" by such a frank discussion of color, which had never before taken place in her presence. The next day, she overhears a follow-up conversation between Mr. Millburn and his son to which she "didn't mean to listen" but had to recall, because "he was harpin' on that color question again." Mr. Millburn tries to explain to Junior that "Charlie is a very good, nice person, but not white . . . and therefore not in the same class." Junior doesn't understand, so he proposes another scenario:

> FATHER: Let me put it this way, son. How would you like it, if I took Martha to the movies tonight?
> JUNIOR: What's playing?
> FATHER: [*Raising voice*] Now, what difference does that make?!—if I took a Negro to the movies, we would be ostracized by polite society! Nobody would play with you anymore.[52]

These dispiriting impressions combine to persuade Howard to quit her job. When Millicent questions why, she responds, "Ask Mr. Millburn . . . he can tell you. Or talk to your son . . . Junior will tell you." Unbeknownst to her employers, Martha Howard's position in the household has made her intimately aware of the bigotry that members of polite society attempt to cultivate in their children. Like any woman subordinated to the role of "Mammy," she accepted the limitations on her opportunities in life, but the confrontation this episode stages reveals that as an "American woman," her tolerance has limits, as well. Her exit culminates with a defiant statement of solidarity and affection.

> MARTHA: [*Choked up*] I have worked for you for ten years to the day. I never got too much pay. I came here in the depression 'cause I couldn't do no better. I stayed on and did my work—and you all seemed to like me. . . . Workin' here, I couldn't look after my own son right. I gave you most of my time . . . day and night . . . whenever you asked me to do extra things like that dinner last night and even when you didn't ask me. I wasn't in love with the work . . . but I tried to do a good day's work an' not complain.
> MOTHER: Yes, we're perfectly satisfied with you, Martha . . .
> MARTHA: [*Continuing as though uninterrupted*] I always liked your boy. He's a good boy. I treated him like I did my own . . . But after what I just heard Mr. Millburn tell your boy . . . I don't belong here!
> FATHER: [*Amazed*] You heard what I told Junior?
> MARTHA: Only by accident. I was comin' up the stairs, the door was open . . . anyway, I'm glad to know how you feel.
> MOTHER: What now, what did you tell Junior, Frederick?

MARTHA: You had nothin' against me, Mr. Millburn, but the things you told your son only helps to turn his mind against me an' my race . . . people who's done nothin' wrong to you.

FATHER: I only tried to show him . . . to try and explain to him . . . Well, you know, Martha . . .

MARTHA: Yes, I know, Mr. Millburn. An' *I'm* sorry for you because you're teachin' your own flesh and blood to have prejudice.[53]

Martha holds her ground despite self-centered interruptions from the Millburns because communicating her dissatisfaction is more important to the scene than considering their valuation of her place in the household. Ever sensitive to the differential significance of the actors' performances for members of its racially mixed audience, Ottley has structured the Millburns' dialogue to expose fault lines within their domestic sphere. Frederick is amazed to realize that the woman working in his home hears his conversations; Millicent is suddenly forced to reckon with the knowledge that the household help she relies on constitutes an alternative frame of reference for lessons about socialization that are taking place within her home but outside of her influence.

Martha Howard leaves without explaining herself further to the Millburns or their child, leaving them to discern what to do with her judgment. The drama concludes after Martha Howard informs the audience that she has found a job sewing in a parachute factory. She encounters Junior again when he comes to visit the house she has rented with her newfound earnings. He compliments her fine dress, and she invites him into her home with the acknowledgment, "In my house friends are always welcome."[54] Although their reconciliation might appear foreordained by Junior's youthful egalitarian idealism, the details about his parents to which Howard has borne witness suggest that the child would have to resist considerable normative pressure to work toward a relationship of mutual respect with a woman like Martha. When she invites him into her own home as a friend, Howard is exercising the autonomy she enjoys in a state of freedom from economic dependency and domestic security. She frames the implications of her departure from the Millburns' household on similar terms with respect to her son, noting that, "I think he must have known, though, that something was wrong. You can't fool bright young people. And even if I must say it myself, Charlie is a bright boy. I told him that I wanted a job in a war plant, that I wanted to be part of this war too." Interpolating Georgette Harvey's rendition of the anti-Mammy in this episode into the wider narrative of a multiracial working class fighting to redefine democracy marks it as an iconoclastic performance worthy of the new world.

No Green Pastures

The appearance of *New World A-Coming* on the radio integrated the audience, in a way, by exposing listeners and readers from different segments of the public to aspects of culture that were of mutual interest. Two episodes demonstrating this effect were "The Story of Negro Humor," from April 1944, and "The American Negro Theatre," from December of that year. These programs synthesized different modes of writing, music, and performance to showcase Black artists fulfilling Horace Cayton's urgent demand to bring the concerns of the race to white folks' attention.

"The Story of Negro Humor" dramatized a piece by Langston Hughes that had first appeared in *Common Ground* magazine.[55] Ottley was credited with adapting the script, and Mitchell Grayson directed. Canada Lee acted as the narrator, speaking in the first person, as Hughes. *Common Ground* was a publication of the Common Council for American Unity, a group, founded to facilitate the assimilation of European immigrants, that promoted the same agenda of multiethnic unity as the Citywide Citizens' Committee on Harlem during the war.[56] With this dramatization, *New World* traded on the reputation of one of the most successful Negro authors of the era. The original title was "White Folks Do the Funniest Things," but the content of the episode preserves the relation at the heart of Negro humor: Black folks laugh at the irrational situations that arise out of segregationist social conventions. The series of vignettes making up the story lampoon white people for going to ridiculous lengths to avoid social proximity with Negroes, from a Virginia roadside shop that cut a hole in its wall to sell to Black patrons, which Hughes describes as "so absurd as to belong in *Alice in Wonderland*," to an incident when a white man sat opposite Hughes in a train's dining car only to leap from his seat and flee the car "as though he had sat down in front of a lion by mistake."[57] Stringing together these moments with his own baritone version of the author's wry chuckle, Lee connects such seemingly trivial indignities to others that betray their underlying significance as sequelae of second-class citizenship.

Like the poignancy of the blues, the dark humor of Jim Crow emerges when suffering gives way to amusement. Hughes sources a particularly affecting story to the late Negro scholar Robert Moton, the president of the Tuskegee Institute. In the radio version, Lee digresses from the presentation of Moton's account to provide context that Hughes hadn't included in print:

> LEE (AS HUGHES): Before I retell it, I think that certain factors should be explained. You see in the south, if a white woman were to be seen shaking hands with a Negro, the Negro might worry he'd very well be whisked off to jail and tried on all sorts of false charges. That is the unwritten law of the south, and that is the fact.

As the story goes, Dr. Moton had just deboarded a train when he heard a woman's scream—she was falling from the train to the platform! The radio episode verbalizes her plaintive cry: "Help! I'm falling!" The action continues in the text thus:

> Naturally his first impulse as a man was to reach out his arms and catch her—but when he looked up and saw that she was a white woman, he dropped his arms. At this point in his story the student audience roared with laughter. Every one of those colored kids knew that for a black man to catch a white woman in his arms in Atlanta might mean a lynching party. . . . The woman landed head first on the concrete platform. At any rate, she did not have a chance to cry, "Rape." So Dr. Moton lived to tell the tale.[58]

While the radio version prefaces the incident to let white listeners know how a Black audience would understand what was at stake, it omits the explicit statement from the text that the woman in question might have accused the storyteller of rape. In both renditions, the injured party falls victim to the conflict between the Negro scholar's "first impulse as a man," on the one hand, and the demands of his inferior social station, on the other.

The episode becomes more than the sum of its written and spoken parts thanks to Josh White and his guitar providing musical interludes throughout the program. An announcement by Gordon Heath at the beginning of the episode invokes the same celebrity status for White as Langston Hughes and Canada Lee. White was a well-known folk singer who had first made his name with the blues guitarist moniker "Pinewood Tom" in the 1930s. His music was successful on the "race records" market, and he made a friend of Paul Robeson while working on a stage production about the Black folk hero John Henry.[59] He played and recorded with antifascist folk singers, bringing him to the attention of New York's avant-garde café society, and he enjoyed both public and personal regard from the Roosevelts; Eleanor Roosevelt was godmother to his son Josh Jr.[60] His musical stylings round out the blend of provocation and entertainment essential to the *New World*'s brand of socially minded broadcasting. It was one of several engagements with radio drama in his career and not his last association with *New World A-Coming*.

Songs by White punctuate the vignettes in "The Story of Negro Humor" and provide transitions between them. After the dining car incident, White strums some alternating high and low notes that begin to gain momentum as they build toward a bass line that will repeat throughout the song. The pattern mimics the chugging exhaust of a steam engine. It is the start of a song titled "Jim Crow Train," featuring the lyrics "Can't you hear that train whistle blow? Oh I wish that train wasn't Jim Crow" and "Stop Jim Crow so I can ride this train / Black and white both riding side by side."[61] This song came from White's 1941 record *Southern Exposure*, which included other thematically appropriate songs like "Bad Housing Blues" and "Defense Factory Blues," which set paradigmatic encounters with wartime discrimination to music, much like Ottley and Hughes had narrativized them. Later in the broadcast, White sings "Freedom's Road," a song written by Hughes that transmits the synergy between the two artists.[62] The lyrics enjoin, "Black and white together, unite and fight!"

The final song in the episode has the refrain "What is America to me? A name? A land? The flag I see? / A certain word / democracy?"[63] Heath identifies the song by its subtitle, with the question it poses, "What Is America to Me," but White recorded it as, "The House I Live In," which was his answer. He repeats "The house I live in" at the start of several verses, detailing that "America, to me" consists of, "The farmer and the worker / the sailor on the sea," "My neighbors, white and Black / The people who just came here / or from generations back." He populates his America with specific historical subjects, such as "The words of old Abe Lincoln / of Jefferson and Paine / of Washington and Jackson / and the task that still remains," incorporating canonical figures into the utopian narrative of an unfinished democratic project whose full enunciation "still remains" to be accomplished. Similarly, by rhyming "Our little bridge at Concord / where freedom's fight began" with "Our Gettysburg and Midway / and the story of Bataan," White emplots the Pacific in the domestic and international construction of American national interests through war, linking his contemporaries in "freedom's fight" to their forebears who won the Revolution and preserved the Union. The assortment of songs in the broadcast complements Hughes's story, which positions the narrator as a reluctant critic of white America disappointed by the betrayal of noble ideals. Rather than expressing their criticism through invective, however, the humorous reveries and blues-inflected folk songs buoy the listener's spirits by coaxing them to laugh and sing along.

Another episode ushers in the *New World* from behind the scenes in the performing arts. "The American Negro Theatre" parlays the popularity of the play *Anna Lucasta* on Broadway into an occasion to relate the history of the Harlem-based troupe responsible for it, portrayed here as a story of democratic progress in the arts sector. *Anna Lucasta* was the American Negro Theatre's (ANT) realization of an unpublished script by Polish American Philip Yordan, transposing economic and moral themes from the immigrant experience to rural and urban Negro life.[64] It was a financial success (leading to controversy over who could claim credit for adapting the original playwright's work) and a critical milestone. In the episode of *New World* that takes up the subject, a fictionalized journalist interviews ANT members after a performance of *Anna Lucasta*. The actors, including Fred O'Neal, Abram Hill, Hilda Simms, and Ruby Dee, portray themselves. The journalist character is named Grace Thompson, and her employer is a generic magazine called *The Digest*. Neither her racial identity nor that of her publication's target audience is specified. But the episode's format constructs the backstory of *Anna Lucasta* and its stars for the interest of the predominantly white Broadway audience and the white majority of radio listeners. It takes the form of a frame narrative, with Thompson observing an emergent phenomenon—a Black presence on Broadway—and delving into its roots in Harlem, the WPA, and American Negro efforts at self-determination.

The episode initially promises intimate conversations in the humble dressing rooms of some overnight sensations, as Thompson asks O'Neal the straightforward question, "How did *Anna Lucasta* happen?" By invoking the title, she leaves its referent open to definition: *Anna Lucasta* could mean the text, the lucrative opportunity for Negro actors and their enterprising producers, the stage production she has just witnessed, the eponymous tragic heroine, or O'Neal's own experience. Like the other interviewees who will follow, he responds to her question by invoking the actions that made the event possible, recounted from his perspective as someone who took part in them. His reply is, "Well, that takes us back to the very beginning, I suppose, to the start of the American Negro Theatre." For his purposes, the interview is an occasion to frame the hit production as a triumph for the ANT and its goals, which he traces to the company's founding. Setting the scene for his early conversations with its co-founder Abram Hill, he explains that they intended to "create the opportunity to show Negro life as it really exists and to overcome the usual lazy, comical, superstitious Hollywood characters." In familiar fashion, their critique cites Hollywood as a source of problems because of its undignified portrayals of Negro life. The ANT, like *New World A-Coming*, seeks solutions by devoting itself to the truth, instead.

When O'Neal revisits the scene of the ANT's founding, he offers some insights into the working conditions of artists in the Black community. Discrimination was a given; roles open to Negro actors were few and far between. However, even if they could obtain a part in a production that welcomed them, showing up to rehearse and perform was no small demand. One woman asks, "You know, most of us have jobs during the day, and how can we work in the theatre at night?" Her frank question is predicated on some structural factors accounting for Black artists' absence from the stage: In the twentieth century, virtually all Black people need to work to sustain themselves and their families. The uncertainty of theater, where productions lose money and performers spend months at a time out of work, made it impractical as a livelihood. It was notable for this recognition to come from a female character in an all-Black setting. Her voice reminds the audience that race differentiates the way gender roles and jobs map onto class and culture. Black women's performances continually reinforce considerations like this throughout the series. Abram Hill, to whom the question was addressed, concedes that taking part in the ANT would simply mean "long hours" earning wages and then "perfecting ourselves as actors, directors, technicians, writers," in succession, on a daily basis. Committing to such an arduous way of life with no respite from the demands of everyday labor distinguished the ANT's members from their bohemian and bourgeois counterparts in the theater world.

The practical aspects of their working-class background linked the ANT with other elements in the arts in the Popular Front era, while their racial separatism, born out of necessity, gave them an intracommunal ethos characteristic of the Black radical tradition.[65] Rather than digressing from his story to inform Thompson about its intellectual and social contexts, however, O'Neal continues to narrate the ANT's story from the same grounded, intimate setting. At their first gathering to consider starting the theater company, O'Neal and his peers agreed that they would have to raise "a few hundred dollars" by themselves. Rifling through their pockets and purses, the eight of them pool their money and count it: six cents! A chorus of laughter gives way to a jaunty musical transition. The brass instrumental that plays is the chorus from "The Gold Diggers Song," wordlessly evoking its refrain: "We're in the money . . . " The allusion to the Depression movie musical *Gold Diggers of 1933*, a mainstay of mass entertainment in the era, invites the audience to share the ANT founders' downtrodden but plucky sentiment.

Other subjects of Thompson's twice-told tale reiterate the pattern of using personal anecdotes to appeal to universal values. When she speaks with Hilda Simms, the star of *Anna Lucasta,* Simms presents her with the story of a crew member, to whom she refers as Joe, who works on lighting and electricity for their productions. To explain who he is, Simms relates a conversation between Joe and Fred O'Neal that subsequently plays out as part of the program. O'Neal asks where Joe learned his trade, recalling that he came aboard with prior experience in electrical work. "Yeah, it had something to do with electricity,"

Joe leads. He reveals that he'd come from Cleveland, where he repaired and collected coins from pinball machines in establishments around the city. While it may sound innocuous today, the machines were one of many revenue streams for "a mob of gangsters in Cleveland," as Joe describes them. His employers would, in his words, "just as soon shoot your head off as say good morning to you!" Though he earned far more money before, the young man cherished the legitimate occupation that stagecraft provided.

> SIMMS: Imagine, a boy like that being rescued from a criminal environment and adjusting himself into a well-balanced life for the future. Isn't that something?
> THOMPSON: Where is he now?
> SIMMS: Where are all the healthy young men today?
> THOMPSON: In the service?
> SIMMS: Yes, overseas. He's in the medical unit in the South Pacific! He writes to everybody at the theatre all the time and we send him all the news of what we're doing, it's remarkable . . .

Placing Joe on a path to redemption that ends with wartime service renders his story as heroic as possible for public consumption. When Simms shares this parable with Thompson, she is portraying the ANT in the best possible light by demonstrating its positive impact beyond the arts. While Thompson came seeking to extol the good fortune of Negro actors, her subjects consistently associate themselves with a higher moral purpose than their own prosperity.

Recreating Simms's imaginary dressing room in the WMCA studio facilitates visits by certain other interviewees who just happen to be in the wings while Thompson is present. Her conversation with Simms gets interrupted by a man's voice calling, "Hilda?" Simms replies, "Oh, that's Canada!" to which Thompson responds, incredulously, "Canada *Lee?!*" The contrived spontaneity of this encounter encourages regular listeners to forget, momentarily, that they are hearing a broadcast in which Canada Lee appears every week. Instead, like new audience members, they can indulge in the fantasy that Thompson's reporting represents: a behind-the-scenes discussion with celebrities from stage and screen. Rather than talk about himself, Lee defers to his comrades with the endorsement, "The American Negro Theatre is the star of this show, and that's as it should be!" Though *Anna Lucasta* was the initial spark of interest for her assignment, and an interview with Canada Lee would be a story in itself, by the time she meets him, Thompson concedes, "I see you're not going to talk about *Anna Lucasta* either." Accordingly, Lee asks her a question, instead: "Did Hilda tell you about the case of the broken record?" Intrigued by the phrase, Thompson asks, "What's that, a new detective story?" Though the title evokes a shift in genre, the vignette that follows is not a mystery but rather, as Lee describes it, "it's a story of a girl's sacrifice to keep the theatre going."

As Lee launches into the story in question, he explains that the girl's name was Georgia Wilson. His voice, in the present, becomes softer and softer, just as another speaker becomes audible from out of the past. Wilson's first words take the form of a crescendo repeating the name, "Fred, Fred . . . " She is attempting to get the attention of Fred O'Neal. The two of them play themselves reenacting a crisis in the early days of the American Negro Theatre. The are fretting over what to do upon noticing that some records have fallen from a shelf and broken into pieces. Those records were the sound effects for that evening's show. Wilson warns they will have to buy new records, or the play would be incomplete. O'Neal laments, "New ones? You know how much money there is in the treasury? Nothing. Not a dime. In fact we owe everybody." Wilson professes to know where they can obtain duplicates at a cost of six dollars—a hundred times the initial endowment of the entire theater company. Fred replies with what he takes to be a rhetorical question, since he knows everybody in the company is flat broke: "Where are we going to get six dollars?" But Wilson, defiant, gestures to the antique ring she is wearing: a bequest from her mother and grandmother before her. She ponders, suggestively, that the pawn shop will not close until six o'clock. Over O'Neal's protestations, Wilson insists, "We don't get those records, Fred, we can't give a performance tonight, and the theatre will get a bad name! No, I won't have any more nonsense from you, Fred, I just won't have the theatre get a bad name . . . I know I don't have to do it, but I want to do it!" O'Neal calls out, not believing that she is actually headed to the pawn shop, but she marches out of the scene. Trumpets flare in appreciation. Trailing the quick brass salute, as if they are scoring Fred O'Neal's emotions as he witnesses his friend's self-sacrifice, clarinets repeat a romantic phrase adagio. The show must go on.

The episode follows its conceit to a logical conclusion by portraying Thompson's decision to publish a story about the American Negro Theatre's treasured principles rather than their exceptional Broadway hit. The episode maintains *New World A-Coming*'s weekly affirmation of Negro character by using fictitious news coverage of a cultural breakthrough to frame a set of personal reflections in which pillars of the community perform decency on a quotidian level. Whether the war occupies the foreground or the background of its constituents' lives, the Negro citizenry envisioned in the series abounds in steadfastness and self-esteem. Black America endures hardship without resignation and expresses a sense of entitlement to a future free from persistent injustice.

Through the radio broadcasts examined throughout this chapter and reinforcement in the Black press, the vernacular of a "new world a' coming" tapped into a broader sentiment than any single publication or performance. On Monday, June 26, 1944, Madison Square Garden played host to tens of thousands rallying in the name of Negro freedom and victory for Roosevelt.[66] Its goals included reelecting the president, making the FEPC permanent, eliminating the poll tax, and desegregating unions, all under the banner of defeating the Axis. The Negro Labor Victory Committee, a coalition with membership representing CIO, AFL, and railroad workers, had designated June 18 as "Negro Victory Sunday" a year beforehand and planned an annual parade. They had launched a campaign to register fifty thousand Black voters by Negro History Week of 1944, and in January they took part in convening an interracial symposium in Mount Vernon, New York, on the topic of "The Negro's Place in the New World A-Coming."[67] Their spectacular plans only gained momentum with the coming of D-Day. The centerpiece of the rally was a dramatic presentation on a star-shaped stage, titled "New World A-Coming: An Original Pageant of Hope." Houghton Mifflin granted the rally organizers permission to use the title of Ottley's book free of charge.[68] Moran Weston, the "Labor Forum" columnist for the *Amsterdam News* and field secretary of the Labor Victory Committee representing the Newspaper Guild, was responsible for organizing the rally.

To write and direct the pageant, Weston identified Owen Dodson, a Yale graduate and veteran of the Federal Theatre Project who had contributed poetry to *Opportunity, New Masses*, and the post-Harlem Renaissance literary magazine *Challenge*. Dodson had also produced plays to boost Negro sailors' morale during his brief time in the Navy. He would go on to become a beloved director of theater at Howard University. Following a Broadway salute featuring Paul Robeson and cast members from his *Othello*, the pageant would showcase scenes and songs on the braided themes of unity and victory. The presentation featured Canada Lee; Will Geer, a star of NBC's *Cavalcade of America*, who had also appeared in early episodes of *New World*; Pearl Primus, a pioneering interpreter of African dance; Josh White and his guitar; and Marie Young, a singer and actor who had appeared in WPA productions of *Androcles and the Lion* and Orson Welles's *Macbeth*, as well as Broadway and cabaret shows.[69] After the opening number, the ensemble enacted their roles as soldiers for the allies advancing on the enemy. Three soldiers representing China carried three Chinese flags; four soldiers representing Great Britain carry its flag and those of Canada, Australia, and South Africa; three Russians carry three Russian flags; and for America, "One Negro, one white, and one Mexican with American and Mexican flags run through the spot." The Negro soldier recounts a dream he had to his peers: "Last night after the battle I dreamed about a good world. A new one."[70]

The Negro soldier's dream throws the setting into a musical, transhistorical reverie. Depredations of racism, war, and alienation play out before the audience, and figures from the past and present appear onstage to mete out justice against them. A mob in Klan robes calls for book burning, lynching, and denigration of Jews. Relief comes in the form of a "council of the common man" assembled to pass judgment on the vandals who desecrate churches, synagogues, and cemeteries. When crowds of common folk demand their reward for turning in the perpetrators, the character designated People's Leader proclaims, "Freedom. Freedom to worship, freedom to speak, freedom from fear and want. The Freedom promised at Teheran. Freedom to build the new world that's a-coming!" Apparitions of Sojourner Truth and of the naval cook who became a hero at Pearl Harbor, Doris "Dorie" Miller, "in a white sailor suit," invoke their heavenly camaraderie with John Brown. The chorus sings a refrain that Dodson has titled "Dorie Miller":

> There are millions of Dorie Millers living
> And millions of Dorie Millers dead;
> They are signs, signals, tokens that free men
> will rise and claim this earth again![71]

The choir is joined by Thomas Paine rising from the grave. The Negro soldier remembers aloud that Paine had said, "'Where freedom is not, there is my country.'" And Paine affirms, "I tell you freedom must be renewed in every age, must be fought for, must have enemies in order to see itself clear. Black soldiers who are forbidden to salute their own flag in some parts of their own land must believe this." Cementing the association of patriotism with antifascism, the action culminates in a mock trial at which the Judge decrees a sentence: "White Supremacy, Jim Crow, Jew-Murderers, you are dying every minute. I condemn you to die now!"

The dream sequence occupies an allegorical time and space onstage, where living and dead figures articulate the Negro soldier's desire for justice. Before the pageant transitions back to a setting consistent with the circumstances of the present, however, the characters portraying ancestral figures summon contemporary artists to sound the death knell to the old world. The narrator bids, "Now, Tom Paine, walk out of your grave. Sojourner Truth, climb out of your grave. Dorie Miller, swim out of your grave." The physicality of the manner of movement attributed to each character's return from the grave heightens attention to their deaths and burials. In the liminal role assigned to her, Sojourner Truth directs the in-scene and offstage audience alike to "Look yonder, there Pearl Primus come to dance the evil down in good." Scripted directions indicate that her dance occupies the stage. Afterward, Truth declares, "And there Duke Ellington come to praise freedom." Ellington's orchestra would play the theme "New World A-Comin.'"

Like the radio series and the pageant that both used its title, Ellington never intended for "New World A-Comin'" to reproduce in musical form the book that had inspired it. Instead, he described his composition as an "anticipation." It was his gesture of appreciation for the hopeful reflection of history and everyday life that he found in the book. He wrote it in 1943, the year that elapsed between his first and second concerts at Carnegie Hall.[72] He had begun that year with the premiere of *Black, Brown, and Beige*, which he described as a "tone parallel to the history of the American Negro."[73] His homage to Ottley's text followed, in part, a strategy he had innovated with this earlier work. It was emotionally and rhythmically responsive to its source material, subjective, and moody. There were no vocals, although Dodson would write lyrics for a separate piece by the same title in the 1944 pageant:

We've buried Jim Crow. We'll keep him down;
White Supremacy has no crown.
with hand matching hand against the foe
We'll rise in a brighter world we know.
We know,
We know
There's a new world a-coming,
Come on,
Come on,
Come on
And on and on and on![74]

Whereas *Black, Brown, and Beige* spread its three named phases over an hour's duration, Ellington devised "New World" as a "twelve minute performance for piano with band."[75] Regarding "New World" as a tone parallel to Ottley's book, as the *New York Times* did in one announcement of Ellington's December concert, encourages the listener to compare it to *Black, Brown, and Beige.*[76] After hearing its debut, Dan Burley, in the *Amsterdam News*, surmised that "'New World A' Comin' was spotty . . . although the theme has infinite possibilities, if developed further. As it was, it didn't compete with 'Black, Brown, and Beige.'"[77] Insofar as they recognize its inspired approach, the comparisons weigh in favor of using the tune as a theme for the radio series and as a praise song in the pageant.

Ellington quoted the closing lines from Ottley's book in his memoir, *Music Is My Mistress*: "Ottley looked forward to better conditions for the Negro after World War II, his final optimistic statement being: 'In spite of selfish interests, a new world is a-coming with the sweep and fury of the Resurrection.'" Those words, "With the sweep and fury of the Resurrection," commenced each episode of the radio series, accompanied by the melody that repeats throughout Ellington's theme to trumpet the arrival of something much anticipated. In the orchestra leader's words, "I visualized this new world as a place in the distant future where there would be no war, no greed, no categorization, no nonbelievers, where love was unconditional, and no pronoun was good enough for God." Years later, while dedicating a performance of the song to his compatriots rebuilding a cathedral in Goutelas, France, he invoked the same utopian sentiment: "The title refers to a future place, on earth, at sea, or in the air, where there will be no war, no greed, no categorization, and where love is unconditional, and where there is no pronoun good enough for God."[78] Though they differed with respect to how far away the new world might be and how to present it to the public, Ellington, Ottley, and Dodson all endeavored to close the distance.

This chapter has considered the intellectual and rhetorical approaches to attaining double victory that *New World A-Coming* realized in radio drama. The research and reporting that formed that text and the creative interventions that followed its example attest to the immanence of critical consciousness in African Americans' social and political attitudes. The project of a new world rooted in freedom for Black America appealed to communists, millenarians, cynics, and stalwart believers in the doctrine of American liberal democracy. The war that brought them into a mass coalition aligned with the American state would not sever them from their ultimate strivings. The future called them, and their answers resound throughout the passage to utopia.

2
Silence Is Golden
Samuel Delany in The Star-Pit

Samuel R. Delany is among the living authors recognized by his peers in the Science Fiction and Fantasy Writers of America as a "Grand Master" for his lifetime contributions to the field.[1] He has written dozens of novels and short stories; autobiographical works including a memoir in graphic novel form; literary essays and social criticism; pornography; published diaries, letters, and interviews; and a few issues of *Wonder Woman*, and he has taught at universities. *The Star-Pit*, subject of this chapter, is a Delany novella that first appeared in the February 1967 issue of the science fiction magazine *Worlds of Tomorrow*. It was reprinted in Judith Merril's *SF 12* in 1968, an anthology that brought it to more readers' attention, and Delany would include the story in *Driftglass*, the first collection of his fiction, in 1971. But before those reappearances, Delany shared the magazine featuring *The Star-Pit* with his friend Baird Searles, who worked at the Pacifica radio station in New York. Searles was impressed enough with the story to enter into conversation with Delany about adapting his work for the program of dramatic productions he was directing for the station. They embarked on an exciting collaboration, drawing in performers from the bohemian Greenwich Village artists' scene where Delany lived at the time, with the young author himself cast in the leading role as the story's narrator and protagonist.

This radio play is a rare sample directly out of the formative environment that produced one of the twentieth century's most exemplary writers. Readers can debate whether science fiction is the proper registry for Delany's continuing contributions to literature; it is not adequate, according to the author himself. Yet this play, like the man behind it, contains multitudes: It includes many voices, relies on many technical skills, draws in a diverse audience, and opens

Figure 3: Samuel Delany (standing), in 1966, at the World Science Fiction Convention in Cleveland, Ohio. Photographed by Jay Kay Klein. Robert Silverberg seated next to Delany. In next row, from left: Karen Anderson, Norman Spinrad, Poul Anderson, unidentified woman, and Alva Rogers (dark glasses). *Source*: Jay Kay Klein photographs and papers on science fiction fandom, University of California, Riverside, Library, Special Collections and University Archives.

onto multiple futures in the arts, science, and commerce. In addition to indexing these many repertoires of meaning—far beyond the genre in which the story was written and published, and beyond the medium in which it was broadcast—*The Star-Pit* invokes a variety of overlapping, structured interpersonal contexts as its social milieu. As part of the broader assemblage of literary adaptation, performance, broadcasting, speculation, and utopian thought that I am calling *Audiofuturism*, it is a notable document of multidisciplinary artists and audiences actively reimagining social relations through historically specific modes of mediation. The same is true for all the works in this study. In this instance, the story and its mediation tell us about queerness, dis/ability, and the challenge of reckoning with human difference before the availability of adequate language to describe it. *The Star-Pit* employs language and other sounds to posit ways of being human that might elude language as their condition of possibility.

The Star-Pit, as a print narrative and radio play, is a slice of life portraying the experiences of an Earth-born, heavy-drinking Black American spaceship mechanic named Vyme as he moves through radically different but intersecting social circles on the space colonies that have become the home of the human race in the future. The Star-pit is a place on the proverbial edge of the galaxy where Vyme has found work tending to vessels that he and most of his peers can never fly. It is a setting for people who have exhausted their social mobility; on the margin between everything and everywhere else, it is possible to come from anywhere and enter into new relationships with anyone. This makes it an ideal setting for people to test their presumptions about one another and learn from their differences.

In an essay titled "Notes on *The Star-Pit*," Delany recounts his novella's publication in *Worlds of Tomorrow* and the subsequent casting, recording, editing, and broadcast of the radio play on WBAI 99.5 FM.[2] After discovering that essay online, I followed its leads to the Pacifica Radio Archives, where the radio institution disseminates the product of a GRAMMY Foundation grant to preserve their unique recordings, including those produced from 1966 to 1969 for a program called the Mind's Eye Theatre. This series included original works on contemporary themes, poetry and experimental wordplay, dramatized readings of historical documents like the letters of Julius and Ethel Rosenberg, and adaptations of other speculative fiction texts by Theodore Sturgeon, Arthur C. Clarke, and Mervyn Peake. Delany's work fits comfortably among their eclectic offerings. The audio that was originally broadcast for the Mind's Eye Theatre program on November 26, 1967, appears online in two parts.[3]

At the time Delany wrote *The Star-Pit*, Soviet and US rivals were scrambling into low-Earth orbit with chemical propulsion and nuclear ulterior motives. Within a couple years, thanks to the genius of human computers, astronauts would land on the moon and return safely to Earth. As we took that small step in real life, Delany's protagonist, Vyme, was building the machine that would represent another giant leap in the future: a spacecraft capable of traveling to other galaxies. The epigraph to the original print publication of *The Star-Pit* reads: "*We were trapped in the tiny, billion-star backyard of our own galaxy—while the golden roamed the universe!*"[4] This line never appears beyond the story's title page in the magazine, nor is it present in Merril's anthology, nor in Delany's short story collection *Driftglass*. However, a version of the statement appears on one paperback edition of the novella: a 1989 Tor "double" in which it's packaged with John Varley's novel *Tango Charlie & Foxtrot Romeo*.[5] These peritexts indicate that the novella's editors and its potential readers could identify "golden" as the name for some persons who enjoy a sort of privilege that instills envy. During the narrator's lifetime, a new facet of human difference, correlated with mental health but not quite congruent with it, would come to eclipse the race and gender and even the home planets of the persons capable of intergalactic travel. Those who could make the journey into intergalactic space were called "golden."

The plot of *The Star-Pit* involves Vyme's relationship to golden from outside their ranks. He is a member of a society that depends on intergalactic commerce, and the presence of golden is uniquely valuable. Yet he is not the principal source of the story's strong impression that golden evoke a sort of jealousy. That sentiment is most pronounced with one of Vyme's intimates, Ratlit, a prodigious teenaged writer and social misfit who reminds Vyme of his long-lost son. While Vyme grew up on Earth before golden were discovered and never developed an appetite for their exotic travels, Ratlit wants to explore the great expanse of intergalactic space that has unfolded within his short lifetime. He desires the unlimited liberties that golden seem to enjoy, and he feels they do not deserve it. He will stop at nothing to obtain their freedom for himself, even though he is not one of them.

The unattainable status of golden only adds to the fascination quotient of the trope. The plot of the novella revolves in part around the tension between its desirable and undesirable implications, and the radio play seizes on this tension to dramatic effect. Virtually all the characters we meet in the story regard golden with a mix of pity and disdain. Underlying their attitude, however, is the wish to do what only golden can: to know what it is like to travel between galaxies and live to tell the tale. When Vyme first learned of the possibility of intergalactic travel and the people who could accomplish it, the announcement came in the form of a mixed message. The scene might have helped convince Delany and Searles that *The Star-Pit* was ripe for adaptation to radio, because it involved Vyme listening to a news broadcast. In a flashback to his education on Earth, Vyme recalls hearing the voice of a scientific commission say:

> "As a ship leaves the galactic rim, 'reality' breaks down and causes insanity and eventual death for any crew. . . . Yet, just when we had to face the black limit of intergalactic space, bright resources glittered within. Some few of us whose sense of reality has been shattered by infantile, childhood, or prenatal trauma, whose physiological and psychological orientation makes life in our interstellar society painful or impossible—not all, but a few of these golden . . . " at which point there was static, or the gentleman coughed, " . . . can make the crossing and return." The name golden, *sans* noun, stuck.[6]

Through this incomplete trumpet of revelation, the initial naming of golden confers them a sense of opportunity burdened with mystification.

The irretrievable origin of the term "golden" persists throughout the story and into its adaptation for radio. No character finds the noun that golden modifies or even so much as looks for it; we never hear from the head of the commission again. It feels fitting to withhold the unutterable referent to which the descriptor applies: Being golden is a miracle, but it is also a curse. It coincides with disadvantages in psychological and emotional well-being that limit the life chances of members of the larger group to whom all golden belong. As the announcement made clear, golden are a fraction of that segment of the population "whose physiological or psychological orientation makes life in our interstellar society painful or impossible." Vyme refers to the first golden identified in the media disparagingly as "psychological freaks with some incredible hormone imbalance in their systems." The circumstances of life among the stars, for the vast majority of people like Vyme and Ratlit who are not golden, brings them face-to-face with the limits of humanity and the costs of straining against their boundaries.

The broken syntax that gives rise to "golden" as a fictitious epithet for potential space travelers makes this act of naming especially compelling to hear in the radio play. According to his recollection, Vyme is not sure whether "there was static" or "the gentleman coughed" between using "golden" as an adjective and completing his sentence:

> *Not all but a few of these golden* ________ *can make the crossing and return.*

In the broadcast, Delany and his collaborators reproduce the ambiguity that prevented Vyme from hearing what golden refers to. The spokesman was already a bit congested when he began reporting the discovery, and he clears his throat a few times. Then, adding to the uncertainty of his statement, the speaker's voice devolves into a coughing fit while both static and the voice of Vyme, saying the line "there was static *or* the gentleman coughed," compete for intelligibility—as we hear static *and* the gentleman's coughing.[7] Even though the story takes place in the distant future, persistent problems of communication place the listening public of Vyme's era in the same predicament as listeners to the WBAI broadcast, then, or the recording, now. The unreliability of transmitting sounds and their meanings leaves us all wondering why the newly defined idiosyncrasy that will characterize representatives of the human race to other galaxies should be called golden.

This Place Which Is Not One

Gold is an element. Golden is a descriptor denoting a figurative or literal association with gold's properties: its color, rarity, luster, fungibility, its comparative, ideal, or superlative value. In *The Star-Pit*, golden is a *catachresis*: a figure of speech that transfers the meaning of a word or phrase in its proper context to an unfamiliar situation where there is no equivalent term. As the modifier for a subject that can never be named any other way, golden communicates the unspeakable peculiarity of the circumstances to which it applies.

As Lisa Freinkel, glossing her extensive explorations of rhetoric via Shakespeare, defines the term, catachresis is "the use of a borrowed word for something that does not have a name of its own":

> Catachresis . . . invokes a world whose contours and contents are already shaped, but not yet named, by language. This is a world that comes to us already articulated and processed by trope, a world chewed up by language before we meaning-makers even arrive on the scene.[8]

The leaves of a book, the heel of a loaf of bread, and the tail of a comet are all catachrestic figures. They appropriate words from the contexts where they seem to occur naturally into others where their appearance is unanticipated, because the context of their application has no suitable terminology except what it can borrow from elsewhere. This form of catachresis makes an association that calls attention to its own imprecision in order to disabuse itself of the task of precision. In a systematic account, "Catachresis—a Metaphor or a Figure in Its Own Right?," Elzbieta Chrzanowska-Kluczewska describes Freinkel's definition as one of several varieties of catachresis: "lexical."[9] Calling this usage "Catachresis One," Chrzanowska-Kluczewska differentiates it from more incongruous turns of phrase that tend toward malapropism. "Catachresis Two" consists of metaphors "marked by the feature of illogicality, often close to absurdity, and generates far-fetched, strained associations."[10] This phenomenon necessarily consists of strikingly uncommon juxtapositions, and it is more likely to be identified with unique turns of phrase invented for poetry than in everyday prose. If Catachresis One verges on "dead metaphor," wherein an expression has become so conventionalized that most speakers can scarcely imagine its meaning literally, Catachresis Two poses the opposite problem, when "it is difficult to find an exact point at which non-catachrestic metaphoric quality ends and Catachresis Two begins."[11] It is our familiarity with the contexts out of which these tropes emerge that lends them dramatic effect when they are transposed into an unexpected, even off-putting frame of reference. For that reason, catachresis is sometimes described as the trope of abuse.

In the late twentieth century, the impropriety of catachresis was subject to reevaluation as part of the transformation of philosophy and rhetoric provoked by critics like Roland Barthes, Jacques Derrida, and Paul de Man. Insofar as catachresis connotes the "misuse" of words, "as in a mixed metaphor, either in error, or for rhetorical effect; this 'misuse' can thus either be deliberate or mistaken."[12] An emphasis on the deliberate misappropriation involved in catachrestic figuration leads critics such as Sianne Ngai, James Berger, and Callie Gardner (quoted here) to recognize that "catachresis, which can be defined as deliberate error put to a rhetorical purpose, might also function as an aesthetic value."[13] The aforementioned critics apply this insight to poetry and to the historical specificity of artistic judgment. They assess how the referents of signs are determined to be appropriate or inappropriate under different social circumstances and what effects result from using a word against its ostensibly "natural" purpose. As artistic experimentation and critical exploration move readers' expectations away from rhetorical conventions respecting the notion of natural, proper meanings in language—figurative language in particular—catachresis has come more sharply into view.

Since his participation in critical debates on speculative fiction in the 1970s, as his writing emerged in multiple genres and across strata that are separated in the marketplace by boundaries of class and education, Delany's reputation for playfully, deliberately recombining mundane vocabulary in order to produce novel meanings has been a hallmark of his creative output.[14] *The Star-Pit* exemplifies this play of invention in its print and audio forms. The radio adaptation amplifies some of the story's most salient catachrestic images by making them audible. In turn, I will discuss how *The Star-Pit* uses choice words to establish a hypothetical frame of reference for meaning making that allows for and even requires phrasing that its readers would regard as catachrestic, but for its genre context. The double-take that ensues when listeners interpret these constructions in the story, and on the radio, is a characteristic experience of the science fiction writing that Delany rehearses throughout his contributions to the genre and its criticism. Closing in on the figure of golden, as an imaginary human variation specific to this fictitious future society and uniquely inflected by the circumstances of its naming, I explain how *The Star-Pit* posits catachresis as instrumental to the way speculative fiction constructs imaginary forms of social difference. The invention of fictitious beings like golden redeploys the language of actually existing forms of identity in order to preserve and simultaneously to undermine their familiar meanings. This deconstruction of the relation between identity and words persists through the double presence of catachresis in writing and sound.

Place has a powerful semantic role in fantastic literature. Tolkien's maps of Middle Earth, Jemisin's geomancy, Lovecraft's multidimensional stratigraphy, and the space Diasporas of Herbert and Le Guin: Each generates an assortment of linguistic innovations for readers to apprehend as we navigate and historicize their respective story-worlds. To some critics, as Tom Shippey points out in "How to Read Science Fiction," these neologisms and "*nova data*" (new information, known by the singular term "novum" from the influential writing of Darko Suvin) are the sine qua non of science fiction.[15] When a novum does not consist of new words but a textually specific novel use for existing words, however, it can take the form of catachresis. Examples abound in the literature: Shippey refers to the "depilatory soap" a character uses instead of shaving in C. M. Kornbluth and Frederik Pohl's *The Space Merchants*, and there are space elevators in Isaac Asimov's *Foundation*, dragonriders in Anne McCaffrey's Pern novels, a heroine with a full-body prosthetic in Masamune Shirow's *Ghost in the Shell*. What links catachresis to these genre-specific innovations, including the figures introduced in *The Star-Pit*, is a sense of place invoked in figurative terms.

The notion that language organizes itself into bounded places—rhetorical situations; speech genres; interpersonal, historical, and political settings; disciplines; categories of subject matter—where some words belong and others don't is foundational to the significance of catachresis. The fantastic constructions of science fiction draw terms with known uses into as-yet unknown applications, projecting them into contexts that have yet to be seen, have never been, or may never come to be. James Berger writes of catachresis that "if one's primary desire is to conceive an unthinkable, to bring an alterity into the lexicon, then one must first build a terminal where all the trains for the unspeakable can discharge their passengers"; that is, the speaker must establish a place at which the as-yet unthinkable can be thought.[16] Catachresis is the expression of that desire, of "the wish enacted in language . . . to reach toward some place, some piece of consciousness or non-consciousness, outside of language."[17] Speculative fiction might invoke a place outside of actually existing language when it invents a neologism, but when it employs catachresis, it locates the referents of the language it uses (abuses, misplaces) outside of actually existing language.

Delany's theoretical and pedagogical work displays assiduous attention to the discursive construction of boundaries—between segments of the literary marketplace, social classes, and speech codes—and he suggests that certain exceptional spaces are intrinsic to reading and writing science fiction.[18] As he discusses in an interview with the SF critic Takayuki Tatsumi for *Science Fiction Eye*, "Science fiction has often taken new ideas of conceptual space, then inflated them with language."[19] Innovative verbalizations of conceptual space form a common ground linking the state of mind where the protagonist of Alfred Bester's *Stars My Destination* experiences synaesthesia (rendered typographically distinct on the printed page), the cyberspace of Gibson's *Neuromancer* and *Count Zero*, the interdimensional "hellrides" of Roger Zelazny's Amber novels, and iconic representations of outer space by Algis Budrys, Robert Heinlein, and A. E. Van Vogt. Outer space in fiction, Delany notes, "began as a kind of subspace that sat next to . . . well, planetary-surface-space."[20] Tatsumi and Delany discuss a similar space constructed by a Zelazny novella, "He Who Shapes," which posits a technology allowing psychoanalysts to participate in their patients' dreams therapeutically. Delany observes that language, or, more precisely, the rules by which language is used, differentiates these subspaces (to which he will subsequently ascribe the name "paraspace") from ordinary space represented in the text:

> The language with which Zelazny talks about the dreams that Render can control is very different from the general narrative voice of his tale in the same way that the language that Gibson uses to discuss moving through cyberspace is different. . . . The original title for "He Who Shapes" was "The Ides of Octember"—which is to say, a figure of rhetorically distorted language. The ides of Octember, you'll recall from the story, is a time whose possibility or impossibility we can only even talk about when we are in the dream space . . . created by the Ro-womb. That beautiful, poetic, and ultimately noncommercial title was taken off the story by its initial editor, Cele Goldsmith, because it did not name the subject (in either sense) of the story. It was rather a verbal tag for a pertinent subspace—the space that the story was about. It was a sign of a space in which language could be distorted in a certain way, giving us access to certain purely verbal constructs.[21]

The "figure of rhetorically distorted language," used to invoke "a space in which language could be distorted in a certain way," is catachresis.

The renaming of "Ides of Octember" to "The Dream Master" is comparable to Delany's story "We, in Some Strange Power's Employ, Move in a Rigorous Line," which was originally published with the title "Lines of Power."[22] These poetic constructions and their signal value for the stories they name participate in a common tendency to elevate catachresis to a more formal level, from an occasional possibility to a generic expectation. In response to Delany's explanation of why he preferred Zelazny's original, catachrestic title, Tatsumi replies, "It reminds me of one of your own verbal constructs, your title *Starboard Wine*. Even the title *Dhalgren* is a tag for a particular process, created of expectation and verbal highlighting, rather than a name for a person or a place that the book will then observe, explore, or circle in on."[23] The title of *The Star-Pit* does designate a place within the story. Yet because it is a place where the reader will encounter verbal figures particular to the story's contrived circumstances, "golden," "world-wind," and "keeler intergalactic," to name a few, attention to catachresis facilitates understanding the story's language. When Chrzanowska-Kluczewska argues for a third, metatextual form of catachresis in her schema, she describes it as "a text-forming (or rather, text-disrupting) strategy" associated with poststructuralism and postmodernism.[24] She identifies its workings with Michel Foucault's analysis in *The Order of Things*:

> Seventeenth-century rationalism already had to cope with all kinds of errors, illusions, madnesses and logically ungrounded patterns of thinking. We can observe that these features mark the beginning of *catachrestic discourse*. . . . Foucault invokes catachresis as a figure whose defining properties are *incongruity, juxtaposition of incompatible entities, and distortion of categorization*; in a word, catachresis is defined by what Foucault calls *atopia* (or *heterotopia*): a displacement that provokes the most remote things to approach one another, "a worse kind of disorder than that of the incongruous, the linking together of things that are inappropriate."[25]

In keeping with other scholars who appreciate Delany's Foucauldian tendencies, informed in part by other evocative titles he employs such as *Trouble on Triton: An Ambiguous Heterotopia*, it is no great leap to conceive of *The Star-Pit* as a heterotopia: a tale told in part through catachrestic discourse.[26] The conceptual space it inflates with language occupies the galaxy's edge and what lies beyond.

In Space No One Can Hear This Broadcast

Delineating a space of representation where distorted language becomes necessary is a key expository task for the radio version of *The Star-Pit*. As the Mind's Eye Theatre began on November 26, 1967, at 5:00 pm, the first voice to speak, as usual, was Baird Searles apprising listeners of the evening's program. In a nasal baritone, he announced:

> Samuel R. Delany's *The Star-Pit*, directed by Daniel Landau, with Randa Haines, Walter Harris, Jerry Matz, Joan Tanner, and Phoebe Wray. The narration is by the author. The music for *The Star-Pit* is composed and performed by Susan Schweers. "The Star-Pit" first appeared in *Worlds of Tomorrow* published by the Galaxy Publishing Corporation.[27]

The War of the Worlds had exposed listeners to the rare hazard of confusing the production's verisimilitude with a factual report. *The Star-Pit* presents no such risk—except at the moment when the broadcast represents Vyme hearing the word "golden" used in its uncharacteristic fashion for the first time: The voice from the commissioner who coined the term through memorable interference on Vyme's radio is the same announcer, Baird Seales. He is otherwise only heard as an extradiegetic presence before and after the dramatic presentation. By associating the term's coinage with the sonic identity of the figure who sets the boundaries between the time and place inside the narrative world and the time and place outside, the production calls for attention to how uses against convention—catachresis—take on a pivotal role in this play.

After Searles's introduction to the program and its cast, the first sound in the production is a musical overture. Delany's "Notes on *The Star-Pit*" reveals that Schweers produced this melody on a homemade instrument fashioned from "a length of industrial hosing with an inch and a half bore and arbitrarily cut-in fingers [*sic*] holes."[28] Schweers was one of Delany's many housemates and collaborators in her capacity as a musician during the period when he wrote several novels in succession, including *Babel-17* and *Nova*. He recounts this era in his memoir, *The Heavenly Breakfast*. Of all the musical interludes, background noises, and sound effects Schweers provided for the production, the only ones produced by a "classical silver flute" accompany the public psychedelic reveries of a character named Alegra.

In addition to the overture and interludes, Schweers is responsible for diegetic and atmospheric sounds perceived by the characters and audience alike. The most significant of these sounds has a puzzling name: the "world-wind." In the story, The Star-pit is a floating space station of sorts located far, far away from Earth's solar system, and it is never associated with any identifiable stars or constellations. It is situated in relation to other points by its remoteness. When Vyme's spacecraft crosses paths with an intergalactic vessel elsewhere at one point, a crewmate exclaims, "This far into galactic center? . . . They should be hanging out around the star-pit!"[29] Vyme recalls arriving at the Star-pit for the first time: "From the view deck we watched the immense artificial disk of the Star-pit approach."[30] From these descriptions and the characters' observations as they live and work at the Star-pit, it evokes the image of a megastructure akin to the titular cylindrical vessel in Arthur C. Clarke's *Rendezvous with Rama* or the great circumstellar strip of Larry Niven's *Ringworld*, but perhaps closer in size to the asteroid belt settlements of television's *The Expanse* or the eponymous space station setting of *Star Trek: Deep Space Nine*. Amid the hangars for intra- and intergalactic spacecraft, residences and leisure sites for the denizens of the Star-pit are located on streets with names like "Calle-D," "Calle-G," and "Calle-K," suggesting an urban grid.[31] Streetlamps light their paths. There is no star close enough to function as a sun. But the inhabitants of the Star-pit enjoy a breathable atmosphere and simulated gravity, and they also experience weather in the form of the "world-wind." As Vyme and Ratlit sit on the edge of the neighborhood:

> Star-flecked infinity dropped away below our boot soles, and the wind created by the stasis field that held our atmosphere down—we call it the "world-wind" out here because it's never cold and never hot and like nothing on any world—whipped his black shirt back from his bony chest as we gazed on galactic night between our knees.[32]

The world-wind provides local color to the story's far-fetched setting. It comprises a touchstone for the work's technologically augmented future. For it to fulfill these functions in the radio play, Schweers and the sound engineers employed by WBAI (including David Rapkin and Ed Woodard) had to overcome the technical and artistic challenge of representing a sound that does not exist in nature.[33] As the example of the Martian heat-ray in *The War of the Worlds* demonstrates, technical devices contrived in writing can astound the reader. Achieving the equivalent effect through recorded sound requires highly original performance and presentation in order to avoid too close a resemblance between the sound effect and anything identifiable to the listener. Catachresis is an appropriate classification for such an unprecedented, jarring sound/image: "like nothing on any world."

Delany reports that after rehearsals and marathon studio sessions to record the action of the radio play, "the editing and the placing of the music and special effects took almost ten times as many studio hours to put together and lay in as had the editing of the dialogue."[34] The result was a series of textured, internally consistent settings within the play that differentiates between "windy" streets, cavernous hangars, buzzing cockpits, cloistered offices, and an apartment that plays host to cacophonous hallucination in one scene and quiet deprivation in the next. The dialogue, including its normalization of catachrestic figures, slowly reveals how Vyme arrives at the outpost where all ventures, save golden, end.

When Vyme first learned of golden's existence, he was working toward the possibility that would make them necessary. At the time of the flashback during which he remembered the radio announcement, he had been a student.

> I was a drive-mechanics major, on scholarship, living in and studying hard. All morning in Practical Theory (a ridiculous name for a ridiculous class, I thought then) we'd spent putting together a model keeler intergalactic drive. . . . I had been silently cursing my teacher, thinking, thinking, about like everyone else in the class, "So what if they can fly this jalopy from one galaxy to another. Nobody will ever be able to ride in them. Not with the Psychic and Physiologic shells hanging around this cluster of the Universe."[35]

The words in young Vyme's complaint invoke the psychological and physiological nature of the barriers to intergalactic travel that he would soon learn were not insurmountable after all. Several other turns of phrase in his recollection, however, foreshadow the first encounter he would have with golden, many years later. "Practical Theory" is an oxymoron, a ridiculous name indeed. Its objective seemed equally ridiculous at the time, because no pilot or crew could ever utilize a "keeler intergalactic drive" for its intended purpose. Despite the theoretical possibility of a mode of propulsion (the drive) that could sustain travel between galaxies, such an invention remained impractical so long as no human being could physically or psychologically survive such a voyage.

The tell, in this formulation, might be the peculiar word order of "keeler intergalactic drive." Although ships are thoroughly associated with transportation across water in human history, "space ship" has become a standard enough metaphor, thanks to science fiction, that it passes for a compound word. "Ship" typically denotes a spacecraft by default in the genre, for any narratives in which space travel occurs. The actually existing space shuttle spent many years shuttling people and payloads back and forth between Earth's surface and outer space. "Keeler" is an even more concrete image, transforming a synecdoche for the central and lowermost part of a ship into a verb that communicates its orientation and movement. The significance of the figure's orientation also implies its size. The position of the modifier "intergalactic" makes for an atypical construction. Like "postmaster general," "body politic," or "accounts payable," it is a postpositive adjective. Though they are conventional in Romance languages, postpositive adjectives are uncommon in English syntax.[36] Taken together, the cumulative implications of this exceptional usage for Vyme's classmates portray assembling the model drive as a wholly academic assignment, a task they could never expect to undertake in their vocation, rather than an artifact of hands-on experience. Only when Vyme has a fateful brush with golden in real life are the contradictions of Practical Theory finally put to rest.

Years later, as copilot of a ship close to the galactic center, Vyme recounts, "Something I'd never heard of happening, happened. We came *this* close to ramming another ship. Consider how much empty space there is; the chances are infinitesimal."[37] To his surprise, "This big, bulbous keeler-intergalactic slid by so close I could see her through the front viewport. . . . I slammed on the video-intercom and shouted, 'You great big stupid . . . *stupid* . . . ' so mad and scared I couldn't say anything else." The incident gave him firsthand experience with unfathomably improbable phenomena: a spacecraft he'd studied in school far from the vicinity for which it was designed, a gap merely a hundred meters wide between vessels that had traveled millions of kilometers, and golden. Delany's line reading, as Vyme in the radio play, was a sputtering jumble, with the redundant second "*stupid*" achieving emphasis through repetition of the insult in the absence of any adequate word for its subject.[38] The two iterations of the word nearly collide, like the ships that narrowly survived the near-miss. He was still dumbfounded as he tried to explain to his copilot, moments later, "'Damn it,' I shouted, 'it was one of those . . . ' and lost all the profanity I knew to my rage, . . . 'golden . . . '" For that line, Delany had to pause with bated breath so as to indicate his character's inability to summon the words for his contempt. The copilot was incredulous, since golden belong in the far reaches of space, where their keelers intergalactic arrive and depart from other galaxies and where no one else can venture. But Vyme clearly recalls his own reply, "'It was a keeler drive,' I insisted."[39]

Finding golden out of place, so unexpectedly close that their appearance defies description, represents the fulfillment of a prophecy of sorts. Like the educational exercise that scarcely prepared him to observe a keeler intergalactic drive operating in the real world, Vyme discovered the difference between the knowledge that golden exist in the abstract and the concrete evidence of their presence in a situation that was too close for comfort. Reflecting on his stupefied silence as he looked through the viewport, he remarks, "The golden piloting the ship stared at me from the viewscreen with mildly surprised annoyance. I remember his face was just slightly more negroid than mine."

Misappropriation

The golden who almost crashes into Vyme is phenotypically Black, just like the author/narrator. Though it traffics in pseudoscientific terms, i.e., "negroid," the description emphasizes similarity rather than difference. The physical descriptions of all golden in the story elicit the same manner of banal, even disappointing familiarity. The pilot is not the only one for whom the story invokes a superannuated vocabulary of racial identity along with an off-putting sentiment like "mildly surprised annoyance." When Vyme recalls the first golden identified to the public, he remarks on their features and their attitude in similar terms: "They were both psychological freaks with some incredible hormone imbalance in their systems. One was a little oriental girl; the other was an older man, blond and big boned, from a cold planet circling Cygnus-beta: golden. They looked sullen as hell, both of them."[40]

One of the effects of Vyme's internal monologue in the story and play is reassuring the audience that racial identity has not disappeared from view in the future *The Star-Pit* represents. Readers at the time might have found the terms "oriental" and "negroid" unremarkable, and listeners to the radio adaptation of *The Star-Pit* may have only momentarily acknowledged that such epithets were giving way to new ones in the late 1960s. "Negro" remained in common parlance, alongside Colored, while only a fraction of people of African descent signaled the nationalism and militancy associated with identifying as Black, with others adopting the hyphenate Afro-American.[41] Yet "negroid," coming directly out of nineteenth-century race science, was a relic of comparative anatomy as deeply associated with discriminatory biological determinism as phrenology. Meanwhile, US participation in the Vietnam War had exposed more English-speaking Americans to Asian terms of ethnic and national self-identification, but the reductive and reifying force of "oriental" had not yet come under the intense scrutiny that would eventually displace its use as a facile stereotype. Reductive language with respect to matters of racialized description bespeaks impropriety rather than disrespect, in this context. By projecting these comparatively disfavored terms into the human future, Delany suggests that the language of race might retain some of its denotative value while shedding its offensive connotations. In the novella and its adaptation, the racial epithets in question, though hardly benign, at least function more referentially than golden, whereas the latter is invariably freighted with some defect in character or disposition.

The first two golden Vyme knows about are "sullen as hell," the next reacts with only "mildly surprised annoyance" during a life-threatening crisis, and yet another diminishes his livelihood with a rhetorical question. When Vyme arrived at the Star-pit for the first time, one of his fellow travelers was "a golden who, as golden go, was a pretty regular gal," he recalls.[42] "We'd been discussing inter- and intragalactic drives. She was impressed I knew so much. I was impressed that she could use them and knew so little." Vyme's training placed him among the minority of drive mechanics who could understand the means of intergalactic travel, but his supremely improbable counterpart could actually *do* it without any thought as to the reason why. As they reached their destination, "she turned to me and said, in a voice that didn't sound cruel at all, 'This is as far as you go, isn't it?'" Vyme calls attention to the lack of cruelty in her voice to underscore the devastating effect of her remark. Like her incurious mastery of intergalactic travel, the golden's matter-of-fact acknowledgment of Vyme's permanent limitations made him seem insignificant. The actor who delivers this line from the narrator's formative recollections in the radio play is Randa Haines, who also plays Alegra, the ethereal hostess with whom Vyme and Ratlit visit frequently at the Star-pit.[43] The memorable exchange, associated with a familiar voice, contributes to the lingering sense that golden are as blissfully detached from the norms they violate as they are from the emotional impact of their obliviousness on others.

Golden invite widespread alienation through the double bind of their status as outliers to the norms of mental health and their misunderstood comportment as ostensibly privileged space travelers. This social marginalization raises the quandary of why anyone in their fictitious society would want to occupy the place reserved for golden. Yet Vyme's young companion, Ratlit, is consumed with jealousy when it comes to golden. His resentment toward them manifests in every interaction Vyme witnesses as well as in his repetition of the reductive rhetoric that summarizes prejudice toward them.

> "They're only two types of golden . . . Mean ones and stupid ones," He was repeating a standard line you heard around the Star-pit.
>
> "I hope yours is stupid," I said, thinking of the two who'd just ruined Sandy's day and upset mine.
>
> "Which is worse?" Ratlit shrugged. That is the rest of the line. When a golden isn't being outright mean, he exhibits the sort of nonthinkingness that gets other people hurt.[44]

This dialogue follows a gruesome scene in which one golden has just murdered another in the hangar where Vyme, Ratlit, and another mechanic, Sandy, work. That the episode merely "upset" Vyme's day attests to his learned indifference. He and Ratlit have shifted their focus to the fortunes of another golden whom they came across staggering through the streets and carried to their friend's home to convalesce. When Vyme suggested they should leave him to "sleep it off" on the street, Ratlit feigned concern. "Leave him so somebody can come along and steal his belt?"[45] he'd asked. Golden wore yellow belts as a badge of status. They were easily appropriated, in theory, but Ratlit explains what makes the threat of theft an idle one: "I'd be nasty to whoever stole the belt and wore it. Nobody but a golden should be hated so much."[46]

Taking the golden to Alegra's home was no great act of mercy. Alegra's defining character trait is a congenital, lifelong addiction to a powerful drug that combines narcotics with psychedelics.[47] This character's background was a representation of shifting mores giving way to politicized anxiety over fetal and neonatal health in the 1960s. Some policy factions and their constituencies depicted innocent babies as victims of sexual and psychoactive experimentation among the poor and in the counterculture. Numerous medical studies from the late 1950s to mid-1960s warned that "babies are born addicted" and tracked children born to mothers showing signs of addiction and withdrawal.[48] However, Delany imagines several inventive sequelae to this predicament through Alegra. In a conscious homage to Bester's *The Stars My Destination*, the character was a "projective telepath," able to implant her thoughts in others' minds. These would include fantasies, hallucinations, and her best conscious approximations for images that others could relate to her verbally. Delany also employed an allusion to Zelazny's *The Dream Master* by making Alegra's talent part of her occupation as a psychiatric aide to patients with mental illness. She worked with golden; she could "concretize their fantasies and make them work 'em through. In just a couple of hours I'd have 'em back to their old, mean, stupid selves again."[49] Alegra's disdain for her patients was understandable: She was tragically conscripted into this service at only eight years old. Her employers had prolonged and intensified her addiction during childhood, "withholding her drug to force her to work harder, then rewarding her with increased dosage," in order to continue exploiting her abilities. The drug she could not live without was easy to obtain at the Star-pit. "Golden don't use it," Vyme explains.

Unlike Ratlit and Vyme, whose discontent appears highly subjective and world-weary, Alegra is predisposed to empathize with golden. "Prenatal or infantile" causes outside her determination make her both socially useful and irredeemably strange. When he enters her home, Vyme declares, "I can't describe Alegra's place." He means it literally:

> I can describe it before she moved in because I knew a derelict named Drunk-roach who slept on that floor before she did. You know what never-wear plastics look like when they wear out? What non-rust metals look like when they rust through? It was a shabby crack-walled cubicle with dirt in the corners and scars on the window pane when Drunk-roach had his pile of blankets in the corner. But since the hallucinating, projective telepath took it over, who knows what it had become.[50]

He could make comparisons, but they would never be accurate. Alegra's distorted perception allowed her to remake the premises in her mind's own image for any observer, but that also rendered it impossible to detect the deterioration that had undoubtedly taken place. No one could observe any features in the environment besides what her mental projections caused them to perceive.

This conceit meant that every scene in Alegra's home would require a virtual symphony in the radio play. When they arrive at her apartment, a single woodwind accompanies the narration, "Halfway up the tilting stairs, Ratlit said, 'She's in a good mood,'" before the pair go inside. Once they enter, the volume of the high-pitched musical track overwhelms Delany's low narration, and the dialogue becomes hard to hear. "Ratlit opened the door on an explosion of classical beauty. 'Come in,' she sang, accompanied by symphonic arrangement scored on twenty-four staves, with full chorus." As they laid down their burden, "the golden lay on orange silk pillows in a teak barge drawn by swans, accompanied by flutes and drums."[51]

The primary soundtrack to these actions emulates strings and flutes simultaneously playing at least two looping, unsynchronized melodies. As the three conscious people in the room converse about where the golden has been, Alegra's florid mind illustrates the places they mention. "Mosquitoes darted at us through the wet fronds," Vyme says, and a whizzing sound whistles after the word "darted." Moments later, a plaintive squeal rises and falls as he says, "I back-paddled frantically to avoid a hippopotamus that threatened to upset my kayak." When Alegra mentions that golden have come down with an illness after recent visits to some distant galaxy, to a place as humid as the river into which her apartment has transformed, a scraping, twisting, noise begins, piercing as feedback, to punctuate her use of the word "sick." It persists. Vyme remarks, "I dug my fingers against my abdomen trying to grab the pain." Then, the rattling rhythmic clap of some makeshift tambourine occurs over a dozen beats, as Vyme mentions "fever heated blood-bubbles in my eyes," and Ratlit coughs.

After some pleading from Ratlit, they settle in for conversation. They agree to wait until the golden regains consciousness. Alegra says, "We can talk. That way it won't seem like such a long—" and the music stops. The pause in the music continues just long enough for Vyme to resume the narration by interjecting with an explanation, "and hundreds of years later, she finished." When Alegra resumes speaking, she completes her sentence "—time." The brevity of the pause in the music, which had accompanied the past four minutes of the scene, jars the listener back to attention. It is a masterful editing trick that returns the listener after an interval so short they would fail to measure it, in order to convey the sense that it felt interminably long to the characters. Vyme leaves his companions to talk among themselves.

The unspeakable excess of Alegra's state of mind makes it futile to attempt any mimetic representation of her presence. Accordingly, Randa Haines's soft-spoken, earnest delivery allows the overstimulating flourishes of music accompanying her every word to stand in for the sheer abundance of expressive content she impresses on her interlocutors. Sound can convey the experience of conversation with her, but language cannot. After Vyme departs and the golden wakes up, Alegra and Ratlit spend hours listening to the tales of adventure he has to share while she "concretizes" the details for their entertainment. A progression of fantasies and persuasion leads the three of them to reach fatal conclusions. The next time Vyme and Ratlit visit Alegra, the golden has left. But he has convinced Alegra, in the meantime, that she, too, is golden.

> Something in my medicine kept it from coming out until now, until a golden could come to me, drawing it up and out of the depths of me, till it burst out, beautiful and wonderful and . . . golden! Right now he's gone off to Carlson Labs with a urine sample for a final hormone check. They'll tell him in an hour, and he'll bring back my golden belt. But he's sure already. And when he comes back with it, I'm going to go with him to the galaxies, as his apprentice. We're going to find a cure for his sickness and something that will make it so I won't need my medicine any more.[52]

Incredulous and seething, Ratlit assents to do Alegra two favors before she leaves him behind. She asks him to obtain the last dose of the drugs she needs and retrieve her new yellow belt, which will guarantee her passage aboard an intergalactic ship. It makes sense to reveal that Alegra, the most technically demanding character to portray in the drama, is golden. She is the only sympathetic example of the type and, in the end, the most tragic.

Alegra's tasks go unfulfilled. Instead, Vyme witnesses Ratlit taking off with the golden for intergalactic space. Ratlit picked up her belt, but he stole it for himself. He has blasted off to certain doom by the time Vyme returns to find Alegra, abandoned, in acute withdrawal.

> The translucency of her pigmentless skin under how-many-days of dirt made my flesh crawl. Her face drew in around her lips like the flesh about a scar. "My medicine. Vyme, is that you? You'll get my medicine for me, Vyme? Won't you get my medicine?" Her mouth wasn't moving, but the voice came on. She was too weak to project on any but the aural level.[53]

With her strength depleted, the only sense Alegra can affect is hearing, and its only contents are feeble words. Vyme's description enables us to imagine this eerie ventriloquism as her last act of self-definition. Ratlit's departure left no one willing and able to retrieve her drug from the dealer; Vyme knows the hour is too late for him to try now. She promises him, "If I were well, Vyme, I'd fly you there in a cloud of light pulled by peacocks and porpoises, and you'd come back to hautboys and tambourines, bringing my beautiful medicine. . . . But I'm sick now. Sick."[54]

In the radio play, we hear hollow wheezing from one of Schweers's flutes as a subpar accompaniment to Alegra's last words about "peacocks" and "hautboys." In her times of good health, Alegra's references would have cued the carrying "may-awww" of the male *Pavo cristatus,* the Indian peafowl, and the long Baroque melodic lines of the *hautbois,* or "oboe."[55] Her delirium is usually louder and sharper than the actors' voices. Now, the music sounds as she describes: sick. Ratlit's betrayal frustrates Alegra and Vyme, and they exchange insults over what it means for her to be golden:

> "You mean you didn't know what you were doing to Ratlit by leaving, Alegra? . . . You couldn't see what it would do to him if you deprived him of the thing he needed and rubbed his nose in the thing he hated both at once? . . . Oh, kid-girl, you talk about golden. You're the stupid one.'
>
> "Not stupid," she projected quietly. "*Mean,* Vyme . . . I was cruel. I had the chance to do it and I took it."[56]

Vyme and Alegra's reaction to Ratlit's betrayal forces them to reflect on their shared expectations about what golden means. Outside the language community invented for this narrative, the characters' exchange is nonsensical. Readers and listeners can follow it only by appreciating the relationship between the words "mean" and "stupid" in this particular speech context. Adapting this story for performance requires the actors to infuse arbitrary words with unmistakable emotions. They can only do so insofar as their dialogue falls into discernible patterns—including uses that they know listeners will find incorrect or unintelligible based on their prior experience—within the play.

A Marriage of Convenience

For better or for worse, the adaptation demystifies some of the text's conceptual innovations. In "Notes on *The Star-Pit,*" Delany writes about some discrepancies between the novella and the radio play:

> In 1967, two years prior to Stonewall, on the written page the most notable thing about "The Star-Pit" had been its gender skewing. . . . Jerry Matts—that *rara avis,* a twenty-nine-year old straight male actor—was

> particularly tickled with it. "Now here, Chip, I'm playing your . . . husband? Wow!" . . .
>
> The greatest gender skewing in the printed version is, of course, the penultimate scene's revelation that Poloscki is a woman—which revelation does not arrive on the page until halfway through her dialogue with Vyme. But even though we'd picked Phoebe [Wray] for her somewhat masculine voice, because it was a radio play there was no way to preserve the ambiguity till the proper dramatic moment. As soon as Phoebe/Poloscki spoke her first line ("Who's over there?") her gender was clear—and we had to let the effect go.[57]

"Poloscki" appears dozens of times in the text, often in the possessive in order to designate a place, i.e., "Poloscki's," where mechanics work. However, only after a character enters a scene by addressing Poloscki formally as "Ma'am?" does the text subsequently refer to her with any pronoun rather than her name.[58] To her fellow actors and listeners at the time, Delany suggests, Wray's voice was insufficiently androgynous. Using a proper name where a pronoun could perform the same task preserves a capacity for the sign in one form to withhold something that it would otherwise give away. By "adding" the dimension of sound, the adaptation "loses" something from the original.

The "gender skewing" involved in casting husbands for male characters is a different grammatical sleight of hand. Such a role features in the story because the people of *The Star-Pit*'s future live in "procreation groups." Humans populate many planets living in large reproductive collectives where love and the duties of parenting are shared among the participants. Both Vyme and his coworker Sandy once belonged to such groups. In this context, marriage is plural, and the fine distinctions between paternity and other forms of filiation diffuse. Vyme remembers when he was "the proud father of three and expecting two more. The hundred and sixty-three of us had the whole beach and nine miles of jungle and half a mountain to ourselves."[59] Later, Sandy shows Vyme a picture of his seven children, then explains that tensions among the twenty-three adults in his family had become "pretty rough on all our kids, thirty-two when I left."[60]

Vyme's wanderings begin when he exits his procreation group after one of their children becomes injured; he remains heartbroken in his attempts at mentoring Ratlit. Sandy tries to warn him:

> Boss, Ratlit is the kid your own could be. You want to give him the advice, friendship and concern he's never had, that you couldn't give yours. . . . Until I admit to myself what I can't do, it's pretty hard to work on what I can. Same thing goes for Ratlit. You too. That's

> growing up. And one thing you can't do is help Ratlit by giving him a ship he can't fly.[61]

Vyme feels paternal, and he has his heart broken again when he meets another golden toward the end of the story. The youth explains that Sandy has sent him to Vyme in search of a job: "Brother-in-law Sandy and I got to talking, so I asked him about working here."[62] Until they have a disagreement, the golden, Androcles, refers to Vyme affectionately as "cousin" and "brother," which Vyme obligingly reciprocates, calling him "kid-boy." Vyme attempts to give him fatherly advice, only to be rebuffed:

> The psychotechnicican who made sure I was properly psychotic *wasn't* a golden, *brother!* You *pay* us to bring back weapons, dad! *We* don't fight your damn wars *grampa! You're* the ones who take us away from our groups, say we're *too* valuable to submit to *your* laws, then deny us our heredity because we don't *breed* true, no-relative-of-mine![63]

Pretending at kinship is routine for golden. Androcles's vitriol throws the terms of endearment back in Vyme's face, casting off the irony that was a blanket of familiarity between them and raising it into a wall.

When Vyme reports back to Sandy, he asks, "So how do you like my brother-in-law, Androcles?"

> "Brother-in-law?" I remembered An using the phrase, but I'd thought it was part of the slang which is golden. Something about the way Sandy said it though. "He's your *real* brother-in-law?"
>
> "He's Joey's kid brother."

When Vyme asks who Joey is, he replies, "He's one of my husbands." Sandy's reference to one of many husbands is consistent with the plural parenting arrangements in the story. It was uncharacteristic, however, for Androcles and Sandy to employ such terms for their relationship precisely, given that they are typically used in a colloquial fashion. Sandy's choice of words takes on greater significance when he explains, "An and Joey were pretty close, even though Joey's my age and An was only eight or nine back then. I guess Joey was the only one who really knew what An was going through, since they were both golden!"[64]

Vyme enunciates the impact of this revelation twice: first, as a question, and then, as an affirmation.

> Surprised and shocked, I turned back to the desk. "You were married with a golden?"
>
> "Yeah," Sandy said, surprised at my surprise. "Joey."

So I wouldn't stand there gaping, I picked up Alegra's letter.

"Since the traits that are golden are polychromazoic, it dies out if they only breed with each other. There's a big campaign back in galactic center to encourage them to join heterogeneous proke-groups."[65]

When Androcles cursed people who would "deny us our heredity because we don't *breed* true," he was referring to the eugenic pressure to propagate golden by isolating them from one another and compelling them to reproduce with others instead. That pressure produced groups like the one to which Sandy and Joey belonged, allowing for the potential distribution of Joey's heritable status as golden among the group's children. As Sandy explains this fact about one of his husbands and their children, an incongruously cheerful voice from the "portapix" device announces news for Alegra. The message did not confirm that she was golden. It advised that she was pregnant and that Ratlit was not responsible:

"If you are interested, for your eugenic records, in further information, please send us other possible urine samples from the men in your group, and we will be glad to confirm paternity . . . "

In the radio play, Vyme interrupts the recorded voice with a rhetorical question for Sandy:

"You were married with—you loved a golden?"

Unbidden, the portapix began again. I flipped it off.

Vyme's decisive action to interrupt the delivery of information pertinent to the plot shifts the focus of the scene back to Sandy's personal history and its significance for understanding the nature of relationships in the story.[66]

The prepositional phrase Vyme uses, "married with," rather than "married to," sounds incorrect the first time he says it, but because he interrupts other speech to pose the question a second time with the same phrasing, its construction sounds intentional. Like making the term "husband" plural and using it in the possessive, i.e., "my husbands," the expression "married with" in this context transposes the role of a spouse from a phenomenon that is dyadic (like boxing or ballroom dancing) to the conceptual space of an activity (like membership in a band) with a finitely many quantity of participants. When Vyme changes the inflection of his question midsentence by rephrasing its predicate, he brings what his conversation with Sandy has been implying into the open. Just like being married *to* someone, according to the proper phrasing, to be married *with* someone also means to love them. Through the painstaking rehearsal of language that establishes that a man might have husbands he would love, which is unremarkable in the story but novel for the audience, the narrator conveys the strangeness of the notion that someone could love golden.

Delany advises that "not only was this a time (two years prior to Stonewall) without any notions of 'gender skewing' or 'gender bending,' along with the word 'gay,' the word 'gender' itself was rarely or never heard."[67] Contemporary readers might describe what he is referring to as queerness. Notwithstanding the legacies of homophile movements and the publication of Alfred Kinsey's research in previous decades, readers of *Worlds of Tomorrow* were as unlikely as a casual WBAI listener to hear the terminology Delany references in everyday conversation. However, the tactics the story and radio play employ to introduce the notion of group marriage, which are largely the same as those used to recount the fictitious travails of golden, proves that even unspeakable realities are not unthinkable. When certain configurations of intersecting social forces arise before the time has come to name them, catachresis can be a constructive way to hold open space in language for them.

Until recently, it was uncommon to hear the term "neurodiversity" as a conception of dis/ability that might situate what golden represent. Like its queerness, the text's treatment of dis/ability is inexact and anticipatory, but it is full of irresistibly labile metaphors. Positing golden as the neurotypical's Other might construe it as a constituency including persons subject to diagnoses of schizophrenia, autism spectrum conditions, and neurodevelopmental disorders, as well as what's summarily called psychosis or madness. Sami Schalk observes that "[dis]ability, race, and gender often operate as mutually constitutive discourses that inflect texts even in the absence of explicit embodied representations of these categories."[68] *The Star-Pit* and its mediation for radio demonstrate how portraying a sensible (if not mimetic) rendition of socially consequential human differences in narrative—whether they are real or imagined—produces speech associated with dis/ability, race, gender, and sexuality. This language might be mistaken, and it will often reveal or enact prejudice, but it may be useful even when it is not proper to its subjects.

As a Set of Fragments

In an effort to reconcile Delany's speculative fiction with his approach to memoir, Tavia Nyong'o writes, "The heterotopic spaces Delany constructs within his writings . . . resonate to sounds that cannot always be straightforwardly understood as belonging to our aesthetic continuum."[69] Delany's experimentation with fact and fiction alike revel in deconstruction, displaying a preoccupation with undermining dualisms and casting doubt on deterministic models of interpretation. Just as he manipulates language to refract the characters and events in his imaginary settings through the prism of their far-fetched temporal and spatial circumstances, Delany displaces and recombines personalities and observations from his life to emphasize how narrative and memory themselves are susceptible to the sanctions of discourse. His work famously resists associations between racial identity and expressive style, in particular. Nyong'o is among the critics who take seriously the proviso in Delany's memoir, *The Heavenly Breakfast*, that he represents his experience with what he calls "distortions for essentially musical reasons."[70] I recommend adopting this attitude toward interpreting Delany's writing in the manner he suggests, which includes acknowledging the possibility that the nonverbal sounds in music have idiomatic rather than universal significance.

In a literary biography of Delany from the 1980s, as part of a series of short volumes on authors including Bradbury, Sturgeon, Fritz Lieber, and Ursula Le Guin, Seth McEvoy mentions the time Delany spent on the radio adaptation of *The Star-Pit*. He situates it at the beginning of a period when Delany disassociated from his identity as a science fiction writer. Although he does not make the work of creating a musically rich, aural production involving complex sound editing in a radio studio an explicit part of this transition, McEvoy argues, "To understand what happened next, we must go back to a thread of Delany's life that has only been touched upon lightly before: music."[71] In retrospect, *The Star-Pit* represents a thematic connection between the different modes of creativity in Delany's career. One of the most important insights he communicated in his reflections about working with the Mind's Eye Theatre, which he offered as guidance for future productions shortly after *The Star-Pit* was finished, focused on how to learn and rehearse the music.

> Because the score has to be recorded in non sequential fragments, if the musician(s) have only rehearsed the piece linearly, all hell will pop up in the studio. The musician(s) must spend their time learning what the overall shape of the score is, rather than concentrating on how to get from one section to the next. . . . The musicians must know the score as a set of fragments; otherwise when they first encounter the dislocated sections, they lose confidence, want to re-write, and this—in the midst of a recording session—is the way to total insanity.[72]

Like his poetic approach to coining phrases for science fiction stories, Delany's attitude toward the role of music in a radio play—undoubtedly informed by Schweers and other bandmates—involved a conscious effort to delink parts from the whole in the interest of reconsidering how those parts might fit together. Knowing what the available range of instruments, motifs, melodies, and effects making up the soundscape would be was important, but it was equally critical to plan for the enunciation of each of these elements at different moments: a transition between scenes, an atmospheric element such as the world-wind or engine noise aboard a spaceship, or the execution of Alegra's psychic projections in a heightened or attenuated form. Recording the sounds in ways that would allow them to create impressions that were predictable in some instances and striking or mystifying in others required a certain versatility that musicians could cultivate in the service of different creative visions. Relinquishing the notion that any one part of the whole stood in relation to the others in a way that could be understood in advance allowed for musical and verbal performances that only attained their meaning for the narrative after it was assembled into its final form. No matter how strangely the parts fit together.

To suggest that music functions in a fragmentary and catachrestic fashion in *The Star-Pit* removes it from a relation to reality that is anything other than speculative. Just like the figures of speech distinct to the work, its music strikes the listener as resonant or inappropriate to varying degrees based on the context in which it is heard, rather than any objective standards of usage. Catachrestic images disorient through their imperfect appropriation of intelligible forms and thereby orient us to new possibilities. Recognizing in language as well as music the power to mystify, err, and correct (according to its own contrived principles) dispels any notion that nonlinguistic expression is inherently more apt to provide insight into what is natural or possible. Expressions that sound inappropriate here and now belong to some other time and place; speculative fiction and radio drama allow us to read and to hear what this other place is like. To play the discordant sounds of another world and call them music is to remember that we never know the entirety of a language that presents itself to us in pieces. We can rehearse it as a set of fragments.

3
The Audible Epigraph in Octavia E. Butler's *Kindred*

> I must be fired this week. I must be fired Friday. I must be fired so that on unemployment, I can finish my novel.
>
> —OCTAVIA E. BUTLER, JOURNAL ENTRY, DECEMBER 10, 1974 (OEB 999)

We are currently in the midst of a renaissance for academic and popular interest in the work of the late Octavia E. Butler, the first science fiction writer to win the MacArthur Foundation fellowship (or "genius grant") and one of the most prominent African American authors of the late twentieth century. This resurgence is taking place through further scholarly legitimation, in works like Lynell George and Gerry Canavan's exemplary biographies of Butler, as well as artistic and activist projects spearheaded by the likes of Ayana Jamieson, founder of the Octavia E. Butler legacy network, and adrienne maree brown, who coined the term "emergent strategy" to describe how Butler's dynamic, attentive, revisionary humanist approach to narrative inspires her approach to political mobilization.

Butler's last novel, *Fledgling*, was published in 2005, the year before her untimely death. In addition to uncovering her fiction writing, people are returning to Butler now in the way that a great deal of literature reaches contemporary audiences: through adaptation across a range of popular media. The coming reappearance of Butler's authorship in visual media invites comparisons with Philip K. Dick, whose work was ubiquitous in film and television for a while, recently. Projects adapted from *Wild Seed*, by the Kenyan filmmaker Wanuri Kahiu, and *Parable of the Sower*, from A24 studios, respectively, are on the way as of this writing, and the graphic novel versions of several of Butler's books have won Eisner and Hugo Awards for comics creators John Jennings and Damian Duffy. In 2022, Butler's novel, *Kindred*, was adapted for television by the Obie Award–winning playwright Branden Jacobs-Jenkins, with an updated contemporary setting.

The subjects of this chapter are two versions of *Kindred:* an Octavia Butler novel in which a Black woman from California in the 1970s finds herself repeatedly wrenched backward in time to antebellum Maryland to ensure that one of her ancestors is born. The protagonist's ancestor is the progeny of a white slave-owning family's ne'er-do-well son and a free Black teenager. In both versions of the story, the protagonist, whose name is Dana, is married to a white man in the present. For *Audiofuturism*, I examine the radio play based on *Kindred* produced for the online arm of television's SciFi channel (now SyFy), in 2001. The Seeing Ear Theatre was an internet radio platform linked to the channel (at SciFi.com) in the early years of the World Wide Web, when streaming audio was a fairly new entertainment format. Amid the current resurgence, this prior adaptation offers us a rare glimpse of Butler's attainment of the vision she had for herself as a writer within her lifetime. The radio dramatization also leveraged the wider and more diverse audience attending the emergence of online entertainment to foreground the novel's concern with the memory of slavery in the present.

Butler worked on *Kindred*—which she described as a "grim fantasy" involving morally impossible but irresistible decisions—for years before publishing it in 1979. Her thinking took shape amid the development of some of her major interconnected novels, but it also grew out of her intermittent studies in the Southern California community college and public university system. Butler's speculative research habits yielded awesome imaginings and prescient warnings in the Xenogenesis trilogy and the two Parable novels. *Kindred*, however, required her to cultivate an extensive factual background for its historically realistic setting. The inexplicable time travel at the core of its plot, for which she never attempts a metaphysical explanation,[1] stages a reckoning between a present her readers can know and a past they can only know about. From its inception, the text gestured toward some possible multimodality that would complement the sensory and temporal experience of reading it. Butler's notes on writing and publishing *Kindred* and the novel's evolving place among her intellectual property underscore her constant awareness of the economic, racial, technological, and gendered dimensions of her work as a writer.

My analysis of *Kindred* in this chapter reads the adaptation in relation to the novel through their different approaches to representing the life-threatening

Figure 4: Portrait of Octavia E. Butler with illustrations representing Patternist novels and *Fledgling*, by Dr. Melanie West.

situations that enslaved people survived. While Butler emphasizes the way the depredations of slavery bring an individual's struggle for survival to the fore in a first-person narrative, the radio play employs a more didactic approach to making present-day audiences aware of the institution's ignoble circumstances. Adapting *Kindred* into a play of two-and-three-quarter hours' length was a challenge. Not every word Butler wrote appears in the radio play: In audiobook format, the novel is nearly eleven hours long. Butler researched the local setting meticulously, she reserved some details about the characters for flashbacks, and she relegated the causes behind some dynamics evident in the text to background knowledge rather than making them apparent to Dana (or the reader). However, the adaptation also includes elements that are not present in the novel: Multiple actors, rather than a single protagonist, attest to different perspectives on their circumstances through dialogue. Most notably, between the play's scenes, quotations from enslaved women's autobiographies invoke historical precedents for situations represented in the narrative. By overlaying the educational aim of informing the audience about slavery from eyewitness accounts onto the already psychologically intense story of Butler's novel, the radio adaptation underscores *Kindred*'s contribution to what Ramón Saldívar, after Jacqueline Rose, has called "historical fantasy." Here, "fantasy is not therefore antagonistic to social reality; it is its precondition or psychic glue."[2] By staging the protagonist's return to past moments that are hard to imagine using our present-day sensibilities, *Kindred* and its adaptation delve into the fears, painful compromises, and irreparable harms that are the premises for storytelling within an American history that confronts slavery.

After a brief recapitulation of the novel's plot and its intertwined settings, this chapter recounts how Butler published *Kindred* as part of her lifelong struggle to turn her passion for writing into viable employment. Crafting an irresistibly compelling novel and selling the rights to produce adaptations of it in other media formed part of her plan to escape economic precarity. Rendering Dana's experience into a harrowing, morally challenging struggle for survival was Butler's way to arrest her reader's attention. I discuss the radio adaptation as the fulfillment of this goal and as a work with its own agenda grounded in the text's historical setting. The production redoubles the effort at enabling present-day audiences to revisit slavery that *Kindred* achieves via time travel with a literary device of its own: It interpolates the story with audible epigraphs drawn from the slave narrative tradition. By constructing parallels between Dana's fictionalized travails and the women who survived them in real life, the adaptation insists—whereas Butler does not—on the factual basis for the events of the narrative.

Like Octavia E. Butler, *Kindred*'s protagonist and first-person narrator, Dana, works menial jobs in Southern California while pursuing a career as a writer. Dana met her husband, Kevin, who is also a writer, on the site of one of her temporary clerical jobs. Kevin's growing success at publishing his fiction has allowed them to buy a house. The couple is moving in as the story begins. Dana is Black, and Kevin is white. In the early days of their moving-in process, Dana vanishes from before Kevin's eyes and sees herself transported to nineteenth-century Maryland, where she unexpectedly has to save a white child from drowning. She returns to the present just as suddenly. Over the course of the novel, readers learn that the white child, Rufus, grows up to be the father of one of Dana's distant ancestors: Hagar. The child's mother is a free Black woman, Alice. Rufus is the scion of plantation owners in Maryland who enslaved Dana's ancestors (Alice's extended family) in the past. Dana is continually pulled back to the past, sometimes with Kevin, to save Rufus from life-threatening situations, and she learns that she must ensure her distant ancestor is born. In the process, she must survive slavery and face the fear that she may never return to her life as a free, literate Black woman married to a white man who respects her as an equal.

Rendering the setting in a convincing fashion served Butler's goal of writing an appealing novel, but even as she researched antebellum Maryland in meticulous detail, Butler remained focused on what she saw as the most important means to her ends: "I need first, a plot."[3] The success of the narrative, from conception to completion, depended on a compelling story, which for Butler consisted fundamentally of character in conflict. With this foundation intact, the story could translate to any medium and, indeed, any combination of geographies and time periods. As the text took shape, with working titles from *Switchback*, to *Canaan*, *To Keep Thee in All Thy Ways*, *Guardian*, and finally, *Kindred*, its abstract remained grounded by one contrast: "This is the story of a modern day black woman who is thrown back in time and must struggle to survive antebellum slavery. The story of a person taking some action that leads to some result. Not the story of a person who is something. 'Is' stories bog down. Go nowhere, ramble, remain unfinished."[4]

By placing the protagonist's motivation at the core of the story, Butler set the stage for *Kindred* as an odyssey. Any reader following the heroine's journey and any actor taking on her role would immediately and constantly focus on the task she had to complete. This attitude empowered Butler to finish writing the book, and it inspired later writers, as she had hoped, to adapt it for performance. A succession of readers, including those who read the paperback novel as well as agents, publishers, filmmakers, playwrights, and eventually, actors and listeners, who would encounter it in different forms, followed Dana through the obstacles she faced until her journey reached its end.

Reading *Kindred* as the story of a woman who "must," whose story is defined by what she *does*, rather than a woman who "is" brings us closer to understanding the performance common to the novel and the play. Each iteration of the story relates Dana's actions toward her objective. To maintain the coherence of the story's settings, including the relationship between what happens in the past and what happens in the present, Butler prescribes the meaning of Dana's story in a form that retains its truth value across its different contexts. Like an epigraph, any declarative statement about Dana's undertaking ultimately emerges out of the space in which her story is told and thereby frames its telling: Butler's statement of what Dana must do sets the story's agenda and thematizes each stage in its accomplishment.

Although *Kindred* uses the fantastic device of time travel as well as flashbacks to Dana's own memories to emplot events in a complicated order that could have yielded multiple renditions of the story, the novel consistently rehearses a sense of urgency that Butler communicates through different synopses she wrote in the process of developing her drafts. In the note to herself quoted earlier, Butler summarizes Dana's story without reference to her ancestors. On another occasion, she writes, "Dana's purpose is to survive and save Rufus's life while resisting Rufus's subterfuge and refusing to betray herself or her people."[5] These formulations characterize Dana differently in terms of who she is and what she does. The earlier statement defines Dana on her own terms, as a "modern day black woman," and the later one implies that who she will be depends on what she does in relation to Rufus. The multiple clauses in the latter synopsis compound Dana's responsibilities: to survive, to save Rufus's live, to resist subterfuge, to refuse specific hazards that would cause her to betray herself or to betray her people.

Insofar as "Dana's purpose" in the novel is plural rather than singular, i.e., "to survive and save Rufus's life," the two objectives are never quite equal in importance, nor are they independent of each other. Protecting Rufus from harm, whether external or self-inflicted, proves instrumental to Dana's own survival once it becomes clear that he is her ancestor. Rufus's self-interest is consistently at odds with that of Dana's Black forebears, because his prosperity comes at the price of their suffering. For Dana, then, "refusing to betray herself or her people" amounts to a check on Rufus's self-indulgent and exploitative tendencies. His "subterfuge" affects both of their prospects for survival. Over the course of the narrative, Dana recognizes that Rufus's survival is meaningful to her if and only if it allows her ancestors to leave a legacy that will make her own life possible. This often requires her to make choices that prolong their suffering rather than allowing Rufus's egotism, ineptitude, insecurity, and self-destruction to defeat them both.

The Working Day

Other scholarly readings of *Kindred*, such as those of Ashraf Rushdy and Timothy Spaulding, understandably focus on Dana's inexplicable time travel as a gesture by which Butler "illustrates the fact that the past asserts itself in the present in a material and a physical way."[6] Insightful critics like Katherine McKittrick and Sami Schalk highlight what *Kindred* says regarding dis/ability as a modality of Black life, as well.[7] The novel seizes readers with an opening sentence that reveals how the story to come will leave Dana permanently altered: "I lost an arm on my last trip home."[8] This foreshadowing by Butler apprises the reader that the trials the protagonist is about to face can and eventually will permanently change her identity, and she will not make it through without an unmistakable reminder of her loss.[9] I think it important, however, to devote a separate analysis to the realities of the protagonist's everyday life before her journey alters them or casts their significance in a new light. Readers cannot ignore the gendered, racial, and class perspectives in the text that emerge from its author and narrator being Black women writers in the late 1970s. Butler has inflected *Kindred* with her own critique of social mobility in contemporary

America as well as her research into the antebellum past, and the transformative events that ensue in the novel are all the more dramatic in contrast with the tedium of the narrator's everyday life.

Dana and Kevin's household, the home of an interracial married couple just over a decade after the Supreme Court legalized unions like theirs nationwide in *Loving v. Virginia*, is a more remarkable and exceptional feature of the novel's present setting than the unimpressive circumstances under which the couple pursued their relationship. Reading *Kindred*, a thinker as astute as Karla Holloway examines the legal significance of the couple's marriage in its own time period as well as the past, whereas Dana's and Kevin's jobs generate little to no critical discussion.[10] However, their working-class backgrounds play an integral role in the story as it unfolds. Dana's point of view reflects Butler's class consciousness as an aspect of her construction of the vantage points from which contemporary Black and white Americans perceive slavery.

In the beginning of the second part of the novel, titled "The Fall," Dana recounts how she and Kevin met at a warehouse where they were both working at the time and came to view each other as kindred spirits. The flashback invokes one of the blue-collar jobs that both characters have held down to subsist while they've pursued their common vocation. At the time the story takes place, Dana works for a temp agency that places employees in positions for a limited time at low-to-moderate pay. While the differences of race and gender between Dana and Kevin are consequential, their quotidian reality as members of the same class dealing with precarity and striving for security brings them together. They are also separated by age—Kevin is twelve years older than Dana in the novel—but this difference garners little significance. They share a common present while working toward a shared future as authors. Dana learns that Kevin has published three books by the time they met, but "they'd brought so little money that he'd gone on taking mindless jobs like this one at the warehouse, and he'd gone on writing— unreasonably, against the advice of saner people. He was like me—a kindred spirit crazy enough to keep on trying."[11] Butler knew that being a writer could mean struggling for years to make ends meet through unfulfilling jobs, even with intermittent publications. Kevin once offered to support Dana financially if she quit temp work to write full-time, but she reasoned, "The independence the agency gave me was shaky, but it was real. It would hold me together until my novel was finished and I was ready to look for something more demanding. When that time came, I could walk away from the agency not owing anybody."[12] The events of the novel commence when the couple has become secure enough to buy a modest home, between Kevin's book sales and Dana's sale of a story to *The Atlantic,* a publication with a household name that would be recognizable to Butler's readers. Escaping the doldrums of the working day was a tantalizing goal that they had only just begun to realize.

At the time she wrote *Kindred,* Butler knew this struggle all too well from years of excruciating efforts to craft short fiction, essays, or salable pitches for movie-ready novels that might provide enough money to live on, all so that she could dedicate herself full-time to the expansive writing projects that sustained her mentally and emotionally. Knowing that magazines for general audiences would pay more per word for short fiction than science fiction magazines, Butler (unsuccessfully) submitted a short story with no discernible tropes of the fantastic genres, "Near of Kin," to *Redbook* in 1977.[13] She'd recommended this strategy in a letter to her close friend Victoria Rose (to whom *Kindred* was dedicated) by suggesting Victoria submit a story she'd shared with Butler to *Cosmopolitan.*[14] In her journals, Butler recounts her efforts to translate her talent for writing into nonfiction articles that might yield consistent remuneration; with anguish, she reckons that her inhibitions with regard to interpersonal conversations would make it impossible for her to succeed at a form of writing that required interviewing people.[15] Perhaps, like N. K. Jemisin, she thought her skills simply operated on a scale more suited to novels and even multivolume sagas than writing in shorter forms. In the introduction to an anthology of her short stories, *How Long 'Til Black Future Month?,* Jemisin writes that she had once found the format challenging: "Short stories were a completely different art form from novels, so shouldn't I spend my limited free time refining the thing I wanted to do, rather than learning this other thing that honestly seemed kind of boring? Also, I knew that the pay rate for short stories was abysmal; this was in the days when the SFWA [Science Fiction Writers of America]-acceptable rate for pro-level markets was only three cents per word. . . . Short stories, assuming I sold any, wouldn't even cover the cooking gas."[16] Working according to one's own inspiration, without constant deference to market expectations or genre conventions, is a privilege for writers and artists fortunate enough to enjoy it. Butler knew from experience that a career driven by deferred gratification would provide a familiar backdrop into which she might introduce spectacular developments like time travel for two characters she intended to portray as common folk.

The difference between writing as an ideal career and temp work as an unsatisfactory everyday reality is perceptible; the difference between freedom and bondage is immense by comparison. By starting the chronology of the novel with a change in the couple's standard of living, Butler set a gauge for how Dana would experience minor and major shifts in her material circumstances. When Butler was young, as she recounts in an interview, her family advised her to undertake writing as a hobby rather than a career. She came to view creative work as a form of "gambling"—speculation—because it never promised the predictable return on investment that even the most undesirable daily job would provide.[17] She struggled to internalize these values and live the kind of life to which women like Dana usually resigned themselves. But in 1974, Butler reached a point where there were not enough hours in the day to get writing done while working full-time. "I knew I had my chance right then to finish my novel without starving," she wrote in her journal, "if only I could find a way to be fired or laid off."[18] Butler negotiated her circumstances strategically: Positioning herself to be laid off, rather than quitting her job of her own accord, was a means to an end. She calculated that she would earn just a dollar less per week from unemployment assistance than she had on the job she held at the time, which was better than the total loss of income that quitting would have meant. If she quit the job, she'd be ineligible for the assistance, but once she was laid off, the meager income benefit she could draw from California's unemployment insurance would be enough to pay her modest bills while she completed a manuscript. The palpable necessity of food and housing, as well as transportation, paper, a working typewriter, and postage—costs that she added up in the margins of her notebooks—occupied Butler's mind to a degree that influenced Dana's characterization as well as Kevin's in the novel. Dana's relatives, oblivious to the fact that she hates typing, expect her to abandon her aspirations and enroll in secretarial school to obtain reliable employment.[19] The couple's newfound relief from these expenses on a day-to-day basis was one small measure of freedom within their modern lives. While the subject of freedom takes on much greater proportions in *Kindred*, the very form of the text that Butler strove to complete, as a salable novel with a marketable story amenable to adaptation, attests to her determination to attain that small measure of liberty for herself.

In April 1986, after publishing several novels, including *Kindred*, with Doubleday, Butler wrote to herself, "It is possible that I will receive $30,000 for the *Kindred* film. This is a distant thing."[20] She was hard at work on closing the distance. In 1987, after years of frustration with her original publisher, Butler sold the trade paperback rights for *Kindred* to Beacon Press and redoubled her efforts to realize residual income from her prior books. By that time, with the extraordinary success of George Lucas's *Return of the Jedi*, Stephen King's fusillade of books and adaptations, and Frank Herbert's *Dune* (reinvigorated by David Lynch's quixotic 1984 film) in mind, she wanted more than ever to see her productivity pay dividends.

The possibility for a film version of *Kindred* first paid off in 1997. Through Butler's new agent, the writer/director Nicholas Brandt entered into an agreement to pay Butler $18,000 for the option to sell the production rights for his *Kindred*-based screenplay to a Hollywood studio, with the promise of delivering Butler a portion of the film's eventual budget and net profits once it was sold and released.[21] The project retained momentum as Sigurjon Sighvattson (a co-founder of the successful early-1990s independent studio Propaganda Films) and his Palomar Pictures joined with Brandt to renew the option through May 2001, increasing their payment to $35,000.[22] As she strived to do throughout the 1970s and 1980s by taking on temporary jobs, diverting her energies to work that could be sold to magazines, and positioning herself to take advantage of the unemployment insurance that she and millions of other wage earners were paying for all the while, securing new life for her extant published works through the promise of future adaptations enabled Butler to continue writing productively in the 1990s without the hazard of diminishing returns.

While film and television adaptations of her work never entered into production within her lifetime, the path that Butler started with her new representation by Writers' House represented an unparalleled milestone in her efforts to make her writing a hot commodity. An update, in May 2000, to the film rights agreement just described introduced a crucial distinction into the possible future forms in which *Kindred* might appear. While Paragraph 7 of the 1997 film option agreement had indicated that Butler, identified as the work's "Owner," would reserve "the following rights: live television rights, live dramatic stage rights and radio rights," the new agreement went into much further detail.[23] It altered the corresponding paragraph to specify that "Owner hereby reserves the following rights: Live television rights, live dramatic stage rights, radio rights, and all Internet broadcast rights. Owner reserves all Dramatic Audio Rights and live dramatizations and all rights pertaining to the dramatized audio, digitized audio, and electronic transmissions."[24] This clarification carves out a set of modalities in which a performance in audio format based on the novel, whether live or recorded, might appear. By amending the existing agreement to delineate the probable characteristics of an audio version of *Kindred* from the property over which the prospective producers of any motion picture based on the novel could claim ownership, Butler carved out the space into which that audio adaptation would develop and accrue value of its own. The renewal and clarification of the film rights is dated May 16, 2000. Another agreement in her correspondence, dated the very next day (May 17, 2000), demonstrates why Butler had described the audio version of *Kindred* as a form of property separate from its film adaptation in such specific terms: so that she could dispose of it in exchange for consideration in the form of money. The letter from USA Networks, the parent company of the SciFi Channel and SciFi.com, reads:

> This will confirm the agreement reached between you and USA Networks with respect to the dramatic audio rights for "KINDRED" for use in an audio drama to be adapted and produced by USA. . . . In full and complete consideration of the above license hereunder, USA shall pay to you the sum of Twenty thousand Dollars ($20,000) . . . in addition in the event that USA sells at least 5000 unites of audio tapes or CD's, USA agrees to pay Contractor a 10% share of USA's net profits of those audio tapes or CD's sold in excess of 5000.[25]

The foregoing agreement governed USA and Butler's respective rights to the proceeds from an audio adaptation of *Kindred* based on a script by screenwriter Tony Daniel. Television and film star Alfre Woodard would lend her voice to the character of Dana, with Lynn Whitfield, Caroline Clay, and Ruby Dee in supporting roles. As she prophesied in 1986, *Kindred* had fulfilled its potential to bring Butler the remuneration she was hoping for as an adaptation.

I would argue that the strategic aspiration that Butler enunciated in figures of ten, twenty, and thirty thousand dollars at a time in her journals—her strategy to create saleable intellectual property—was integral to her work to become a bestselling author rather than separate from it. Selling the products of her writing in a way that allowed them to become something other than the books she had written enabled Butler to maintain her prolonged, disciplined writing habits even when sales were slow, work of any kind was scarce, and forms of work available to her other than writing were scarcely tolerable. While Butler's novels are a treasure trove today, the remuneration she received during her lifetime was less like a windfall and more like a wage for her years of diligent practice as a working writer. With that material understanding in mind, this chapter now turns to the way *Kindred* and its radio adaptation employ divergent strategies that link the story to its literary and historical precedent: the slave narrative tradition.

Busy Trying to Do a Marilyn Durham

Like speculative fictions from the nineteenth and early twentieth century, the print and radio versions of *Kindred* introduce a somewhat typical narrator transported, through inexplicable or occult means, to an unfamiliar world. Travel narratives bequeathed the shipwreck as a device for displacing characters to uncharted territory, and tales of dreamers and sleepers awakening to new realities date back to antiquity (e.g., the biblical Sleepers of Ephesus). Irving's Rip Van Winkle (1819) falls into a drunken sleep in the eighteenth century and awakens after the American Revolution, Edward Bellamy's *Looking Backward* (1887) places its protagonist under hypnosis, Rokheya Sakhawat Hossain's *Sultana's Dream* (1905) removes the heroine to Ladyland as she sleeps, and George Schuyler's *Black Empire* (1936) sees its chronicler kidnapped.

Though Butler may not have known or valued all of the aforementioned precedents, Solomon Northup's *Twelve Years a Slave* (1853) was a direct influence on her rendition of a free Black author reduced to slavery. She records her search for this text in the extensive research she conducted to write *Kindred*, and she recommends it in the course of her publicity for the novel.[26] Northup's true story recounts how he, a New Yorker who had been free from birth, took a trip to Washington, DC, during which white men deceived, poisoned, and captured him in order to sell him into slavery. Northup survives his ordeal in the dystopian South, but it never relents once it has begun. Dana, on the other hand, suffers the horror of being torn away from her waking life at unpredictable intervals to participate in the recurring nightmare of life on the Weylin plantation.

Elements from the slave narrative tradition in African American literature that recur throughout *Kindred* account for its frequent uptake by scholars and educators outside the fields of science fiction and fantasy. These influences resurface in the audio adaptation in amplified form. The directors of the radio play, Brian Smith and Jacqueline Cuscuna, a married couple, prioritized the narrative's relationship to historical reality. In a coauthored directors' note, they write, "Our first thought, even prior to 'How to adapt such a work?' was that we wanted to figure out a way to incorporate the voices of African American women who lived, struggled and survived the time of institutionalized slavery."[27]

The radio play reenacts statements that enslaved women made to amanuenses or represented in their own writings, whereas the novel left the voices of actually existing historical individuals unheard, echoing them only implicitly. Just like Butler when she was researching the text, however, Smith and Cuscuna regarded their forebears with awe. Enslaved persons who spoke in public or in private, especially those who recorded their experiences in writing, established the conditions for the reception of Butler's narrative in its print and audio forms, acting as silent partners to the storytelling process in the former case and forming an offstage chorus in the latter.

Although Tony Daniel follows Butler's example by drawing from early African American writing and contemporary film and television, respectively, to stage scenes that juxtapose representations of slavery with Dana's everyday life in the present, it is only the radio play that includes moments unfolding wholly separate from its narrative. These interstitial moments form the space for Smith and Cuscuna's desired voices from the past. Both texts rehearse the conventions of the slave narrative: the abolitionist potential of literacy, the innocence that children born into slavery lose, spectacles of violence, and—with particular deference to slave narratives by women—endemic sexual harassment. The inclusion in the radio play of certain scenes from *Kindred* that illustrate each of these themes demonstrates the indelible imprint of slave narratives on Butler's novel. The parallel space of representation within the radio play, however, makes the paradigmatic value of those conventional scenes explicit.

Butler situates enslaved authors outside of the text, absenting them to a history that precedes the reader's present, in order to delimit Dana's journey through time and space as a fantasy. They are neither seen nor heard on the pages where Dana exists; there is, literally, no sign of them within the semiotic boundaries of the text. Dana acts as a surrogate for Harriet Jacobs, Mary Prince, Elizabeth Keckley, or any living person who may have been present at the times and places that coincide with *Kindred*'s setting.

Butler did not conceive of the novel as a dramatization of historical events so much as an inquiry into history: She distinguished her aim of creating believable characters from any claim that they could plausibly represent actually existing historical individuals. At the time she was working on the book that would become *Kindred*, she described herself in a letter to Victoria Rose as "busy trying to do a Marilyn Durham—writing a novel almost entirely from research."[28] Durham's western novel, *The Man Who Loved Cat Dancing* (1972), had recently become a Hollywood hit starring Burt Reynolds. Just as Durham set a satisfying romance on her dramatized frontier, Butler hoped to recreate the antebellum eastern seaboard as a backdrop for the execution of a successful approach to crafting a story: "character in conflict with a twist."[29] In her notes from the same period, she gave herself the assignment to "behave as though I was planning a nonfiction book on Maryland—1830 to 1840. I could take notes for research as though for a term paper. I could . . . to gather my thoughts, actually write such a paper. I could also be working on the character of the people involved—getting to know them."[30] For Butler, Durham, and many other authors, fictionalized members of social formations such as slave owners, free Blacks, and enslaved persons could populate times and places drawn from the real world without the proper names that identify them with particular individuals in the historical record.

Critics categorize *Kindred* as a neo–slave narrative: a contemporary novel that adopts the forms and devices of the autobiographical tradition of enslaved Black authors in order to revise perspectives on the antebellum past and influence the function of its memory in the present. In the company of Margaret Walker's *Jubilee*, Ishmael Reed's *Flight to Canada*, and Sherley Anne Williams's *Dessa Rose*, *Kindred* recognizes the power of the slave narrative tradition to illuminate obscure spaces in history, but it also interprets that tradition as a creative and rhetorical enterprise. Neo–slave narrative authors negotiate the perception of historical reality in the present, just as their forebears intervened in contemporaneous understandings of the peculiar institution. Writing in the first person enabled enslaved authors to present their readers with impressions of the slavery that emphasized the urgency of abolition in their time. The neo–slave narrators invented by later writers take up their progenitors' positions to rehearse their roles as the arbiters of what is meaningful about the historical setting.

Contemporary authors benefit from treating the slave narrative as a rhetorical mode in which writers bend the presentation of reality, if not its substance, to their purposes. While we might make accurate inferences about the historical situation in the aggregate and afford veracity to accounts by known individuals, the author of a neo–slave narrative imagines scenarios for which enslaved people are uniquely credible informants in order to confront characters and readers with revelations, some harrowing and some anticlimactic, about slavery as a condition of subjective experience. Rather than simply compiling a catalog of the hardships endured by enslaved persons and the cruelties enacted by their antagonists as if these facts were inherently dispositive toward abolition, the slave narrative tradition relied on readers to form the association between cause and effect, between the harm and its remedy, through interpretation. Neo–slave narratives enlist readers who no longer live in the same world as the people depicted by the text in resolving its lingering dilemmas. Butler redoubles this effort in *Kindred* by representing the protagonist as a writer—someone keenly aware of how the presentation of information affects its use—and situating her alongside her ancestors in the past. Dana's perception, shaped by the experience of freedom and other aspects of the present, corroborates but also differs from that of characters representing enslaved persons. Butler engages Dana in slave narrative practices selectively, placing her in representative historical contexts while simultaneously insulating her account from certain interpretations. The reader can infer that the challenges Dana and her fictitious peers face belong to the era without entertaining the heavy-handed fantasy that they might encounter known historical figures by coincidence. The characters' distance from notable contemporaries in the period as they traverse verifiable place names and landmarks and witness typical events lends a sense of spaciousness to the world to which Dana has traveled. At the same time, the text's freedom from representation with respect to characters limits the suspension of disbelief required to associate the plot with its historical conditions.

What the novel signals through exclusion, the adaptation achieves through repetition with difference. Tropes and devices derived from the primary sources Butler has consulted inform her rendition of Dana's first-person narration and the dialogue of her nineteenth-century counterparts. Though the voices in the novel belong to fictional characters, their diction, attitudes, and tones frequently emulate those of persons whose speech and writing are documented in the slave narrative tradition. The radio play makes their latent influence manifest. The adaptation casts actors in the roles of actually existing historical persons to indicate that enslaved persons belong to a part of reality continuous with the present in which the audience lives—albeit separated by the passage of time. When these actors address the audience from a frame of reference external to the narrative, their statements prime the listeners for the kind of dramatic confrontation Dana experiences: Voices from the past are made to live again.

We Wear the Mask

An epigraph read by Caroline Clay opens Scene 19 in the play:

> The white folks didn't allow us to even look at a book. They would scold and sometimes whip us if they caught us with our head in a book.[31]

The epigraph concludes with Clay naming its source: Mary Ella Grandberry. In 1937, Grandberry spoke about her life to Levi Shelby Jr., an interviewer with the Great Depression–era Federal Writers' Project.[32] Her recollections form part of the WPA Slave Narratives, a body of recordings, transcripts, and publications that collect oral histories from survivors of American slavery. Grandberry was around ninety years old at the time she delivered her recollections, but in Clay's voice, her words live again. She had expressed the same wish that the character named Sarah shares with our heroine in the novel: that she could learn the written language she speaks, in spite of the surveillance, control, and punishment meted out by the plantation class and their agents. The WPA narratives are a vital resource for accounts of everyday life under slavery. For teachers like Jacqueline Cuscuna and me, they can make history personal in the classroom; for authors of narrative fiction, like Butler and Daniel, they provide a representative vocabulary for firsthand accounts and dialogue set in the context of slavery.

Along with the audience, characters from the present must adjust their habits and expectations to the perilous circumstances of plantation society. When Dana inadvertently pulls Kevin into the past with her for an extended period, the couple adapts to ensure their physical safety and livelihood under perilous circumstances. White and male privilege make Tom Weylin, owner of the plantation, more inclined to believe Kevin's account of where they come from than any explanation Dana could provide. Dissembling, Kevin explains that he is a writer from New York, and Dana is his property: a slave whom he bought because she could read to assist him in his work as well as satisfying his intimate needs.[33] Kevin's story is even more believable because it confirms Weylin's suspicions about Dana: "He was already pretty sure you could read and write. That's one reason he was so suspicious and mistrustful. Educated slaves aren't popular around here."[34] Dana agrees, noting, "So Nigel has been telling me." Repressing literacy was a measure of social control within the white supremacist slave society. As Butler discovered in her research, house servants in particular subverted the tactics their enslavers used to withhold knowledge from them while working in close proximity to educated members of the white household. On a photocopy from the book *The Negro in Virginia*, Butler drew a star above a passage about the way enslaved children took advantage of their school-aged white counterparts' access to books. A quotation from a formerly enslaved narrator reads, "Marse used to warn them about leaving their books around where we could get to see them. . . . All us slaves knew [white] Russell had been going over his lessons with [enslaved] Jerry for a long time, but Marse didn't know it."[35] In the margin of the photocopied page, Butler wrote, "Nigel should know how to read, between Rufe & Dana," referring to the enslaved young boy who was Rufus's age. Indeed, in the novel, Dana leverages her occasional privilege of reading to Rufus into an opportunity to fulfill young Nigel's request that she teach him, as well. "If Rufus had been a better student," Dana thinks to herself, "Nigel might already know how to read."[36]

Literacy was a precarious resource that placed enslaved persons at risk precisely because it could afford them knowledge instrumental to their survival. Understanding the written word was not the only mode of literacy that Butler thought to depict, however. She also noted passages in *The Negro in Virginia* indicating how enslaved persons learned to listen carefully when their captors attempted to conceal knowledge from them. In one reference to *The Negro in Virginia*, which Butler copied in her own handwriting onto a note card, Rawick wrote: "While serving the dinner table, waiting on guests, dressing and undressing master and mistress, house servants learned to appear as automata—not hearing, seeing, or thinking. To many, house service was not a task, but an education. As master and his guest reviled Garrison or Phillips or John Brown and his gang, servants, without twitching a muscle would rejoice silently to know there were such men . . . the thought ever present in the big house as well as in the field was: 'Us gonna be free one o' dese days.'"[37] Even when they did not know how to read or write, references like this demonstrate how enslaved people used listening as a conduit for written information. When they could read, as Frederick Douglass memorably recounts, they might be inspired to use print to find out the meaning of words like "abolition," a term that Douglass learned to associate with slave owners' vocal complaints.[38] No such references to the print culture of the abolitionist movement appear in the pages of *Kindred*. Nonetheless, Tom Weylin displays a violent intolerance toward Dana's efforts to read on her own. When she is caught alone in the family's library, Weylin reprimands her and restricts her access to books to the time she is spending with Rufus on his lessons.[39]

Daniel, Smith, and Cuscuna took the lessons of surreptitious education among the enslaved to heart in their depiction of literacy in the radio adaptation. In addition to rehearsing Dana's efforts to build trust with Rufus by reading to him, the drama also parlays this task into a means for Dana to share the education she is providing him with the people the Weylins have enslaved. The intimacy that Dana must cultivate in the course of teaching Rufus to read becomes a liminal practice that she can manipulate to the advantage of Nigel and his mother, Sarah. I call Dana's teaching "liminal" because the practice brings her (and by extension Sarah and Nigel) into proximity with books: objects from which they are otherwise alienated by their enslaved status. Dana's teaching is also liminal insofar as it renders action at disparate locations sequential in time: The scenes alternate between Rufus's room, where reading is an obligation Dana must perform, and in the cookhouse, where Sarah is typically sequestered. Dana brings these times and spaces together by reading the same book, *Robinson Crusoe*, with her diametrically opposed pupils.

Although he is a reluctant student, Rufus's request to have Dana help him with reading occurs at his initiation, in the play. The script reads:

RUFUS: Read to me from this—
/SFX/ BOOK OPENS, RUSTLE OF PAGES.
DANA: Robinson Crusoe.[40]

After Dana begins reading aloud from a passage, the script signals a transition in the play.

DANA: [from Robinson Crusoe] . . . I had many thoughts of how to do this, and what kind of a dwelling to make—
/MUS/ TRANSITION MUSIC IN
DANA: —and whether I should make me a cave in the Earth or a tent upon the Earth. And, in short, I resolved upon both, the manner of which it might not be improper to give an account of.
/SFX/ AMBIENCE OUT AND
/SFX/ CROSS FADE TO
<u>SCENE 18</u>
SLAVE QUARTERS AMBIENCE—NIGHT IN THE COUNTRY.

Notably, the transition takes place in the middle of lines spoken by Dana, indicating that in all likelihood Woodard read the lines continuously and that the recording was edited to intercut the transition music. The music begins immediately after she says the words "what kind of dwelling to make" and continues as she completes the line. She finishes speaking, leaving only the music playing; when she resumes speaking, reading from the end of the book, the music has been playing for twenty seconds. Her voice is shortly thereafter joined by Sarah attempting to pronounce the word "adventures," and the background music ends to coincide with Sarah reading the phrase "The end."[41] Interpolating language from a well-known text that was available to antebellum readers into the narrative of the play situates it in a historical world where literacy had a differential significance. The words and music linking together these scenes reinforce the fact that slavery and freedom took place on a partially shared soundscape, in contiguous spaces, where slave owners depended on enslaved people's movements and knowledge practices, however controlled, in their everyday lives. Even though the Weylins surveilled their property in many ways, removing Sarah's labor from view in order to bring its products to their table more efficiently provided her with the smallest iota of autonomy. Within this veritable "loophole of retreat," Dana and Sarah seize an opportunity to extend Dana's otherwise circumscribed movements beyond their typical purpose.

Sarah emerges as something of an iconoclast in the radio play by demonstrating attentive management of the limits within which she lives. On the night that Dana first arrives in the past with Kevin alongside her, she's sent to the kitchen to assist Sarah and her children while Tom Weylin entertains her white husband over dinner. Sarah remarks on her conspicuous speech patterns and clothing and clocks her immediately.

SARAH: What cloth is this?
DANA: Polyester double knit.

SARAH: Uh huh. (*beat*) You can read.
DANA: Yes.
SARAH: And write?[42]

Dana contrives a story about her mother teaching at a school for free Blacks back where she comes from, in New York. Sarah remains dubious, but she advises Dana, "All the same, keep it to yourself around Master Tom if you know what's good for you. He don't want no niggers 'round here talking better than him—putting freedom ideas in our heads." At this pronouncement, Sarah's son, Nigel, opines, "(*mutters*) Like we so dumb we need some stranger to make us think about freedom." Evidently, he has learned to pay attention to the way white people censor their speech in mixed company. While the content of his statement conveys the inference he has made about the Weylins' low opinion of their slaves' fitness for freedom, the stage direction in the script, "(*mutters*)," indicates that he has also learned to bear his indignation discreetly. Like Douglass and like the subjects Butler had studied in *The Negro in Virginia*, these characters have "learned to appear as automata," to guard their knowledge and feelings from their captors while subversively learning from them; moreover, in Daniel's rendition, it was important for the enslaved listener to express disdain for the notion that they would not think of emancipation themselves until someone presented the idea to them. Formerly enslaved authors, in the real world, might conceal their resentment toward such condescending whites, perhaps to credit right-thinking white allies for giving them hope and to reinforce the effectiveness of abolitionist propaganda. After all, slave narratives relied on well-meaning white people like Lydia Marie Child and Wendell Phillips for their credibility. As a fictitious reflection on the era many generations hence, *Kindred* could expose its protagonist (and the reader) to some attitudes that enslaved people only displayed among themselves, and the radio play could dramatize their interior lives even more directly, verbally and through performance.

Fascinatingly, Sarah is every bit as perceptive as Nigel and just as affected, emotionally, by reading, but she chooses not to share her strategic interests with the newcomer Dana. After Nigel's statement, Sarah returns to the subject at hand with a decision about how Dana should present herself:

SARAH: I'll get you some Osnaburg.
DANA: Pardon?
SARAH: A dress. So you'll fit in.
DANA: I'm not sure that we're staying.
SARAH: I told you I done heard 'em talking. Master Tom offered your master a job as a teacher to Mister Rufus. He said he'd do it.
DANA: I see. He did, did he?

SARAH: So you'll need a Osnaburg dress if you're gone stay out of Master Tom's gun sights.

Dana doesn't recognize the foreign word, but Sarah is talking about coarse "osnaburg" linen—a cheap export from the German textile manufacturing city of Osnabrück. In her time, the word is a metonym for the kind of fabric dumped in the markets of working-class England, the Caribbean, and the Eastern seaboard of the North American mainland, which was used to clothe enslaved and incarcerated populations.[43] This historical common sense identifies Sarah as a person to whom Dana should be able to turn to negotiate the hazards of everyday life as long as she remains in the past.

This exchange also suggests that the situation Dana might treat as a temporary predicament is a foregone conclusion from Sarah's perspective. When they discuss sleeping arrangements, Sarah leads Dana to question her own presumptions about how people will treat her relationship with Kevin.

SARAH: We can give you a pallet out in the quarters. (*beat*) But he share his bed with you, don't he?
DANA: What? Who?
SARAH: Your Master Kevin.
DANA: Yes. Yes, but it isn't what you think.
SARAH: What do I think?
DANA: (*beat*) I guess I don't know.
SARAH: Mmm hmm. I've see'd how things can get to be with or without somebody wanting them to be so.[44]

At every turn, Dana's efforts to occlude her predicates falter against Sarah's superior discernment. As the voice of an era when resistance was alternately subtle and violent, Sarah represents the tactical inscrutability enslaved women performed in order to negotiate their circumstances. She speaks with the veiled wisdom of the narrators quoted in the play's epigraphs. Dana learns from Sarah's example that she is always being observed and that she must keep her motives concealed without letting on that she is being evasive. Just as Butler read slave narratives and histories to construct the characters Dana would meet and establish the conflicts they would face in her novel, in the play, Dana studies the text of Sarah's everyday performance to determine how her ancestors managed to survive.

The Scene of Subjugation

Across her fiction, Butler depicted physical violence, sexual assault, and other visceral experiences of suffering frankly without allowing them to become gratuitous. *Kindred* was no exception: Its violence remains integral to the plot while never descending into spectacle. Each section of the novel takes its title from a situation that poses a mortal risk to Rufus and his child, Hagar, who is Dana's imperiled ancestor: "The River," where Rufus nearly drowns, "The Fire," which threatens to burn down his house, "The Fall," where he tumbles from his horse, "The Fight," which he instigates, "The Storm," in which he gets lost, and "The Rope." The wonder is not so much that Rufus is unlucky enough to land himself consistently in danger but that his instrumental role in Dana's future existence gives his miserable life enough value to keep her coming back. Although the hazards Rufus invites structure the text by pulling Dana back in time to save him, she is able to return to her life in the present whenever she comes close to dying in the past. Thus, while any rendition of *Kindred* is guaranteed to depict life-threatening violence and its traumatic aftermath, neither the novel nor the radio play can allow these moments to supersede the progress of the narrative.

Of all the violent moments in the novel, the scene in which Tom Weylin beats Dana to punish her for removing books from his library undoubtedly presented a challenge for Smith, Cuscuna, and Daniel to adapt. Using a single narrator, Butler affords violence a systematic function in Dana's experience in order to immerse the reader in her struggle for survival. While she is in the past, abrupt confrontations with life-threatening danger are the only device that can move Dana back to the present. The radio play maintains this structure in the narrative by reproducing Dana's first return to the present the way it takes place in the novel: Tom Weylin points a rifle at her, prepared to shoot, and she reappears before an incredulous Kevin just as suddenly as she'd vanished. The likelihood of violence distinguishes the times and places Dana inhabits from one another in *Kindred*. Violence is a boundary-making device between settings and a differential force in Dana's habitus: The reader can follow her interior monologue as her senses and her comportment shift from one environment to another. As Dana reckons with the reality that slavery is a part of her historical and ongoing experience that is felt and perceived, rather than fantasized, violence takes up a legible place in her consciousness. The reader must rely on her first-person account to share that consciousness to whatever extent is possible. In the radio play, by contrast, Dana's contemporary life and her ancestors' past alike are dramatic situations whose relevance the audience is to apprehend through multiple narrators. Epigraphs from enslaved women orient the audience to violence as a disciplinary feature of slavery before Dana encounters it directly. Several epigraphs precede this scene of Dana's beating in the radio play, and another follows it, by way of explanation. Quotations from Mary Prince, Elizabeth Sparks, and Mary Ella Grandberry convey how the slave owners' society menaced their bodies. Sparks gestures to the harrowing experience ahead of Dana just after the first time she disappears to the past and comes back again:

> ELIZABETH SPARKS: He beat women as well as men. Beat women just like men. Beat women naked and wash 'em down in brine. Sometimes they beat 'em so bad they just couldn't stand it and they run away to the woods. . . . Foreman get you to come back and then he beat you to death again.[45]

The radio play provides warnings like this one, leading the audience to anticipate that Dana will face similar hazards. As Dana witnesses enslaved characters facing beatings firsthand, the audience becomes acutely aware of how the Weylins use violence to control the movements of Black people in their midst.

From Dana's vantage point, while she is indoors with Sarah, we overhear the sound effects of Tom Weylin's whip lashing the flesh of a field hand named Jacob and his cries of pain. The contact takes place at a distance, according to stage directions, which read, "DISTANT—SOUND OF A WHIP BEING EMPLOYED" and "JACOB AND TOM ARE AT A DISTANCE, OUTSIDE IN THE YARD."[46] If the scene hadn't already stoked fear in the audience, Sarah's interpretation makes it clear: "That could be you, girl, if you don't watch out for them Weylins." It's crucial that she says "Weylins," plural, because Sarah has just warned Dana to be wary of both Tom Weylin and his wife, Margaret. Sarah apprises Dana that she described her work as satisfactory to Tom Weylin, who has inquired into the prospect of buying her to add to his own reserves of slave labor. Regarding Margaret, however, Dana remains quizzical.

> DANA: Kevin—Mr. Franklin—won't sell me.
> SARAH: No. Guess he won't. Anyway, Miss Margaret don't want you here.
> DANA: So I've gathered.
> SARAH: Bitch.
> /MUS/ IN—MINIMAL BUT POIGNANT ENOUGH TO MAKE THE POINT
> DANA: Pardon?
> SARAH: Well, greedy and mean as she is, at least she don't bother Nigel. She left me one of 'em.

Dana is taken aback at the unexpected show of emotion from Sarah, and the music that interjects reinforces the shift in tone. Sarah reveals that Nigel is her only remaining child. Margaret Weylin sold the others away to accumulate material possessions. What's more: the play's cast list identifies Nigel as Sarah's son by Tom Weylin. Inscribing the mistress's mercurial jealousy in the historically familiar dynamic of the plantation sexual economy contributes further realism to Dana's predicament. Sarah's withholding demeanor takes on a more threatening cast if we understand them as attributes of a hidden motive awaiting satisfaction; by extension, the open secret of her agenda heightens the stakes of Dana's perceived transgressions. When Dana acts on her own modern impulse to empower Sarah, Nigel, and even Rufus, through reading, it strikes the paranoid Weylins as retaliation for their abusive, dysfunctional paternalism.

In the radio play, when Tom Weylin discovers that Dana has been reading to young Nigel, he storms into the cookhouse to set upon her with a whip. First, he menaces Sarah, whose reaction is unusually credulous: "(*whispers*) You said you wouldn't. You said you wouldn't."[47] Weylin overcomes Sarah and ties Dana to a post. She cries out for help, for Kevin, for God, over the course of as many as forty lashes. This scene affirms Sarah's warning and echoes the epigraph from Grandberry. The joint admonition, from a fictitious and real witness to such a horror, enhances the reality effect of what Dana endures. Weylin shouts, enraged:

> TOM: I treated you good. And you paid me back by stealing from me. Stealing my books. Reading! . . . Niggers don't talk that way. They don't talk like you. They don't act like you. Not *my* niggers!

The threat to her life is so severe that it jolts Dana back to her own time period, and with Kevin too distant to make physical contact, he remains in the past.

Weylin's discovery and his violent reaction also occur in the novel, and they lead to the same consequence in the plot: Dana remains separated from Kevin until her connection to Rufus causes her to return. For Kevin, this means spending five years in the antebellum era. While the epigraph insinuates that Dana's suffering results from the Weylins' obsessive control over the people they have enslaved, the subtext of Tom Weylin fathering Sarah's children complicates the narrative. This particular scandal was contrived for the radio play; in the novel, Butler identifies Sarah as the mother to Carrie, a young girl of unknown paternity who does not appear in the radio adaptation. Distorted through the filters of Tom and Margaret Weylin's petty grievances and sense of betrayal, in the radio play, Dana's beating might be interpreted as a casualty of the personal enmity between Sarah and her captors rather than an element in the structure of discipline that maintains slavery itself. Both versions of the story seem to condemn Dana for doing more than looking at books—for learning from them and teaching others how—but only the radio play situates her injury in the aftermath of Tom Weylin overhearing secrets that were meant to go unspoken among the enslaved. In this way, the drama subjects Dana to unwritten, questionable aspects of slavery that are only corroborated in the dialogue of her fictitious counterparts rather than situations that strictly reiterate the facts of plantation life according to the historical record. Tom Weylin's intimately personal animus toward the Black people under his control is as salient a cause for Dana's misfortune as the institution of slavery itself, in the play.

Dana's defiance during her beating impels the plot in a similar fashion both in the novel and the radio play. It leads to an extended separation between her and Kevin, after which she returns to find him a changed man. In light of the violence Dana had witnessed but not yet experienced up to this point, the scene underscores how sheltered she had been from the psychological and physical ravages of slavery. As the epigraphs portend, enslaved people could expect violence at any time and for any reason (or none that was apparent at all). Dana and Kevin commiserated over this harsh reality while observing children on the Weylin plantation playing games that emulate their role models. The game rehearses a slave auction:

> SAMMY: She young and strong. She worth plenty money. Two hundred dollars. Who bid two hundred dollars?
> THE CHILDREN ARE AT A DISTANCE NOW, WITH DANA AND KEVIN CLOSE.
> DANA: Oh, Kevin.
> KEVIN: I've seen them play this game before.
> SAMMY: Do I hear two hundred?
> GIRL: I'm worth more than two hundred dollars, Sammy! You sold Martha for five hundred dollars . . .
> SAMMY: You shut your mouth. You ain't supposed to say nothing. When Marse Tom bought Mama and me, we didn't say nothing.
> DANA: I've seen them play at field work, too.
> KEVIN: My God, why can't we go home? This place is diseased.
> DANA: Even the games they play are preparing them for the future.
> KEVIN: A future that will come whether they understand it or not.
> DANA: That doesn't make it right.
> KEVIN: No. (*sighs*) Maybe you're reading too much into a kid's game.
> DANA: And maybe you're reading too little.

Dana's expressions of concern regard the children's future, which Kevin agrees is coming "whether they understand it or not." The two of them believe they can relegate the undesirable spectacle to their own historical past. Their fears were immediately realized by Dana's beating, as if to fulfill the prophetic value of the slave narratives that frame these events for the radio play's audience.

Silencing the Past

As she struggles with her displacement in time and space and her separation from the world she knows, including Kevin, Dana performs the incredulity of a contemporary observer reduced to slavery. One benefit of the dislocated narrator in a utopia or dystopia is their capacity to see through the eyes of the reader and speak their language. In the fictionalized historical setting that the neo–slave narrative represents, a woman like Dana is far more like the reader, who is among the author's peers in the present, than any of the people to whom she is bound by the past. In the novel, when Dana interacts with Alice—the free Black woman with whom Rufus will conceive the ancestor recorded in her family bible—Butler ensures that the reader knows that Dana sees a resemblance between them. The physical likeness serves as a connection between Dana and her ancestors, at first, but over time, she gradually comes to appreciate how time has made it impossible for two women with their respective life experiences to think or act alike.

The cover of the original Doubleday hardcover edition of the novel, by Laurence Schwinger, thematizes the characters' divergence in spite of their similar appearance. Beneath the title, the busts of two Black women face away from each other, in profile, with an hourglass between them. Their heads, both hairless, are mirror images in shape. Their color is the same mahogany, but eyeshadow is unmistakably present on one woman's half-closed lids. The same woman wears a glinting earring and thin gold necklace, while the other woman's only adornment is the upturned white lace collar of her garment. The eye of the latter opens wide in the direction she faces: toward the source of light. Dense rows of brushstrokes blend together in the space behind each woman's head and converge above the top half of the hourglass to indicate that the two figures relate to each other across time. The cover is a double image of the same model, but its subjects, within the novel, are far more different than the same woman styled in two ways. The cover becomes legible as a visual index of Dana's relationship to Alice for a contemporary reader who can differentiate the woman made up in accordance with her own daily habits and possessed of simple jewelry, on the one hand, from the woman dressed in the uniform of servitude, on the other.

In the past, however, the features Dana has inherited from her progenitors condense into a controlling image. As Dana begins to piece together the possibility that saving Rufus's life will ensure her own existence, young Rufus is

Figure 5: Cover art by Larry Schwinger for the first edition of *Kindred*, published by Doubleday, 1979. *Source*: Image from the Huntington Library, (c) Estate of Octavia E. Butler.

already able to suggest that she resembles enslaved people in his life: "'You look a little like Alice's mother. If you wore a dress and tied your hair up, you'd look a lot like her.'"[48] Dana dissembles, but when she meets Alice again once the girl is closer to her age, she concurs: "I looked at her in surprise. Tall and slender and dark, she was. A little like me. Maybe a lot like me."[49] After Rufus has taken Alice as a concubine, she and Dana compare their interactions with him. Alice notes, ruefully, "'We're two halves of the same woman—at least in his crazy head.'"[50] Dana fully comprehends her interpretation as a warning, when, at the climax of the story, Rufus attempts to rape her, ostensibly asserting the same control he once held over Alice. In the novel, Rufus complains to Dana, "'[Alice] hated me. From the first time I forced her. . . . She had stopped hating me. I wonder how long it will take you.'"[51] In the play, he declares, menacingly, "You're going to take Alice's place."[52] In both versions of the narrative, Dana's achievement of a final separation between Rufus and herself depends on her denying him the ability to make her submit. After Hagar has been born, while Alice ends her life by suicide in order to escape Rufus's control, Dana kills him to preserve her own autonomy. Rufus's ability to define Dana's existence operates through kinship: a relation and not an identity. She is never identical to Alice, and her survival after Rufus's and Alice's deaths grimly proves the difference.

Dana's resemblance to Alice and her family members is one of many visual impressions that the radio play must translate from the novel's language, which consists entirely of the first-person narrator's thought, speech, and perception (including her perception of others' speech and actions), into its multiperspectival dialogue. The radio play dramatizes Dana's experience of sights, sounds, and other sensations by conveying information within different actors' dialogue and inscribing nonverbal elements from the text as sound effects. The speech genres and sound sources that comprise the radio play help the audience perceive its different time periods, geographical locations, and built environments. For instance, horses' hooves and turning wheels denote carriages, a mode of transportation from the past, while electronically filtered voices from the radio indicate that Dana is listening to them in the late twentieth century. When Dana moves between the present and the past for the first time, a sound effect labeled "HEARTBEAT" rises and falls rhythmically in the background.[53] Horns blow suspensefully to introduce the inexplicable change in environment, and they clash together with a drum once Dana is thrown into the action of her first effort to rescue Rufus. The next time the heartbeat occurs, a sound effect that Daniel labels "SEVERAL STINGER BEATS" announces menacingly that these disappearances will be a repeated event as Dana is pulled back to antebellum Maryland once again. This motif accompanies Dana's trips across time, gradually rising from the background to drown out the characters' fearful, astonished, and exclamatory expressions. Because violent threats to her or Rufus's life trigger Dana's movement through time, the heartbeat sound is always part of a cacophony including screams, blows, curses, crashes, and cries for help. These sonic elements are instrumental to the narrative shared by the novel and radio play. However, they also work in conjunction with other sounds, such as the epigraphs, that are liminal to the text.

Music augments the transitions between certain scenes. The primary motif in the production is an instrumental theme that Tony Daniel's script names "SAGA." It plays for the first time while Dana and Kevin are separated, as she wonders aloud to Rufus if she will ever see him again.[54] It recurs, with the added note "BECOMES WISTFUL," in Daniel's text, as Rufus commiserates with Dana over his longing for Alice. Several times before the play's climax, the SAGA theme plays to suggest parallels between Dana's desire to be reunited with Kevin, on the one hand, and Rufus's manipulative desires, on the other. While Dana yearns for the authentic love of the only living man who sees her as an equal, Rufus acts possessively toward her, Alice, and his newborn daughter, Hagar. When the SAGA theme accompanies epigraphs between scenes, the words of enslaved women relate their awareness of the same disparate tides of love and control that Dana's ordeal rehearses for the audience.

Before the first scene where the SAGA theme can be heard, the voice attributed to Elizabeth Keckley reads, in part:

> ELIZABETH KECKLEY: I can remember the scene as if it were but yesterday; how my father cried out against the cruel separation; his last kiss; his wild straining of my mother to his bosom; the solemn prayer to heaven; the tears and sobs—the fearful anguish of broken hearts. The last kiss, the last goodbye; and he, my father, was gone, gone forever. (*beat*) The shadow eclipsed the sunshine, and love brought despair.[55]

Her father's sale shattered Keckley's family. It also shook her faith in love. The subordination of familial ties to commerce on the Weylin plantation mirrors this historical reality. It begins to take its toll on Dana, as she fears her relationship with Kevin might never be restored.

Later, we hear the SAGA theme in the aftermath of a quotation from Harriet Jacobs.

> HARRIET JACOBS: It was on a lovely spring morning, and when I marked the sunlight dancing here and there, its beauty seemed to mock my sadness. For my master, whose restless, craving, vicious

> nature roved about day and night, seeking whom to devour, had just left me, with stinging scorching words; words that scathed ear and brain like fire.[56]

This passage refers to James Norcom, known pseudonymously as "Dr. Flint" in Jacobs's narrative: the cruel slaveowner who harassed her relentlessly until she made her escape. It represents the dread the audience may come to ascribe to Rufus as he redoubles his efforts to impose his will on Dana. In the final act of the play, like the novel, Rufus begins to leverage his control over Dana's livelihood in the past to close in on her sexually, as well. The audience may not know that Jacobs conceived children with Samuel Sawyer, an attorney, whose property rights as a white man shielded them from Norcom's ownership and may have preserved her life.[57] Butler and the directors responsible for the adaptation, however, studied Jacobs's narrative and took her decisions into account when depicting Dana's efforts to evade Rufus's clutches. In Kevin's absence, there was no white male rival for Rufus's designs. In each version of *Kindred*, by the end, Dana fears that even after Hagar has been born to establish her free Black heritage in the past, she may never return to her own time. Dana's reluctant adjustment to her surroundings threatens to give way to hopelessness. Epigraphs remind us that in spite of how impressive Dana's survival may appear, at any moment the "shadow" might eclipse "the sunshine," or a glimpse of "beauty," such as Hagar's birth, would "mock" her sadness.

Amid these implicit and thematizing elements that adapt the story's historical and psychological concerns, the radio play lacks one of the novel's nonverbal presences that Butler used to offset the past from the present. In the novel, Sarah has a daughter, Carrie, who does not have the capacity to speak. Dana's first-person perception and the observations shared by other characters verbalize Carrie's actions in the text. In the novel, it was Carrie who felt the texture of Dana's clothing and brought its unusual quality to Sarah's attention, prompting her to obtain osnaburg to help her fit in. And in the novel, Carrie helps Dana cope with Margaret Weylin's imperiousness while serving the mistress in the house. She communicates through gesture. She never speaks, and Butler's enslaved characters have no access to sign language to communicate with their Deaf or nonverbal brethren. Yet Carrie imparts wisdom to Dana when the feeling of kinship that has helped her survive life among the enslaved frays under the weight of her obligations to Rufus.

> "I was beginning to feel like a traitor," I said. "Guilty for saving him. Now . . . I don't know what to feel. Somehow, I always seem to forgive him for what he does to me. I can't hate him the way I should until I

> see him doing things to other people." I shook my head. "I guess I can see why there are those here who think I'm more white than black."
>
> Carrie made quick waving-aside gestures, her expression annoyed. She came over to me and wiped one side of my face with her fingers—wiped hard. I drew back, and she held her fingers in front of me, showed me both sides. But for once, I didn't understand.
>
> Frustrated, she took me by the hand and led me out to where Nigel was chopping firewood. There, before him, she repeated the face-rubbing gesture, and he nodded.
>
> "She means it doesn't come off, Dana," he said quietly. "The black. She means the devil with people who say you're anything but what you are."[58]

Carrie even helps deliver Hagar—the child who ties Dana to the generations between them.

Butler provided Dana with an unforgettable ally in Carrie. While the character's distinguishing feature proved prohibitively difficult for Daniel to adapt for radio, maintaining an explanation for Carrie's inability to speak had presented Butler with a challenge of her own. In a photocopied page from a textbook she undoubtedly obtained from a public library, which she identifies as Eric Lenneberg's *Biological Foundations of Language*, Butler wrote, "Here is Carrie's problem: Dysarthria—caused by a lesion to the grey matter."[59] Butler has underlined a full paragraph on her copy of a later page from the same book. The paragraph describes the congenital brain anatomy of children diagnosed with dysarthria, and it ends with a sentence directly applicable to Carrie's relationship to speech in the novel: "Children may acquire a complete understanding of language without ever having been able to produce intelligible words." In the margin next to these words, Butler has written, "Dana will finally settle on some kind of brain damage. She cannot know, of course, but she can question intelligently." This research that Butler conducted not only establishes a realistic basis for the representation of Carrie's disability in the text, but it also contributes to Dana's characterization as a rational person of her time. She could recognize that modern medical knowledge had answers to some questions of profound importance in people's lives. Crucially, Carrie was an active participant in the day-to-day reality that Dana experienced in the past, alongside the likes of Alice, Sarah, and Rufus, but she could not have left a record of her life in the same form that they might have if they had existed. In light of her absence from the play, her presence in the novel underscores the determinative power of speech in the memory of slavery. When present-day actors perform the words of women who lived in the historical conditions that *Kindred* fictionalizes, they immortalize voices that were first heard centuries ago. Those voices were heard by people like Carrie, who understood every word, and people like Rufus, who did not.

> It's not that we haven't always been here, since there was a here. It is that the letters of our names have been scrambled when they were not totally erased, and our fingerprints upon the handles of history have been called the random brushings of birds.
>
> —AUDRE LORDE, "WILD WOMEN IN THE WHIRLWIND"

When Smith and Cuscuna brought the text of slave narratives into their version of *Kindred,* they completed a circuit in American memory. In the present, historical fiction can represent the past in terms intelligible to contemporary readers. Butler took this practice a step further in her novel by using the speculative device of time travel to depict experiences so painful that surviving them nearly defies comprehension. In Butler's effort to represent the awesome significance of that survival, she could not reproduce the past, but she could make it perceptible—known, and felt, if not understood. The words of survivors incorporated in the radio play as epigraphs perform the same task. They stand outside the story while grounding the realism of its setting in their own lives. With so much of her time and thought occupied by the demands of survival in her own reality, the circumstances under which Butler could write were governed by seemingly inescapable material constraints. But speculation was her loophole of retreat. After she confronted the risk inherent in writing for a living and embraced the life that writing could provide, her investment accrued meaningful value. The returns were neither immediate nor intangible but in between: *Kindred* did not become profitable as an uncompromised realization of its author's vision, but rather, it succeeded at fulfilling its purpose for Butler insofar as she imbued it with the potential to change. In no small part because of its reliance on areas of historical knowledge that can never be fully known from the present, *Kindred* could approximate reality in more familiar ways or deviate further from what the record shows.

By constructing the narrative in a form that complemented its intangible value as an affirmation of our enslaved ancestors' hard-fought survival with its appeal as a piece of alienable property that could be rewarding for her as well as useful to others, Butler placed *Kindred* into the domain where slave narratives, radio plays, and historical lessons perform their vital work.

4
Haunting and Futurity in the *Woman's Hour*
Toni Morrison's Beloved

> I like the feeling of a *told* story, where you hear a voice but you can't identify it . . . So you have this sort of guide. But that guide can't have a personality; it can only have a sound.
>
> —TONI MORRISON, "THE SITE OF MEMORY"

While its popularity has waxed and waned in the United States, radio drama has enjoyed a virtually uninterrupted presence on the BBC. From its earliest days, radio has played host to an ever-evolving array of living soundscapes through which British listeners know themselves and the world. Drama figures centrally in British broadcasting. The dramatic works heard on British radio represent a repository of the public's cultural heritage from which artists draw inspiration and a reservoir that is constantly replenished with new interventions. The integral function of radio in discourses of national, racial, linguistic, and geographic subjectivity affords it a place of significance for investigations into modern and contemporary Black British cultural life. The relevance of what happens on the BBC for African American culture is oblique, at best. In the literary and media context of *Audiofuturism*, however, a Black British rendition of African American literature offers compelling insights into the shared imaginary of readers and listeners haunted by the legacies of slavery.

This chapter analyzes the 2016 BBC radio adaptation of Toni Morrison's *Beloved* by the playwright Patricia Cumper. In the words of the Radio 4 copy associated with the program, the narrative "melds horror and poetry" to relate Black American women's negotiation of a life in freedom that is relentlessly haunted by slavery. The performance uses sound to preserve and reframe what the novel accomplishes in text: a powerful demonstration of haunting as the modality through which the memory of slavery influences the present and future of American culture. The format of the radio play presents a challenge within this task by dividing the adaptation into ten fifteen-minute episodes. Accordingly, I examine how each episode of the ten-part serial and the production as a whole reiterate the novel's dilemma of haunting on structural and stylistic levels. To evaluate the radio play as a distinctive sound artifact while maintaining consideration for its relationship to the novel, I employ a framework of *audionarratology*. This approach emphasizes those features of the sound work constitutive of its narrativity and highlights the ways in which sound proves central to understanding the original text. In addition to enlisting Morrison's reputation in the fulfillment of longstanding objectives of BBC radio—to entertain, educate, and provoke reflection—the adaptation affords Cumper a unique role in that endeavor as a Black British author. The unique history of British broadcasting sets a distinctive task for the playwright as well as the cast. Surmounting the differences of nation and medium, however, sound and memory combine in the dramatization to hold out the possibility that Black readers and listeners on both sides of the Atlantic might claim radio drama as part of a shared cultural heritage.

Readers may also embrace or reject the application of a liberal definition of "speculative fiction" to *Beloved*. The categorizing logic of genre, which conventionally separates texts from one another, is relevant but insufficient to capturing how the narrative situates haunting and speculation squarely within American social and political life—for Black subjects, at least. As Morrison acknowledges in "The Site of Memory," "The work that I do frequently falls, in the minds of most people, into that realm of fiction called fantastic, or mythic, or magical, or unbelievable."[1] Here, she is speaking to the concerns that connect her work to a broader legacy of Black speculative thought. Whereas plenty of writers, like Octavia E. Butler, Samuel Delany, Frank Yerby, and George Schuyler, published within the confines of genre fiction, I have examined radio drama in part to illustrate how utopian and fantastic tendencies in the work of Black authors persist across medium and genre. Like W. E. B. Du Bois, Pauline Hopkins, Roi Ottley, Ralph Ellison, Alice Walker, and many others, Morrison contributes to the tradition of a Black fantastic in literature from a space of marginality that is as thoroughly racialized as it is characterized by its authors' noncommittal relationship with realism. Insofar as it defies generic expectations rooted in predominantly white canon formations, Black cultural production compels attention to the fantastic in ways that critics have increasingly recognized in the twenty-first century. Recent works by Saidiya Hartman, Jayna Brown, Darieck Scott, Tavia Nyong'o, and

Ekow Eshun represent a school of thought in Black study that places fabulation, fantasy, and utopianism at the heart of different cultural endeavors that exemplify the politics of Black being. According to this reckoning, it is not the peculiarity of the ghost story but its centrality to the social world the text invokes that affords *Beloved* its exemplary place within African American literature. As Morrison writes: "The single most uncontroversial thing one can say about the institution of slavery vis-à-vis contemporary time, is that it haunts us all."[2] Through her adaptation of Morrison's haunting narrative, Patricia Cumper prolongs a tradition of Black speculative practice as "a fantastic, radical epistemological modality through which Afro-Atlantic identity can be lived across time and space."[3]

Avery Gordon's account of the demands that haunting places on the subjects who experience it, first articulated in *Ghostly Matters*, is as much an analysis of our preoccupation with the past as it is an argument for new orientations toward the future. The signature affect of haunting, in her formulation, is a sense of urgency that unsettles familiar perceptions and responses. She refers to it as "something to be done." In both the novel and the radio play, this "something to be done" determines the relation between the past shared by the characters in *Beloved* and their present. Importantly, for the adaptation, it also determines the relationship between the text's historical setting and the present inhabited by its audience. When past violences and their ongoing repression come out of their seemingly settled place in discourse and irrupt into the present in a new way, as a haunting, new possibilities emerge in the form of "something to be done." The presence of this demand displaces the otherwise reliable sense that nothing *can* be done about the past. Gordon describes this something to be done as remembering, i.e., the demand to pay attention to what repressive forces compel us to forget. She also defines it as a quality of futurity. The futurity that is integral to haunting lends to memory "a certain retrospective urgency: the something-to-be-done feels as if it has already been needed or wanted before, perhaps forever, certainly for a long time, and we cannot wait for it any longer."[4] When haunting disturbs the status quo, urgency arises, because "when the repression isn't working anymore the trouble that results creates conditions that demand renarrativization."[5] The urgency is retrospective because it returns our faculties of contemplation and judgment to a moment of determination we believed to be finished. The urgency is futuristic for the same reason: It leads us to believe it is impossible for things to go on the way they have been. Invoking her work with the highly experimental *Hawthorn Archive*, Gordon refers to the future state that haunting brings to its subjects' attention as the possibility of "being-in-difference," which she describes as

> a political consciousness and a sensuous knowledge, a standpoint and a mindset for living on better terms than we're offered, for living as if you had the necessity and the freedom to do so, for living in the acknowledgement that, despite the overwhelming power of all the systems of domination which are trying to kill us, they never quite become us.[6]

The renarrativization occasioned by haunting compels us to assign new significance to the past by insisting that we have not accounted for everything it makes possible in the present. The possible futures that emerge from being-in-difference will seem unprecedented and even unbelievable. They redefine the relation between past and present without disputing what the past has been. This redefinition engenders narratives that deviate from our common sense about what is historically possible, especially when it takes place in light of indisputable structural violence, such as the events portrayed in *Beloved*.

Finally, this chapter maintains *Audiofuturism*'s engagement in sound studies through its exploration of audionarratology. Sound is indelibly inscribed in Morrison's writing, and of course, it is the intended vehicle for Cumper's script. Radio drama lends itself to multiple theoretical currents at work in sound studies, from the poststructuralist and jazz-inflected interpretations that predominate in Black studies to phenomenology, new materialism, and Peircean semiotics.[7] This chapter's focus on narrative emerges out of a concern with the episodic structure of the radio production and the metatextual function of the narrator. As I will discuss, the careful orchestration of sounds ensures that each episode reiterates the exigency of haunting as the central preoccupation of the story as a whole. In both the novel and the radio play, the narrator's "voice" is a perceptible effect of tactics employed by Morrison and Cumper, respectively, to construct a position for the reader/listener. Like other treatments of Morrison's work, my analysis remembers that the reader is already implicitly a listener for the purposes of the text. Other approaches may take greater interest in the construction of the acoustic apparatus and the specifically nonverbal elements of radio drama in order to differentiate the art form from literature.[8] In keeping with a Black Diasporic discursive repertoire indelibly marked by sound, my interpretation underscores how thoroughly sonic the source text has always been.

Woman's Hour

I can no longer recall exactly how I learned that BBC radio had produced an adaptation of *Beloved*, but a long time elapsed between my realization that it existed and the first time I listened to it. In the summer of 2016, I contacted Patricia Cumper, and she graciously accommodated my request to obtain the scripts for the radio play after confirming with its producer, Sasha Yevtushenko, that this would be permissible. The author's gift revealed to me that the play had been structured into ten episodes that were recorded in October 2015 at the BBC Broadcasting House in Westminster. It was edited in November and broadcast for the first time in January 2016. The call sheets for each episode were an impressive array of talent: the names of Adjoa Andoh, Gugu Mbatha-Raw, and Pippa Bennett-Warner stood out. Yevtushenko had provided a link to the audio via the cloud-based file-sharing service Box, but I did not access it before the link expired. Meanwhile, I commenced work on other parts of this study and reasoned that I would return to this adaptation when the time came to compose the book's final chapter.

It would be nearly eight years before I listened to the production and began writing about it. In the interim, Toni Morrison and Queen Elizabeth II died, the United Kingdom left the European Union, I changed jobs, and the play had not been broadcast since 2018. Because the audio from this program was unavailable online, a colleague recommended that I contact the British Library to obtain the recordings. When I did so, I learned that the library had not yet obtained or indexed this program, but they would obtain listening copies of the recordings retained by the BBC that they could make available to their patrons. Before planning a trip to listen in person, I decided to request digital copies. That was in October 2023, when the British Library suffered a significant cybersecurity failure that impeded their ability to fulfill many information technology functions. An archivist thoughtfully suggested that I obtain the files directly from the BBC, which I was fortunately able to do in January 2024.

In January 2016, *Beloved* comprised the 15 Minute Drama segment that concludes the *Woman's Hour* program on weekday mornings on Radio 4.[9] *Woman's Hour* began in October 1946, as part of the postwar daytime programming on the BBC Light Programme. Drama had always been part of the *Woman's Hour* offerings; the first edition included the "daily afternoon serial reading" that listeners had come to expect, along with discussions of householding, childcare, psychology, interviews with prominent women, and issues deemed pertinent to "millions of housewives up and down the country."[10] During the same period, while the BBC launched its Third Programme to appeal to and cultivate avant-garde tastes among listeners, the Light service maintained familiar conventions with a focus on entertainment. *Woman's Hour* formed part of an existing soundscape that was bifurcated into high and low strata, with short-form serial drama situated as a complement to other light fare including popular music. The first selections for *Woman's Hour* Drama were continuations of an ongoing serial, *Under the Red Robe*, a sensational historical romance set in Bourbon France, by Stanley Weyman.[11] Programming that targeted women had been a staple of the BBC since its inception in the 1920s, with slightly different titles and formats and a shifting stable of presenters.[12] As the program and its parent institution evolved and *Woman's Hour's* moved to the all-talk Radio 4 in the 1970s, its dramatic repertoire expanded without abandoning the fifteen-minute serial format. Later works featured on the hour included original works for radio, nonfiction stories drawn from everyday life and history, and adaptations from a broad range of authors: Graham Greene, Margery Sharp, P. G. Wodehouse, Edith Wharton. Speculative fiction accrued ample time in fifteen-minute increments through dramatizations of work by John Wyndham, Jane Rogers, Doris Lessing, and Isaac Asimov at the end of *Woman's Hour.*

The serials associated with *Woman's Hour* varied in tone and hardly hesitated to dramatize the controversial topics the program had addressed over the years. As its longtime editor Sally Feldman wrote, "While most expected to be challenged by us there was a section of the Radio 4 audience who seemed to look out for it, always writing in to complain if items like contraception, or sexy bits of the serial, appeared during the school holidays."[13] A 2016 article in the *Evening Standard* raised eyebrows by announcing that an adaptation of Erica Jong's *Fear of Flying* would be "one of the rudest dramatisations in its history," since BBC radio policies, unlike standards for daytime television, would not bar the use of profanity or sexually explicit language.[14] When the program moved from afternoons to mornings in 1991, Feldman emphasized drama as a source of continuity for the audience: "We'll still offer the celebrity interviews; the long, considered features; the news-reactiveness, the discussions, and of course the drama serial . . . to the regular audience, the changes will be imperceptible."[15] Reflecting on the character of *Woman's Hour* during her tenure, she wrote:

> To be honest, the changes we wrought were cosmetic rather than fundamental. Reflecting the busier feel of morning routines, more short, snappy pieces were injected to punctuate the longer debates and crafted features, as well as more celebrity guests and audience interaction. The daily serial would continue to be a showcase for women's writing. Two other important elements remained intact. One was the weekly editions broadcast from different regional centres, offering unique coverage of women's lives and interests. The other was international items.

The audience stayed with the show at the close of the century, and it grew to include increasing numbers of men, as well.[16] In 2012, *Woman's Hour* Drama was officially retitled 15 Minute Drama.[17] The segment maintained its identity with the range of themes and genres that listeners had come to expect: The last production to air with the old branding was *HighLites*, a contemporary farce set in a hair salon, and the first under the new heading was a World War II homefront thriller, *The Resistance of Mrs Brown*.[18]

Toni Morrison was a known quantity for British readers and listeners. When *Beloved* entered the airwaves as a 15 Minute Drama, it occupied a part of the spectrum delineated by prior interventions from women, speculative fiction writers, and other Black British and American authors. In 1991, the East Londoner Angela Turvey made her radio debut when her play *You, Me, and 12,000 Geese* aired as part of the Young Playwrights' Festival on Radio 4.[19] Turvey continued writing for the stage, radio, and television, and in March 2004 she contributed to *Woman's Hour* Drama with *Venus*, an original work based on the life of Saartjie Baartman, the KhoiSan woman taken captive and made to perform as an exotic fetish object across nineteenth-century Europe.[20] Along with Othniel Smith, Pauline Black, Patricia Cumper, and the American-born

Figure 6: Playwright Patricia Cumper. *Source*: Photographed by Graham Turner for *The Guardian*, 2018.

Cheryl Martin, she was one of five Black writers responsible for a series of dramatic shorts on Radio 4 inspired by Zora Neale Hurston's *Every Tongue Got to Confess* in August that year.[21] Although they were fifteen minutes long, the Hurston-inspired plays did not air after *Woman's Hour*. During the week they aired and the following week, *Woman's Hour* Drama featured Alcott's *Little Women*.[22]

Patricia Cumper had also been a presence on BBC Radio since the 1990s, through broadcasts of her plays *That Man and His Three Ships* (1992), *The Darkest Eye* (1997), and *One Bright Child* (1997). After *Every Tongue Got to Confess*, she returned to Hurston again in 2011, adapting *Their Eyes Were Watching God* for the BBC World Service.[23] *One Bright Child*, an adaptation of Cumper's own nonfiction novel, aired in fifteen-minute episodes outside of *Woman's Hour*. The week it was broadcast, *Woman's Hour* dramatized Kate Atkinson's time travel fiction *Human Croquet*.[24] *Woman's Hour* intercepted a growing and perhaps increasingly diverse audience when it took on the dramatization of Morrison's work. Later, I will discuss Morrison's reputation on BBC radio during her lifetime. It suffices to say that the production blending "horror and poetry" insinuated itself into an hour of the day that had consistently served listeners "a comforting and at the same time stimulating cocktail."[25]

Serial

On Wednesday during *Woman's Hour*, in the first week of 2016, the presenter Jenni Murray moderated a short discussion between writers who could put the *Beloved* serial in perspective for the audience.[26] They included the fiction author Irenosen Okojie, critic Tessa Roynon, and Patricia Cumper.

> MURRAY: What made it such an important novel?
>
> OKOJIE: *Beloved* goes to the heart of what it means to be a human being . . . when there is race-based slavery and when, as a woman, you simply exist as a body, part of an economy, and how do you claim your experience as a human being? How do you assert your freedom in that situation?

Murray asks Cumper why she wanted to adapt the novel.

> CUMPER: It's one of the sort of seminal novels of this time, but also that it gave the women in it agency. They were allowed to make decisions about their lives: they were allowed to celebrate, to love, to be angry, to make wrong choices, and that for me as a woman writer was very, very important.

Finally, Okojie notes:

> It was an incredibly complex book marrying multiple narratives . . . it gives a personal slant to something that perhaps America has distanced themselves from. So, with Sethe, what you get is you're being taken in to her mind and given a psychological insight into what causes this woman to essentially do this horrific act.

This conversation closed the talk portion of *Woman's Hour* in the middle of the first week that *Beloved* was on the schedule. That Monday, at the same time of day, listeners had experienced the new serial for the first time with its more customary, nondidactic introduction. In conjunction with nonverbal sounds, most notably, music, a shift in tone facilitates the transition from the episode of *Woman's Hour* they had just finished to the familiar moment each day when 15 Minute Drama begins.

The penultimate segment of the hour gives way to a musical overture. This signals the beginning and end of each episode of *Beloved*. Strings swell into a resonant, low hum before a length of chain begins to *clink* repeatedly, setting a pace slightly out of sync with the strum of a bass. A timeline was forming in the background, and its counterrhythm emerges from farther away. Another, brighter violin melody rises and falls before the narration begins. The music distances listeners, geographically and temporally as well as emotionally, from the moments preceding it in the broadcast schedule. The first verbal signs enunciated, "One twenty four," are numbers. This could easily be a time check, but these words are taken directly from the novel to name the setting and subject of the story. "One twenty four was," Adjoa Andoh begins, matching the text precisely. In the novel, "124 was spiteful," but here, the narrator specifies that "One twenty four was a spiteful house."[27] This phrasing is one of many turns away from the elliptical manner in which the narrator speaks in the novel. Through its straightforward designation of the house as its subject, the opening line in the play sets a task for the narrator—remembering—that characterizes the adaptation as a whole.

When Andoh speaks, with an American accent suggesting Southern Black melancholy, she is not reproducing the words from the novel's pages. Those words are different from those on the pages of Cumper's script. The narrator is instead constituting the play's discourse by recounting out loud the story that the novel tells in print. Her role is a tone-setting and orienting device, much like the establishing shot of a film or the opening scene of a work on the stage. A later BBC adaptation drawn from African American literature features Andoh performing a similar function. In the dramatizations of Maya Angelou's autobiographies on Radio 4 (also for *Woman's Hour*), Andoh voices the author at the age she was when she wrote her memoirs, while younger actors portray young Maya in the course of her earlier life.[28] The American accent Andoh affects in both roles has a timbre and grain that could have easily taken shape in Angelou's Arkansas or Morrison's Ohio in the twentieth century. Yet she does not perform an impression of either author. She does not affect the cadences of their speech or, for example, raise or lower the pitch of her voice to match them. Rather, she assures the listener that her voice belongs to the time and place from which the narrative derives its discourse. Like the music that opens the proverbial curtain for the drama, the sound of her voice would be out of place during any other part of the broadcast schedule. For the audience of this version of *Beloved*, the connotations of these sounds reside in the American past.

The musical overture that opens each episode and the opening line of the script are among the verbal and nonverbal elements that facilitate an adjustment of the listener's attitude toward the material for the duration of each episode. Extradiegetic signs, such as the presenter's announcement that the series portrays "Sethe, a woman who escapes slavery, but who, eighteen years later, is still not free," also frame the subject matter before each installment begins.[29] Although common sense would assure them that, in the absence of slavery, a person experiences freedom by definition, the listener must tune in to the drama for an explanation of why that isn't the case for Sethe. As in the novel, the ghostly influence of the child she killed in infancy insinuates itself into Sethe and Denver's daily life from the beginning of the drama, well before it takes on substance in the character of Beloved. She appears in Episode 3, but before that, she is the baby whose "venom" fills the house, in Andoh's words in the first episode, and the "baby haint [who] got plans," as Denver reckons in Episode 2.[30] Similarly, as characters (Paul D, Beloved) enter the drama with a mutual desire to seek out each other's company, their relationships are strained in ways that belie their desire to live together. The forces driving them apart and wracking them internally are consigned to a time and place outside the scene of present action. This constant tension between what could be and what has been, which can only be explained through storytelling that the characters undertake, ensures that memory plays a decisive role in the narrative.

The conflicting motivations that cause interpersonal conflict for the characters in the present—Sethe's shame, Paul D's disquiet, Denver's timidity, Beloved's insatiable appetites, and the community's relentless judgment—are symptoms of an underlying conflict over memory. One way of life relies on forgetting, and the characters try and fail to make it livable. Another possibility requires remembering the past, but they fear it will overwhelm them. Even when momentary conflicts are resolved within a given episode, as characters negotiate a painful status quo, the underlying problem persists. Instead of acting in spite of what they know about themselves and one another, the characters must decide, and they must let the audience know, how to use their knowledge of the past differently. Only this movement toward "being-in-difference" will change the conditions of their lives. A fuller understanding of the emplotment of haunting within the adaptation's many parts emerges from assessing the characters' confrontations with the repression that structures their lives.

When Paul D arrives at 124 and crosses the threshold of the house in the first episode, he asks Sethe, "What kind of evil you got in there?"[31] His belief system permits him to acknowledge that the house could be haunted, but the intensely unsettling impression he experiences in the ghost's presence contradicts the only death Sethe has told him about: Baby Suggs, who was mother to Sethe's long-lost husband, Halle. "You said she died as soft as cream," he says incredulously. When Sethe replies that the ghost is "my daughter. The one I sent ahead with the boys," it is the first time she has referred to her journey across the Ohio River, and she withholds any further explanation. The narrator says, "Paul D looked at the spot where the grief had soaked him."[32] This description of his action indicates that he is silently seeking answers from the space itself, because the only person he could ask about that daughter and those boys—Sethe—refuses to speak about them. After Sethe has introduced him to Denver, the girl begs him to stay. She later confides that she feels she can't tolerate living at 124 any longer. Denver fixates on Sethe and herself, rather than the house, however. "It's not the house. It's us! And it's you!"[33] she exclaims. She had begun to identify with the haunting, like her mother, because it was all she had known: "Nobody speaks to us. Nobody comes by," she complains.

In Paul D's presence, Denver recognizes an opportunity to express a sense of outrage and exhaustion at the injustice. Paul D sides with Denver against the pain that Sethe has learned to live with. When the house shakes down to the floorboards in anger, Sethe attempts to placate it like a child: "(IN TEARS) No, no. It's all right. It's all right." But Paul D fights back. First, he pleads with Sethe on Denver's behalf. "You going to tell me it's all right with this child half out of her mind?"[34] The narrator says, matter-of-factly, "A table rushed toward him," with no explanation for the supernatural locomotion.[35] With similar clarity, the narrator relates Paul D's reaction: "He grabbed its leg and bashed it about, wrecking everything, screaming back at the screaming house." By responding in kind and speaking back with righteous anger, Paul D resists the terror of the haunting. He does not know why the child's loss prevents Sethe from knowing peace, but like Denver, he is not resigned to the notion that Sethe and everyone around her should suffer continually. Paul D's appearance has brought possibilities that Denver is newly able to witness, but Sethe is unmoved for reasons the audience has yet to comprehend. Sethe's allusions to the Sweet Home plantation and the whereabouts of her other children raise questions that trouble the characters' lives, but she defers the work of finding answers for them to the remainder of the drama. Thus, when the first episode ends, the haunting persists.

The second part of the drama promises an exploration of the haunting from Denver's perspective. The subject that Andoh summons with the opening line of this episode is "Denver's secret," in the sentence "Denver's secret was sweet."[36] The secret's positive quality contrasts with the "spiteful" subject of the previous chapter, but the pressure of keeping it concealed threatens to compromise its value. Before any dialogue occurs in this episode, the narration and other sounds signifying Denver's interior life—written into the script as "DENVER SINGS SOFTLY TO HERSELF"—bring the girl to the center of the listener's attention. Upon further exposition, we learn that Denver enjoys the scent of wildflowers and perfume. The secrecy applies to a bottle of cologne that Denver once "stole from her mother and hid amongst the wild boxwood in the field behind 124 Bluestone Road" so that she might enjoy its smell within the cloister of bushes by herself. The haunting interrupts her contented solitude with disturbing sensations, "long before Paul D arrived," according to the narrator. The high notes of Denver's voice, accompanied by birds chirping and a gentle breeze, occupy the background as Andoh speaks. When Andoh says, "A thin and whipping snow drove her back to the house," the sound representing the wind rises from white noise and gently swaying branches to a rush of air that moves back and forth amid the soft crush of Denver's footsteps. The narrator says that "Denver saw her mother kneeling in prayer." When Denver bursts into the room with her mother, however, she reveals that she has perceived something subjectively that the narrator hasn't let on.

Denver addresses some listener other than her mother with the shouted demand, "Leave my ma'am alone!" Sethe replies, "Ain't no one here but me, Denver," suggesting that Denver is arguing with someone invisible to everyone but herself.[37] Denver, still breathless from running inside, is compelled to assert that she saw "two women praying together, 'cept one was an empty dress." Sethe's dismissive response is, "Hush, chile," but she acts as if she is taking her daughter's unbelievable report seriously. The narrator says that Sethe wraps a quilt around Denver, "so that the imaginary dress would not come between them." The narrator echoes Sethe's preferred treatment of the event by referring to the dress as imaginary. In the audio format, there is no costume, prop, or effect to demonstrate for the audience whether an empty dress knelt upright where Denver could have seen it or not. There is no evidence to corroborate or refute Sethe's denial that someone was in the room. Pippa Bennett-Warner's voice as Denver is the only sound that gives the apparition substance. While the scene may not convince Denver or the audience that Sethe is being truthful about what took place, it stages a conflict between Denver's ability to rely on her own perceptions and her need to seek validation from her mother. When both characters witness the spirit's manifestations, they can reassure each other in response to their shared observations, but when it affects them differentially, they must choose between assuaging the other's concerns or airing doubts about their own senses.

Immediately after the empty dress incident, Denver asks her mother to "Tell me my story," because, in her words, "It soothes me."[38] The radio play presents the story of Denver's birth in the form that she would have heard it originally. It is a memory that Sethe shares with her daughter to reinforce the sense that their relationship remains grounded in its origins. In the soundscape of this memory, Nadine Marshall, as Sethe, takes on the role of narrator by speaking to Denver. At this point, the drama places the audience in Denver's position by requiring us to rely on what Sethe says and depend on Sethe to invoke different settings and introduce other characters from her past. When the recollection begins, the setting shifts to the South, eighteen years prior. The script marks the scene change with the directions "FX BY THE SIDE OF THE OHIO RIVER."[39] The trilling of birds and insects and the groan of Sethe falling into tall grass coincides with Marshall's narration: "(TO DENVER) I believed this baby's ma'am was gonna die in wild onions on the bloody side of the Ohio River." While the script uses the word "ma'am," the word Denver uses to address and refer to her mother, Marshall pronounces the word "mama" when referring to her character in the third person. This is one of several instances where the broadcast audio differs from Cumper's scripted text, distinguishing the sounds produced by performance from those inscribed in writing.

Eliciting this story yields crucial details about Sethe's understanding of herself in relation to others, including Denver. Sethe feared the worst when she realized someone had heard her groans. The worst would be a "whiteboy" like those who had assaulted her on the plantation, she said, collapsing the words so they flow together the way Morrison had written. Cumper follows this orthographic convention in the script and repeats it with the line Sethe uses to recall that the person she saw "weren't no whiteboy." However, Cumper deviates from Morrison's diction when Sethe recounts how the stranger reacted to seeing her by the riverside. "Look here. A negro. If that don't beat all," says Rebecca Hamilton, playing the role of Amy. Morrison was citing the discourse of the nineteenth-century American South when she crafted dialogue for the novel, and Sethe remembers Amy using the racial slur "nigger" in the novel.[40] Although she is speaking aloud, Amy is not addressing anyone in particular when she voices her discovery. Her next statement, "You 'bout the scariest looking something I ever seen," is directed at Sethe. Hamilton speaks in a nasal voice with an American accent, and her colloquialisms, such as "I like to die" and "I got to eat me something," resemble those of the other characters.[41] She refers to Sethe a second time as a "negro woman," and the *e* in "negro" sounds the same as the long vowel in "here," "me," and "feet," rather than the short *i* of the racial slur. Whether Sethe remembers the woman for whom she named her infant daughter and helped her survive her flight to freedom referring to her with a common epithet or a derogatory one renders the memory of Amy different for readers of the novel and listeners to the dramatization.

Amy's last line as she massages Sethe's wounded feet is, "Anything dead coming back to life hurts."[42] When Andoh resumes the narration, she voices Denver's new thoughts about the apparition in light of Amy's words.

> NARRATOR: And that's a truth for all time, Denver thought as she listened to the familiar tale of Amy, the whitegirl. Maybe the white dress holding its hands around her mother's waist was in pain.[43]

When Denver asks if her mother was praying when she saw the empty dress, Sethe tells her that she was thinking. She goes on to discuss what she was thinking about. She assures Denver that "some things pass on, some things just stay. Places are still there. Out there in the world, even if they are gone, it's still there, right in the place where it happened." In the novel, this is the conversation in which Sethe uses the term "rememory" that Morrison has coined to invoke a concrete, place-based affective experience that confers a transferable meaning on the past.[44] The radio play forgoes the neologism, and in so doing, it tacitly communicates that trauma can silence memory, leaving only a residue of aversion that frustrates interpretation. In another attempt to rationalize what she had seen earlier, Denver asks whether other people can see what Sethe remembers: "Can other people see it?" Sethe can only warn that "Sweet Home ain't never going away. If you go there and stand in the place where it was, it will happen again. . . . It's going to always be there waiting for you." Denver reasons, "If it's still there waiting, that must mean nothing ever dies," and her mother confirms, "Nothing ever does." Denver sees an opportunity to ask why her mother fled Sweet Home while she was pregnant, but Sethe refuses to oblige her: "Enough remembering now, Denver."[45] The haunting persists at the end of the episode as an application of Denver's self-knowledge that is as familiar as her own name. Memory soothes the pain of haunting, to some degree, but encountering the pain from her past also provides Sethe with an alibi against returning to it.

In the third episode, an argument between Sethe and Paul D over Denver's manners yields another instance of Sethe's fraying, desperate insistence on repression as a means of coping with lingering trauma. At the outset of Episode 3, Sethe is "pleasantly troubled by the idea of having a future."[46] The passage of time within the narrative hews closely to the broadcast schedule at this point, as the action of the episode begins with a question Denver poses to Paul D "on the third day as they sat down to eat." A daily encounter with the characters, their speech, and their setting has begun to habituate the listener to their conventions, but now these novelties become unpredictable. Denver asks a question that had been "burning on her lips," according to the narrator: "How long you going to hang around, Paul D?" While Sethe and Denver had struggled to accommodate the constant, isolating influence of the past, Paul D's arrival has invited a shift in the discourse at 124. Sethe reprimands her daughter for the lapse in hospitality. When it was audible only in the narrator's voice, Sethe's future could pose troubling but pleasant possibilities only within her mind. Once another person's speech made the break between her past and future into an objective reality, it could take on eventful significance. Considering the question of whether her life was better, now, than it had been and whether, now, it could become better than it was came at a cost she was unwilling to bear. Adapting to a life where she would never hear or speak about the reasons behind the self-imposed exile in which she had ensconced her living daughter was the painful compromise she had learned to accept. By rehearsing a new manner of speaking in Paul D's presence, Denver was calling into question whether that silent compromise was still necessary, sufficient, or desirable. Sethe is not ready to face these questions, because she is not ready to evaluate whether the pain she has endured is worthwhile.

With Denver dismissed from the room, Paul D asks Sethe, "Did she have to ask that, or want to ask it, of anybody else before me?"[47] Sethe's reply, "You as bad as she is," equates his question's superficial possessiveness with the insolence of a child's prying about an adult's romantic and sexual life. Neither of these chastisements shields Sethe from the provocation she was trying to avoid when she silenced Denver, because the significance of Paul D's presence ultimately resides with Sethe, internally. Sethe says she feels forced to choose between maintaining her lifelong détente with Denver and sacrificing their relationship in order to achieve intimacy with Paul D. He asserts that they might find a way forward together, but Sethe will not be able to impose the same silence on him that she expects from Denver. He insists, "You can't gag me," and again, "Don't put no gag on me."[48] His notice foreshadows later revelations about being forcibly deprived of his ability to speak. Sethe hesitates, wondering aloud, "Maybe I should leave things the way they are with Denver," but Paul D presses her to consider whether this truly works: "What about inside?" She answers, simply, "I don't go inside," revealing that the tenuous concord at 124 is a symptom of Sethe's refusal to expose her unexamined knowledge and feelings. Denver's surprising interjections and the disapproving reactions they have garnered signal that Sethe has inculcated her with the same withholding tendencies to cope with their shared suffering. To do things differently, "making space for somebody along with her," as Paul D proposes, entails undoing Sethe's interdictions, at least in part. Sethe and Denver start to believe, and the audience might expect, that they can keep the haunting at bay as long as Paul D can maintain his loud and angry protestations. His suggestion, "You willing to leave it to me?" holds the illusory promise that Sethe can escape a confrontation with the haunting by surrendering the power of speech to someone else.

In the third scene of Episode 3, Sethe ventures out to the fair with Paul D and Denver. Sethe would never acknowledge it aloud, but the narrator explains that she knew she was "badly dressed for the heat but this being her first social outing in eighteen years, she felt obliged to wear her one good dress, heavy as it was, and a hat."[49] Sethe tolerates the discomfort in order to honor the occasion. Her quiet despair at home and her ceremony in public both emanate from the meaning she has ascribed to her isolation. Feeling responsible for the horrors that characterize her home, she endures without regard for the possibility of a better quality of life, because she fears she does not deserve consolation. She brings discomfort out of her home because she has internalized it, and she reserves her feelings for the inaudible register of her thoughts because she dare not express any sense of entitlement. Paul D and Denver dress comfortably in the heat for the same reason that they vocally protest the difficulty of living in the haunted house. They know of no reason why anyone ought to suffer so, but Sethe is unwilling to tell them why she believes otherwise. Before the end of the episode, she will begin losing her ability to keep this secret because of Beloved's arrival.

Following the day at the fair, Beloved arrives at 124 to initiate the next phase of the drama. For the purposes of my analysis of the serial's structure, I am deferring a more detailed discussion of her presence to the next section of this chapter. More importantly, at this point, the third and fourth episodes demonstrate an established pattern that is beginning to fray. Dialogue between characters and shifting boundaries in their relationships hint at the unspoken causes for the undesirable circumstances at 124. When a sudden apparition or outburst signals the possibility of altering their way of life, Sethe or another character will insist on struggling in silence, instead. The narrator can allude to hidden motivations, but the only eventful developments in the soundscape are those made audible among the characters living in it. If continuing a conversation would have lasting implications for the way its participants relate to one another, Sethe's instinct is to foreclose it. Hence, she tells Denver, "Enough remembering now." If the perception of a supernatural incident is highly subjective, better to bear silent witness to it, since speaking about it will only lend credence to the notion that they ought to do something about it. For instance, when Sethe sees the shadows of Paul D, Denver, and herself holding hands, she keeps it to herself and seeks no confirmation: "Nobody noticed but Sethe and she stopped looking after she decided it was a good sign."[50] After Beloved awakens and Paul D claims to see her demonstrate incredible strength by lifting a solid wood rocking chair with one hand, he attempts to enlist Denver in verifying his account so Sethe will believe him. Although Paul D asserts that she was present for the remarkable sight, Denver claims, "I didn't see no such thing."[51] As in the case of the empty dress, one character's vocal attestation is the only evidence for the act in question; no sound effects simulate the event for the listener, nor does the narrator weigh in to provide an objective account. The episode ends immediately afterward with an assessment of the impasse Paul D has reached because of Denver's unwillingness to join him in a discourse that avers the unbelievable difference Beloved represents: "Paul D frowned but said nothing. If there had been an open latch between Paul D and Denver, it would have closed at that moment." The potential for change has begun to emerge, but the drama will continue without fulfilling it.

Nothing highlights the significance of efforts at repression like their failure. Denver learns to derive a certain sense of agency from her participation in a new ritual of secrecy once Beloved arrives. In Episode 4, the narrator says that Denver, "out of love and a breakneck possessiveness that charged her, hid like a personal blemish Beloved's incontinence."[52] Denver never speaks of the act of concealment. Just as she had indulged her childish love for sweet fragrance, she moves surreptitiously so that she and others can enjoy a salubrious fiction. This ritual, which Denver also undertakes in the novel, signifies poignantly when juxtaposed with Sethe's irresistible compulsion to urinate upon seeing Beloved for the first time. The narrator articulates the urge Sethe feels, but its satisfaction has a sound of its own, scripted as "FX SOUND OF WATER POURING ONTO THE GROUND."[53] Sethe's need to void her bladder could not go unmet. The relief it provides is perceptible to the listener just as surely as it would feel viscerally necessary for the character. Though she tried to act more discreetly by running toward the outhouse, Sethe achieved her objective by running out of sight of Paul D and Denver upon seeing Beloved's face. Her spontaneous decision to determine the meaning of the need she felt by succumbing to it, rather than trying in vain to control it, parallels Beloved's enuresis. It is the expression of an irrepressible impulse. Though it is not yet obvious to the audience, Beloved's insatiable drives will compel other characters to react as if her needs were their own, and their efforts to deny them will always fail.

It Haunts Us All

The audible sign of Gugu Mbatha-Raw's voice distinguishes episodes featuring Beloved as a character from those that came before. Previously, sound effects signifying the scraping movement of furniture or the impact of objects flung through the air, or descriptions, by the narrator, of perceptible phenomena such as "a pool of red and undulating light," attested to the presence of her ghost.[54] Although Raw's performance adds a distinctive voice to the soundscape, her character exerts the greatest influence on the plot of the radio drama by *listening*.

The narrator's function is to guide the reader in discerning what is perceptible and imaginable within the frame of reference the characters inhabit in the text. Whereas literary and film narratology use the visual term "focalization" to describe "the submission of (potentially limitless) narrative information to a perspectival filter," audionarratology scholars like William Nelles and Bartosz Lutostanski employ an equivalent term for the ear: "auricularization."[55] If focalization pertains to the points of view assumed by the narrative, auricularization delimits the reach of the narrator's listening ear.[56] Auricularization is especially salient for comprehending Morrison's literary oeuvre, which is one of the principal sources of evidence among critics for the integral value of sound to African American epistemologies.[57] The emphatically musical and oral devices that characterize *Jazz* and *Sula* are signature examples. Her critical writings and commentary also attest to an aural imagination at work. In the theory of narration she articulates in "The Site of Memory," Morrison states that the narrator provides readers with a vantage point they can believe to be identical with "the characters' point of view, when in fact it isn't; it's really the narrator who is there but who doesn't make herself (in my case) known in that role."[58] I would argue that the listening ear designates the narrator's position vis-à-vis characters in Morrison's writing more precisely than the visual metaphor of "point of view." Cumper's depiction of Beloved as a character for whom listening is supremely consequential preserves Morrison's affinity for oral storytelling in the adaptation.

When characters speak in response to Beloved's questions, they satisfy the listener's desire to know the answers. By enticing other characters to reveal past experiences, Beloved brings the heretofore unspoken *causes* for the symptoms of trauma and discord they display into the verbal record. Episode 4 models how Beloved's presence will unravel the knot of repression that has kept several vital stories untold at 124. The first story she demands from Sethe issues from the question: "Where your diamonds?"[59] Raw's voice is low and monotonous, turning the query into an accusation. Sethe reveals that her erstwhile mistress, Mrs. Garner, had given her a pair of crystal earrings on the occasion of her marriage to Halle. She'd hidden them away during her escape, but they were long gone before Denver had the chance to see her mother wear them. Denver assembles a newly suspicious impression of Beloved from this incident and the one that follows. She thinks, and the narrator speaks for her thoughts, "'Tell me your diamonds.' How did she know?"[60] Beloved also poses the seemingly innocent question, "Your woman she never fix up your hair?" when she sees Sethe drying Denver's hair. Denver surmises that she is asking Sethe whether her own mother performed a similar act of affection. In response, Sethe reveals the only pertinent recollection she has. When Sethe was a child, her own mother taught her to recognize a brand on her flesh, out of the fear that, as Sethe recalls her mother saying, "If something happen to me and you can't tell by my face, you can know me by this mark." Notwithstanding this grim reminder, Sethe's mother was so mutilated in death that no one could identify her body among the corpses of several enslaved women hanged from trees. These moments identify Beloved with a capacity no one else seems to possess: She induces Sethe to remember.

The revelations Beloved elicits from Sethe belie a vulnerability she has been unwilling to demonstrate with Denver or Paul D. Paul D presses Beloved about her origins, leading to a confrontation at the dinner table that spills over into his next conversation with Sethe. He distrusts the new arrival's surpassing strangeness and, above all, "her appearing on the very day Sethe and he had patched up their quarrel, gone out in public and had a good time—like a family."[61] The narrator's enunciation of Paul D's thoughts directs the audience to recall the previous episode's conflict. Just when they were beginning to negotiate the boundaries of their private and public lives, Beloved placed new demands on the household. Sethe makes the connection between the past and present arguments explicit, saying, "We had one good fight about Denver. Do we need one about her too?" To Paul D's mind, she is uncharacteristically willing to meet Beloved's needs, but she is unwilling to interrogate her origins or her motives the way Paul D has begun to do. Sethe gestures toward a basis for her empathy with Beloved with the proposition, "Feel how it feels to be a colouredwoman roaming the fields with anything God made liable to jump on you."[62] But Paul D retorts. He insists that neither he nor Sethe's husband, Halle, had ever taken advantage of any woman's vulnerability, including hers. Yet she has presumed that Halle abandoned her and their children when she fled Sweet Home, because he never joined them.

SETHE: Then why didn't he show himself? Why did I have to pack my babies off and stay behind to look for him?
PAUL D: He couldn't get out of the loft.
SETHE: Loft? What loft?
PAUL D: The one over your head. In the barn.
BEAT
SETHE: He saw? He told you?
PAUL D: You told me.

Unexpectedly, Sethe and the listener learn from Paul D that her husband witnessed the assault that instigated her flight from the plantation.

PAUL D: The day I came here. You said Schoolteacher's nephews stole your milk and opened your back with a whip before you run off from Sweet Home. I never knew what it was that messed him up. That was it, I guess. All I knew was that something broke him . . . whatever he saw go on in that barn that day broke him like a twig.

Paul D provided no indication at the time, but when he heard Sethe refer to what she endured before running away, it filled in a gap in his memory that he had never addressed. He has known for years that Halle had encountered some horror that reduced him to incomprehension, but he has only known for a few days that the very same violence had taken Sethe as its target and precipitated her escape as a fugitive. Sweet Home had severed Sethe's family members from one another physically and severed them from their memories of one another in the process. Paul D's storytelling redresses a small part of the violence done to his and Sethe's memories, but his own incapacitating experience has made it difficult for him to participate in narrating the events. When Sethe asks, "Did you speak to him? Didn't you say anything to him?" Paul D reveals that he literally could not speak: "I had a bit in my mouth."

PAUL D: I didn't plan on telling you that.
SETHE: I didn't plan on hearing it.
PAUL D: I can't take it back. But I can leave it alone.

Even when he was no longer restrained like a farm animal, Paul D retained the diminished capacity imposed on him by the cruel manipulation he endured at Sweet Home. In the course of restoring Halle to a truthful place in their shared memory, they have unearthed yet another impediment to free discourse between them. Concluding Episode 4 with this exchange leaves Paul D and Sethe, as well as the audience, conscious of how thoroughly silence had insinuated itself into everyday life for the formerly enslaved characters.

The radio play does not provide the same extensive exposition as the novel regarding Paul D's travails at Sweet Home and thereafter. However, the following episodes feature other narrators who complement the memory work that commenced when Beloved arrived. In Episode 5, Denver appeases Beloved's desire for stories of Sethe by reiterating the account of her own birth. Listeners know that Sethe has told this story to Denver many times to reassure her, so Denver's belief that it will assuage Beloved's discontent is a credible motive. The story Denver reconstructs from memory requires a change of scene. A few minutes into Episode 5, the instrumental overture begins to play in the background as Andoh says, "And so Denver told Beloved about the whitegirl with thin arms but good hands with hair enough for five heads who birthed her in a boat on the Ohio river."[63] It is as if the episode is beginning again. The sounds of sloshing water mix with a baby's whimper. A breathless voice asks, "Boy or girl?" and for the first time since Sethe conjured her in Episode 2, Amy speaks. The sloshing of the waters and birdsong maintain the setting as the two women swaddle the newborn. Denver's recollection concludes with Amy's instruction, "You going to tell her Miss Amy Denver brought her into this world?" and Sethe's echo of agreement, "Denver. That's pretty. Real pretty."[64]

By recreating Sethe's past experiences through storytelling, Denver acts as a surrogate to temporarily placate Beloved's incessant demand to know her mother. The narrator brings this secondhand reminiscence back to its source with a statement representing Sethe's state of mind: "Sethe too knew that Beloved was hungry for the stories she told." The very next scene relates Sethe's account of her arrival at 124 just two days after Denver's birth. She remembers Stamp Paid, who brought her to the house in his wagon, and she recalls Baby Suggs as "a Holy woman," in terms that slightly modify her honorific in the novel. Beloved is the listening ear for whom all these performances take place. Her presence invites a set of recollections that Sethe previously found too painful to sustain. At first, "she found the hurt in telling them had eased now that Paul D and Beloved lived in her house."

The narrative starts teeming with possibility as Sethe renews old practices and attempts to start new ones. This self-affirmation brings her directly into conflict with Beloved's designs in Episode 5. In a serene clearing with Denver and Beloved, Sethe remembers Baby Suggs, locating her memory of the "Holy Woman" for the first time at the place that best defined her as an empowering influence. The preaching Baby Suggs had conducted there brought free Black women together. The memory of her words encourages Sethe to stop carrying the weight of her suffering and "lay it all down."[65] But Beloved can't abide Sethe's healing. As Sethe longs for the Holy Woman's consoling touch, the phantom fingers on her neck turn from gentle to choking. She is confused, and she can only think to associate the malign presence with Baby Suggs. Beloved kisses her bruised flesh, replacing the anguished manifestation with affection that provides "the peace she had come there to find."[66] With this subversive gesture, Beloved overtakes Sethe's memory of healthy intimacy, a memory guided by the caring voice of Baby Suggs, to instead initiate a seductive and controlling scene of gratification with herself as Sethe's only source of comfort. Beloved keeps kissing her, with Denver looking on, until Sethe's guarded nature reasserts itself. She admonishes Beloved, snapping: "You're too old for that!"[67] She is able to impose a boundary that stops Beloved from acting out by relegating her behavior to immaturity. Yet her next thought, which only the narrator enunciates because Sethe keeps it to herself, betrays how keenly she still feels her unmet need for intimacy. Upon her return from the outing, "she thought about the dinner she wanted to prepare for Paul D, something to launch her newer, stronger life with a tender man."

Just when Sethe begins to inaugurate a new discourse featuring settings and characters that once languished in her memory, Beloved's possessive desire turns all-consuming. The audience is privy to a romantic scene when Sethe enters her kitchen to find Paul D nude, bathing. Yet we are not the only listeners concerned with their activities.[68]

> EVENING. PAUL D IS IN THE TUB AS SETHE OPENS THE KITCHEN DOOR AND WALKS IN.
> SETHE: Summer must be over, you having a bath in my kitchen.
> PAUL D: Come on in the water.
> SETHE: Uh uh. Girls right behind me.
> PAUL D: I don't hear nobody.
> . . .
> PAUL D HOLDS HER CLOSE. SETHE RESPONDS. THE SOUNDS OF THEIR BREATHING AND MURMURING CONTINUES.
> DOOR OPENS

Sethe worries that Denver or Beloved will walk in on their coupling, but Paul D is confident that they won't, because he can't hear them. The audience can participate in their presumption of privacy as long as other characters remain out of earshot. The script suggests breathing, murmuring, and a door opening, but the combination of sounds that follows Sethe and Paul D's dialogue consists of laughter, splashing water, and footsteps.[69] The next word the narrator speaks is Beloved's name, confirming that the footsteps belong to her: "Beloved came through the door and they ought to have heard her tread. But they didn't.

Beloved heard them as soon as the door banged shut behind her."[70] By witnessing their actions, while they remain unaware of her presence, Beloved wrests control of the scene's meaning away from Sethe and Paul D. They believe they enjoyed a moment alone, but the audience knows otherwise, thanks to the narrator's account of Beloved's perception. In addition to the words in the script representing the jealousy she feels, Beloved commands the listener's attention in the scene through nonverbal signs, including the sound of her footsteps and the door she slams upon her exit. Keeping this moment private could have turned the tide of the narrative toward Sethe's hopes for her future. Rendering it as an overheard scandal instead furthers Beloved's interest in determining what will happen next.

When the drama's narrator adopts Beloved's listening ear, the adaptation is rehearsing a key feature from the novel. Throughout the pages of *Beloved*, different characters occupy the position from which readers comprehend the story. Claudine Raynaud highlights the efficacy of this technique for conveying the narrative's approach to memory: "The porosity of the characters' consciousnesses, made possible by subtle transitions from one focalizer to another, the leveling out of different time frames enable the novel to mimic and reflect the process of memory: the actual act of remembering as well as the incorporation of told memories into the oral tradition."[71] The auricularization of different characters, as storytellers and as listeners attentive to the storytelling of others, enables the radio play to emplot their respective memories within the narrative. Who hears is as important as who speaks, and remembered stories are among the most important shared soundscapes in the dramatization.

When multiple characters hear sounds simultaneously, at a moment representing the story's past or its present, they construct experiences in which the listener shares. Raynaud emphasizes the construction of intimacy through a scene in which Paul D and Sethe remember different sensations together: "The text moves from her consciousness to Paul D's through the mediation of Paul D's 'thinking' of Halle making love to Sethe. . . . The unmediated 'shift' from one focalizer to the other leads to a meshing of memories."[72] Though she utilizes the term "focalizer," her emphasis on the senses is transposable to auricularization, as well. As different characters take on the role of the narrator through storytelling and listening, the shift from one set of speakers and listeners to another brings their different memories of the past into the drama's audible present. One of the most consequential demonstrations of this intimate, synthetic process for bringing memory into the present occurs among Sethe, Beloved, and Denver when the three women are alone. Sound is essential to this reckoning in the novel as well as the radio play.

Beloved seduces Paul D after witnessing his coupling with Sethe. The overwhelming feelings the encounter reawakens cause him to banish himself from the house. Beloved then begins to take advantage of unfettered access to Sethe. After a day of joyful recreation, Sethe, Beloved, and Denver return to 124. As they retire, without speaking, Sethe hears Beloved humming. In both the novel and the radio play, the narrator uses onomatopoeia to register Sethe's recognition that Beloved remembers a song she had only sung to her children. The recognition takes the form of a "click":

> When the click came Sethe didn't know what it was. Afterward it was as clear as daylight that the click came at the very beginning—a beat, almost, before it started; before she heard three notes; before the melody was even clear. Leaning forward a little, Beloved was humming softly. It was then, when Beloved finished humming, that Sethe recalled the click—the settling of pieces into places designed and made especially for them.[73]

The novel depicts Sethe comprehending the sign Beloved has given her retrospectively. Within a few seconds, the meaning of the sound coalesces in her mind into a form that was immanent from the moment she began perceiving it. The recognition spurs Sethe to examine Beloved visually, and as she searches the adult woman's face for something familiar, memories of statements from mother figures in her life appear between ellipses on the page. She remembers Baby Suggs and her own mother recounting the sparse signs through which they hoped to form memorable bonds with the children from whom they'd been violently split by slavery. Then, she speaks, inviting Beloved to confirm that the song was a sign of such a bond between them. "Nobody knows that song but me and my children," she says. Beloved responds, "I know it."

The radio play illustrates this moment in a comparatively simpler and more direct fashion. Gugu Mbatha-Raw's singing voice can be heard starting from the moment immediately after the narrator says, "When the click came," and before she completes the sentence, "Sethe didn't know what it was."[74] The interruption, although it lasts only an instant, splits the description of Sethe's reaction much like the ellipses in the text. The tune consists primarily of a high, head-based hum with virtually no recognizable words except "Johnny." Whether it was composed for the play or improvised, the melody is simple and repetitive. It is only represented in the script by the direction "BELOVED HUMS THE BEGINNING OF A SONG."[75] The beginning of the song is enough for Sethe to recognize it. Beloved begins again before Sethe says, "That song you singing, Beloved. I made that song up." The narrator continues accounting for Sethe's perception thereafter: "The click, the settling of pieces into places designed and specially made for them." The sensation the "click" entails has no sonic presence in the play apart from the word the narrator uses for it. Instead, it occurs within Sethe's mind as the conferral of meaning on otherwise ambiguous sounds. When Sethe says, "I made it up and sang it to my children. Nobody knows that song but me and my children," she enunciates the latter as "chirren," situating it in a speech context that would be familiar for the character. Her pronunciation sutures the word "children" to the possessive pronoun associated with it. The dialect choice is consistent with Nadine Marshall's portrayal of a native speaker of African American Vernacular English in the Reconstruction-era South. Whereas Marshall, Cumper, and Morrison would not use the phrase "my chirren" in everyday life, Sethe would. Beloved responds in kind: "I know it." The scene ends with the narrator's confirmation: "The click had clicked." The redundancy of the phrasing underscores a relation of identity between the cause and its effect. The two parts of the call and response, Sethe's invocation of "my children" who know and Beloved's "I know," are complementary.

Until the moment that confirms Beloved is her long-dead child returned, Sethe and Beloved identify each other through implication and allusion. Their elliptical speech creates the impression that they cannot trust explicit language to preserve their relationship. Whereas Denver uses the familial "ma'am" for her mother, and she recounts the story behind her own naming as Sethe told it to her, Beloved refers to Sethe consistently with the pronouns "she" and "her," and she addresses Sethe as "you." Sethe and others had identified the late child affectionately as a "crawling already? baby" to signify that she was a remarkably precocious child. Although the eponymous character adopts it as her name, "Beloved" is a term of endearment and a citation. The gravestone where Sethe's infant child was interred read only BELOVED: the seven-letter word the engraver carved in exchange for the sexual favor that was the only payment Sethe could provide. It was not her child's name but a metonym for the eulogy preached at her funeral, which began, "Dearly beloved."[76] The first time Sethe, Denver, and Paul D ask for her name, Morrison writes, she speaks the word "so low and rough each one looked at the other two."[77] Then, she sounds out each letter of the word. The radio script renders the line Beloved speaks with the direction "(LOW AND ROUGH)."[78] It then instructs her to recite the sounds made by the letters in "rote" fashion, using internal spaces between the capital letters to indicate momentary pauses:

PAUL D: What might your name be?
BELOVED: (LOW AND ROUGH) Beloved.
PAUL D: Beloved. You use a last name, Beloved?
BELOVED: Last? No. (AS IF [BY] ROTE) B E L O V E D

In the novel, Paul D had "recognized the careful enunciation of letters by those, like himself, who could not read but had memorized the letters of their name."[79] His inference about their common relation to literacy goes unspoken, in the novel, and unmentioned, in the dramatization. When Sethe and Beloved acknowledge each other's identities, they do so by remembering a song, rather than reiterating an act of naming.

The use of song to convey what words cannot situates *Beloved*'s characters in a community bound by a distinctly sonic but not necessarily verbal mode of communication. Peter Capuano's treatment of the novel captures this succinctly: "When characters cannot read or write or even talk about the brutality they experience as slaves, they sing to affirm their participation in life and defend their status as human beings."[80] They delineate what matters in life by incorporating it into oral tradition, and they excise what they wish to forget through silence. The wholly acoustic form of the radio play lends significance to the acousmatic, musical, quiet, cacophonous, and indecipherable aspects of the narrative's oral modality alongside its intelligible verbal contents. When Beloved admits that she knows the song Sethe taught her children, the revelation alters the soundscape of the episode so profoundly that it requires citing a phrase that signals a momentous shift in the novel. Just as Part 1 of *Beloved* begins with the phrase "124 was spiteful," Part 2 begins with the phrase "124 was loud." After the previous scene, which rounded out the first third of Episode 8, the narrator says the phrase, "The house at 124 was loud."[81] While the women indoors are sleeping, the listening character at this point is Stamp Paid, standing outside. He says nothing until the next scene, but the narrator follows his thoughts as he contemplates whether to knock on the door and decides to visit the neighbor, instead. The shift from "spiteful" to "loud" signals new ways for the haunting at 124 to manifest. While it may not have been consistently audible before, the haunting is now evident to anyone who can hear. The environment will play host to different sounds, now, and the change in who is listening and what they hear will have consequences for the narrative. Members of the community are no longer able to remain ignorant about the haunting, while Sethe is more motivated than ever to treat it as something she can disregard.

Sethe's last line to Denver, before leaving the house for the day, insists, "Whatever is going on outside that door ain't for us. Our world is in this room.

It's all there needs to be."[82] The narrator describes her attitude thus: "When she left the house, she neither saw Stamp Paid's prints in the snow nor heard the voices that ringed 124 like a noose."[83] For Stamp Paid, "the indecipherable language clamouring around the house was the mumbling of the Black and angry dead," and it made him uneasy. When he came to the door, the voices he was hearing took on the form of overlapping whispers that the audience could also hear but not understand. The sound perceptible to him and to the audience demands reckoning with, yet Sethe is no longer able or willing to address it. The discrepancy between perceiving and reacting to the haunting, on the one hand, or attempting to forget it, on the other, has escalated the conflict to another level. The shift in auricularization allows one episode of the drama to contain a definitive break between parts of the novel and defer further resolution.

The Foreigner's Home

After reading and listening to *Beloved* in multiple forms, I came to the conclusion that the most challenging moments in the narrative occur when a reprieve from suffering is promised but fails to manifest. There are moments when all it would take to diminish the suffering of Sethe's "unlivable life" would be an ordinary gesture, rather than some heroic action, but relief never comes. These moments call for "something to be done," and in many instances, someone could simply make a sound: Stamp Paid could knock on the door, Denver could tell the truth about the rocking chair, the neighbors could announce Schoolteacher's coming. These audible acts would not transform history, but they might make a difference on a scale the characters themselves could perceive. Frustrating moments like this accumulate throughout the novel to cement Sethe's resignation, and they prolong the drama's horror.

The dramatization stages these disempowering scenes faithfully, and it leverages the impact of rhetorical questions to infuse the dialogue with the threat of hopelessness, as well. When Sethe remembers Amy asking, incredulously, "What you gonna do, just lay there and foal?" she recognizes that any agency she could exercise in her life would defy her condemnation to the status of a brood mare.[84] By contrast, when she tells Paul D she had no choice but to remove her children from the risk of living as Schoolteacher's property, he defies her internalized disempowerment by insisting, "You got two feet, Sethe. Not four."[85] When he leaves without saying goodbye, Sethe says aloud, "He must think I can't bear to hear him say it after telling me how many feet I have, that his 'goodbye' would break me to pieces." She voices her refusal to interpret what he has said and what he has left unsaid. Denver struggles in vain to provoke Sethe into treating her as Beloved's equal. In Episode 8, she implores her to give Beloved a share in the chores of everyday life, asking, "When's Beloved turn to dry, ma-am?"[86] Then, she begs to claw back some of the affection she has showered on her rival. In Episode 9, as Sethe fusses over Beloved's hair, Denver implores, "Why don't you braid my hair for a while, ma'am?" When Sethe quits work and spends her meager savings on fabric for new dresses, Denver asks her leading questions: "Who's the yellow ribbon for?" and "Will you sew some of this lace on my dress?" Sethe's answer, unsatisfying as ever, is "for Beloved."[87] When Denver tries to interrupt Beloved's relentless demands, Sethe rebuffs her: "I don't need no rest. I need Beloved."[88] When Denver ventures out to obtain aid from the neighbors, they oblige her out of a sense of charity. However, as long as she withholds the truth about their needs, her efforts to help the household only feed the haunting. The narrator remarks on the unsustainable future as "a doomsday truce. The bigger Beloved got, the smaller Sethe became."[89]

While Paul D was cast out from 124, Stamp Paid attempts to convince him that Sethe was responsible for the death of her own "crawling already?" baby. As evidence, he shows Paul D an eighteen-year-old newspaper article that reads, "A Negro Child's Throat Cut from Ear to Ear by Its Mother," alongside a photograph of Sethe.[90] Paul D cannot read the report, but he will not believe that Sethe is truly its subject in spite of the photograph. As Stamp Paid recounts the story across Episodes 6 and 7, Paul D maintains his disbelief with the refrains "I know her mouth and that ain't it" and "that ain't her mouth." Paul D's rejection is both an expression of doubt regarding the truth claim associated with the image and a statement of epistemic principle. He discounts the resemblance between the image and his own perception of Sethe's facial features; that is, he contends that it is not an image *of* her mouth. Perhaps more importantly, Paul D discredits the claims that the photograph and the article make regarding Sethe's actions because they do not come *from* her mouth. He trusts Sethe's speech about her actions more than any other form of evidence. When he presents the report to Sethe, she does not deny the authenticity of the photograph. Rather, she narrates it for Paul D in a way that he is inclined to believe when no one else could. As she explains her actions, Sethe thinks, "Perhaps it was the smile, or the ever ready love she saw in his eyes that made her go ahead and tell him what she had not told Baby Suggs, the only other person she felt obliged to explain anything to."[91]

The reference to Baby Suggs, which the narrator presents as a necessary consideration Sethe makes in order to speak, connects disparate reconstructions of the same events. Stamp Paid had devoted close attention to Baby Suggs in his reflections for Paul D. When Alibe Parsons delivers dialogue in the role of

Baby Suggs, on the occasion of Sethe's return, she is reenacting speech that Stamp Paid remembers.[92] Like the memories of Amy that Sethe shared with Denver and the memories of Halle at Sweet Home that Paul D shared with Sethe, Stamp Paid's reflection has brought subjects from the past into the present. When Sethe explains why she took her child's life, she elevates Paul D to a role that Baby Suggs once played as a rare worthy listener. The audience thereby hears her disclose truths that would remain hidden, otherwise.

Denver would never hear from her mother's mouth why their lives had been unlivable for eighteen years. When Sethe began to question the inevitability of her suffering by returning to the place where Baby Suggs had coaxed her to "lay it all down, sword and shield," Beloved confounded her efforts. Her presence separated Denver even further from the loss that defined her mother's past. In order to undo the isolation that had engulfed her life, Denver would have to broach a discourse that brought 124 into a new relationship with the entire community. Her initial plea to a neighbor allows much to go unsaid. When Lady Jones asks after Denver's family, courteously, the narrator attests to how guarded she remains: "There was no way for Denver to tell her how the family was, so she said what was at the top of her mind."[93] Later, once she resolves to articulate the depth of her needs by seeking out work for wages, Denver takes part in a conversation with radically different assumptions, boundaries, and implications. Even though supporting Sethe and Beloved is one of her aims, Denver must leave them to their own devices. In the radio play, the only line rationalizing Denver's decision is: "Her father's daughter after all, Denver decided to do the necessary."[94] This line refers to Halle, who worked over and above what slavery demanded in order to earn wages he could use to buy his mother Baby Suggs's freedom. The knowledge of this background provides Denver with an internal motivation to take care of unmet needs in her home.

In the novel, Denver receives additional motivation from an external source. As she leaves a neighbor's house after giving thanks for donated food, a fellow says, "'Take care of yourself, Denver,' but she heard it as though it were what language was made for. The last time he spoke to her his words blocked up her ears. Now they opened her mind."[95] An expression of concern that might be negligible, addressed to someone else, reminds Denver of "having a self to look out for and preserve." The adaptation omits this particular statement. Yet both versions of the narrative depict Denver realizing that she possesses agency when she acts as a member of her community, rather than acquiescing to her erstwhile separation.

The setting for Denver's most consequential negotiation is markedly distinct from others in the play. The script specifies "BUSY CINCINNATI STREET," which the drama evokes through repetitive clanging noises in the background and the loud, metallic hammer of Denver's knock on a door.[96] Denver does not address the white man and woman who own the home, the Bodwins, directly. Rather, she speaks with Janey, a Black woman who works for them. The people Denver is seeking out are so unfamiliar that Janey has to correct her when she asks after a "Mr. and Mrs. Bodwin," advising that they are siblings and therefore "Mister and Miss." Janey, however, recognizes that Denver is "Baby Suggs's kin," and she surmises that the support Denver is asking for must pertain to Sethe. "Now, what's the trouble with Sethe? I heard she took sick," Janey asks. The narrator conveys Denver's thought process as she decides how to respond: "It was a little thing to pay but it seemed big to Denver, but nobody was going to help her unless she told all of it." By framing her disclosure of the troubles in her home as a price, "a little thing to pay," Denver's decision making construes secrecy as something she must give up in order to reenter the community. Although Denver dissembles by explaining "the girl in her house as her cousin come to visit who got sick too and bothered them both," she submits to Janey's informed questioning. As a participant in the speculation that has swirled around 124 over the years, Janey regards the stranger with the same knowing skepticism that Paul D had expressed with his interrogation upon her arrival. Without Sethe's protective influence to hush the inquiry, Janey proceeds to indulge her suspicions. She asks, "Tell me, this here woman in your house. The cousin. She got any lines in her hands?"[97] Denver's response, "No," confirms Janey's inference. Whereas she had once repressed the truth about Beloved's strangeness in front of Sethe, when Paul D asked her to confirm she saw her lift a rocking chair, now she is willing to speak as a witness. With this admission, Denver has joined Stamp Paid and Paul D, and Sethe, on a rare occasion, in sharing her perception through oral testimony. By speaking from memory rather than silencing it, Denver permits another person to make use of the knowledge she possesses.

When she leaves the Bodwins' house with Janey's assurance that she can come back for paid work, Denver has conceded influence over the plot to someone else. Accordingly, Janey's thoughts and actions give voice to the narrator in the final lines of Episode 9: "It wasn't long before the news that Janey had got hold of from Denver spread far and wide among the coloured women of Cincinnati. Sethe's dead daughter, the one whose throat she cut, had come back to fix her."[98] By engaging in a discourse that invites future elaboration rather than foreclosing it, Denver conscripts the listening ears of Black women throughout the community in meeting the challenge Beloved represents.

Numerous scholars emphasize the role of collective action among Black women in Morrison's rendition of the way Sethe's exile begins and ends in the novel. Jonquil Bailey, Peter Capuano, Nancy Jesser, and Roxanne Reed all note how shared resentments and insecurity cause the community to withhold any audible warnings when Schoolteacher and his nephews arrive to claim Sethe.[99] These critics also attend to the way the women coming to Sethe's aid at the novel's conclusion exorcise Beloved's violent influence through prayerful song. The radio drama rehearses the pivotal role of sound in these decisive moments. In Episode 7, as Stamp Paid remembers Sethe's arrest for Paul D, he recounts how the neighbors stood silent while Sethe was carted away to jail: "Outside a throng of Black faces stopped murmuring . . . Sethe walked past them and climbed into the cart, her profile knife-clean against a cheery blue sky."[100] The murmuring never even begins in the broadcast, so only the rustle and creak of wooden wheels can be heard beneath the narrator's voice. Birds chirp as if to evoke the cheeriness of the blue sky.[101] As in the novel, the narrator remarks that, but for the neighbors' umbrage toward Sethe's seemingly prideful posture, "the singing would have begun at once, a cape to wrap around her to steady her on her way."[102] Instead of sending Sethe on her way with a song that could reiterate her connection to them, "they waited until the cart headed West to town, and then no words." Once Sethe rode out of earshot, they expressed themselves by humming. Because the last sound she remembers them making was silence, the sound they make together, in her absence, allows the community members to separate themselves from Sethe. The scene concludes with the wordless humming, performed in harmony by several voices for nearly twenty seconds. Individual inhalations can be heard between some notes. Birdsong continues in the background at regular intervals, suggesting continuity between the time and place where Sethe has departed and the neighbors remain. Three seconds of silence separate the memory from the next scene, which returns to Paul D and Stamp Paid in the present. When the same group of women gathers to act on Janey's news, they have the chance to change their tune.

Thanks to the accumulated context provided in the radio play through scenes depicting characters recounting their memories, audibly, a particular nonverbal sound phenomenon within the final episode takes on decisive significance for the narrative. The women who have heard and spoken about Sethe's daughter "come back to fix her" converge on 124 with a shared purpose. They end Sethe's sequestration of many years and take on her grief as their own by bringing what was secret out into the open. They signal to Sethe that she can once again consider herself a member of the community entitled to its protection and care by engaging in a ritual that sacralizes her subjectivity. The sound of them singing over her attains a profound meaning when it is contrasted with its conspicuous absence at an earlier moment. If the community had chosen to embrace her immediately after she took her child's life, as the audience learned from Stamp Paid's recollection in Episode 8, "the singing would have begun at once." This time, they unfurl the "cape" of sound they had shamefully withdrawn earlier. While the novel does not specify what sort of music the impromptu choir performs, the ensemble in the radio play sings a spiritual, "Swing Low." Replacing their earlier wordless humming behind Sethe's back with a familiar, euphonious cultural touchstone on this occasion signifies a reversal of the attitude the crowd had articulated previously. In addition to its words, which do not appear in the script, the spiritual's sound and its metatextual connotations welcome Sethe back into the fold. The promise "to carry me home" that the lyrics convey portends a future of safety and acceptance she has all but forgotten was possible. Just as the characters and their ancestors performed the song for generations during slavery, they sing it at this moment both to acknowledge their ongoing suffering and to assert a shared belief in its impermanence.

Invoking a well-known African American sorrow song in the radio play situates the climactic scene within the story's historical setting: in the immediate aftermath of slavery. It also correlates the moment with some of the paradigmatic functions of sound in African American literature. Capuano writes, "*Beloved* responds deliberately and exhaustively to the description of slave song that appears at the outset of [Frederick] Douglass's 1845 *Narrative*" through the singing that Paul D, Sixo, and Sethe perform in the novel, and he emphasizes song as "a point of access into the reverberating effects of slavery's horrors" for those who struggle to remember it verbally.[103] While the song cites a culturally specific body of knowledge, the conceit of the performance emerging spontaneously as a manifestation of the community's collective will further authenticates it with the repertoire of African American expressive culture. Just as Morrison has done in the novel, Cumper emplots the act of singing in the final episode in a manner that honors its pivotal role in the narrative as a whole. She and the other parties responsible for the dramatization—the director Sasha Yevtushenko, the performers, the producers, and sound engineers—make the singing audible and intelligible in order to provide the audience with a perceptible impression of its significance. The affordances of radio drama as an art form, and the format of this program in particular, establish a structure wherein the meaning of a particular sound's absence confers unmistakable poignancy to the act of making that sound heard.

The chorus of women who accept Sethe at the climax of Episode 10 serves as an apt metaphor for the coalition constituted among the readers, the listening audience, the performers, and the authors who came together to realize *Beloved*'s adaptation for BBC radio. Each participant in the chorus remembers the past violence afflicting each of them subjectively, but they share in the collective task of determining its significance for their future. Out of their disparate concrete points of departure, they produce something ideal: harmony. Like the members of the choir, the forces involved in creating the adaptation are heterogeneous and linked together only by the shared purpose of the work of art. It may seem impertinent to compare the cacophonous assortment of professions, national origins, racial identities, and genders represented by the personnel responsible for any *Woman's Hour* Drama production to the Black women performing absolution at the end of *Beloved*. Yet each of these parallel assemblages, the fictitious one made up of characters performing within the text and the real one responsible for making a performance audible to actual listeners, contains multitudes. Rather than treating the adaptation as a foreign constituency's effort to simulate the transmission of African American women's subjective knowledge in their own peculiar idiom, I have chosén to regard the playwright and performers as active, critical listeners responding to the call for aural interpretation embedded within Morrison's text. By adapting her work for radio, they are, in a certain sense, singing over her words.

Considered more narrowly, the combination of Patricia Cumper and Toni Morrison represents a nexus of cultural interests among listeners to BBC radio. The overdetermined sight words of "Black," "women," and "literature" are shorthand for the much broader range of phenomena made audible through these authors' contributions to radio drama. Like other works by Cumper and her Black British contemporaries, and the voice of the playwright herself, the broadcast of *Beloved* afforded a substantive presence on the airwaves and digital stream to segments of the British public who seldom heard themselves there. Delivering over *Woman's Hour* to members of the Black British theater community enabled them to assert agency over a discursive site that had historically shaped the meanings of "women" and "drama" for the entire BBC audience.

When the audience experienced *Beloved* as listeners, they were rehearsing the construction of their relationship to everything Morrison represents in a venue where it had already begun. Reading her fiction was only one way that the listening audience could have become acquainted with Morrison. *Woman's Hour* Drama might have been some listeners' first or only encounter with her writing in any form. The adaptation therefore supplements other ways that British radio had established Morrison's persona as an author. She was a subject of interviews and commentary across the service for many years. Her publications engendered lively discussion on programs about literature and culture such as *Book Club* (1998, 2009), *Open Book* (2016), and *A Good Read* (2017, 2020). Milestones in her career, such as the Nobel Prize for literature, made news on BBC Radio. Programs like *Talking Books* (2012) and *Front Row* (2015) would broadcast conversations with her on the sidelines of her public appearances. The sagacious reputation she attained through this discourse within radio, distinct from the content of her writing, led British pundits to solicit her perspective on events of national and global significance such as the inauguration of the first Black president of the United States. Adapting an American author as iconic as Morrison positioned Black Britons as arbiters of the relationship between the countries' respective national literatures. In this cross-cultural transaction, Blackness operates as a conduit between nations. The sound of literature connected their reading and listening publics.

Conclusion

Generative Adaptations

Radio drama brought innovative literary techniques and entire literary traditions to new audiences in the twentieth century. Listeners across the country and the globe who might never study drama or attend a live performance could witness world-class theater in their homes. The benefits were reciprocal. While the audience gained edifying and stimulating cultural experiences, theater practitioners gained broad relevance for work that might otherwise remain cloistered within elite enclaves. As Richard Hand notes regarding Orson Welles's company, "The title of the program *Mercury Theatre on the Air* both reflects the fact that a critically acclaimed New York theater company had been given a radio contract and emphasizes that a live theatrical experience was being created for an audience of millions across the United States. Indeed, the CBS announcer who introduced the premiere broadcast . . . makes this clear when he states that this new series aims to reach 'the Broadways of the entire United States.'"[1]

While radio made authors like Welles and Archibald MacLeish into household names, it also traded on the recognizability of material available for adaptation. While the *Mercury Theatre* brought some works from the stage to the studio, like many pioneering radio dramatists, adaptation was their forte. Even though the mass media of the era invited criticism for falling short of preceding art forms' intellectual sophistication, adaptations on the radio facilitated audience members' initiation into the shared enjoyment of "classic" literature. *Favorite Story* began on KFL in Los Angeles as a way to present listeners with celebrities' cherished reading. Hearing a version of *Alice in Wonderland* was their window into the tastes of Irving Berlin, who made that selection for the broadcast, while Alfred Hitchcock was responsible for the choice of *Dr. Jekyll and Mr. Hyde.*[2] Listening was a way for the everyman to access these artists' cachet from a distance. NBC arranged to make its show *World's Great Novels* into an accredited correspondence course through the University of Louisville as *NBC University Theater* in the 1940s.[3] A critic for the *New York Times* delivered brief lectures during the intermissions of broadcasts on Melville, Steinbeck, and Twain.[4] The same accessibility that enabled canonical literature to reach broader audiences through dramatization made radio an optimal venue for science fiction writers and publishers to extend the life of their work. Meanwhile, Black music entered the homes of millions through broadcasting, but Black authors of speculative fiction and their audiences rarely enjoyed that privilege.

By disseminating an ideal of shared heritage through the literature they chose to adapt, early radio dramas recapitulated the Anglo-American literary canon in the emergent medium. Radio is celebrated in the American and British cultural studies tradition for its heteroglossic and contestatory character, and it certainly engenders diverse imagined communities.[5] But the undemocratic exigencies that some of its proponents brought to the technology demonstrated its potential to forestall democratic futures. The power of radio to foster a particular sort of unity emerged within and across the United States and United Kingdom through the guidance of institutional leaders, like John Reith at the BBC, who espoused the normative aesthetic doctrine identified with Matthew Arnold.[6] According to Duncan Bell, an Arnoldian vision of culture in terms of objective values represented by Western (white) civilization also inspired Reith's fellow travelers, like Cecil Rhodes, W. T. Stead, Arthur Conan Doyle, Rudyard Kipling, and Andrew Carnegie.[7] They all shared in utopian dreams of "racial reunion" between English and American peoples, which Stead defended in the *Review of Reviews* by arguing:

> To oppose the reunion of the English-speaking race is hardly the line which we ought to expect from those who believe in the unity of mankind. What is more natural than that those who seek the larger unity should wish to secure as a stepping-stone thither the union of all those who speak the same language, read the same literature, and are on the same plane of civilisation?[8]

In the minds of these intellectuals, new global connections such as the postal network, telegraph, and "wireless" (radio) would help "repair the sundered bonds of Anglo-American brotherhood."[9]

Scholarship on the ideological and technological developments just described introduces science fiction as something of a Rorschach. Stories attesting to fears of imperial decline, anxieties over the manageability of colonial populations, and prognoses for future war "fictionalized the debates over the possible benefits of an Anglo-American union being played out in the journals and clubrooms of the North Atlantic world."[10] While Anglo-American "reunion" discourse attenuated before the heyday of American and British broadcasting, adaptations of popular tales like *Sherlock Holmes* and H. G. Wells's scientific romances prolonged Victorian intellectuals' race thinking into the age of mass media. While this book is the first study of science fiction radio drama to emphasize racial discourse, the works by Black authors I have brought to the fore stand out against the tradition's stark white background.

Colonial adventure narratives, detective serials, and scientific romances were not the only sources of inspiration for radio drama. It would be simplistic to presume that a shared "racial" heritage compelled listeners to tune in for the *Superman* radio program, *Ray Bradbury Theatre*, and *Hitchhiker's Guide to the Galaxy*. Significant artistic innovations, to say nothing of technical and economic infrastructure, nourished new modes of engagement as radio continued to adapt new and old stories. Political views among the publics for radio drama were as variegated on all sides of the Atlantic as they were within emerging genres. However, as Stuart Hall once wrote, regarding efforts to simultaneously preserve and transform the notion of British identity for the twenty-first century, "The National Heritage is a powerful source of . . . meanings. It follows that those who cannot see themselves reflected in its mirror cannot properly 'belong.'"[11] For Hall, the implications of this axiom about representation reached into and even beyond what he called "the demand to re-appropriate control over the 'writing of one's own story' as part of a wider process of cultural liberation, or—as Frantz Fanon and Amilcar Cabral once put it—'the decolonization of the mind.'"[12] Transforming culture from the outside in, as it were, requires critics and gatekeepers invested in the work of interpreting creative practice that emerges on the margins of the contemporary mainstream and commemorating it for the future. Without this motivated attention, he warned, "Major practitioners surface and pass quietly from view into an early and undeserved obscurity."

The stories that science fiction and radio drama tell themselves about their shared histories will only remain predominantly white as long as we let them. The adaptations I have analyzed in this book do not comprise a tradition for the purpose of literary and media history. They form a pattern in which Black authors and audiences briefly integrate a tradition's process of defining itself and leave it intact with their departure. *New World A-Coming* introduced Black utopianism into a golden age from which it is otherwise conspicuously absent. *The Star-Pit* rehearsed avant-garde artists' desires to escape the hierarchies that formed the basis for their identities by identifying with "something more powerful than any local notion of what creates racial distinctions" or those of gender, sexuality, and dis/ability.[13] The SciFi.com internet radio initiative that announced Octavia E. Butler's novel *Kindred* for Black History Month marketed itself as a continuation of radio's legacies rather than a departure from them, presenting "audio dramas that hearken back to the Golden Age of Radio when the theatre of the mind, the imagination, reigned supreme."[14] BBC Radio 4 adapted *Beloved* in keeping with its long-running *Woman's Hour* programming. The production was never explicitly articulated as a response to concerns about the prominence of American subject matter on the station or its appeal to Black and minority ethnic communities.[15] While the BBC Trust professed support for the "aim" of increasing the popularity of Radio 4 among different demographics, it all but disavowed any commitment to actually achieving that goal: "We recognise therefore that it is not possible for Radio 4 to achieve an equal spread of listening across all age and socio-demographic groups. To do so would require a fundamental change to the nature of the station . . . damaging to the current audience experience."[16] These adaptations came to fulfill the purpose of radio drama, not to undermine it.

Perhaps, in the years since Hall offered his radical critique of cultural institutions' conservative practices, the fundamental transformation required to repair the precarious relationship between postcolonial and Diasporic communities and the notion of heritage in British society has taken place. Maybe radio drama has helped bring about the future he envisioned. Perhaps American culture demanded a similar transformation for different reasons, and maybe it has taken place, here, as well. Do we still hear the "transatlantic accent" when we invoke the phrase "old-time radio?"[17] Or has the listening ear attuned itself to the soundscape of Diaspora, African American literature, and Afrofuturism?

In his 1998 book *More Brilliant Than the Sun*, the Black British cultural critic Kodwo Eshun coined the phrase "sonic fiction" to model a poetics constituted through Black electronic music in the absence (or in excess) of lyrics. Remarkably, this term arose autonomously in Afrofuturist discourse with no reference to science fiction radio drama. Scholars have continued to cite sonic fiction in musicology, science fiction studies, art criticism, gender and sexuality studies, and design, in English, French, Spanish, and Italian, without any attention to radio adaptations of Black speculative texts.[18] The divergent phenomena denoted by the phrases "radio drama" and "sonic fiction" bespeak an underlying split between the way Black authors and audiences have typically utilized sound to conjure alternate possibilities, namely, through music, and the institutional arrangements that enabled science fiction writers to adapt their visions to the airwaves. Eshun argued that his speculative approach provided "a portrait of music today far more accurate than any realistic account has managed . . . because most recent accounts of Black Music . . . are more than anything wish fulfilments: scenarios in which Acid never existed, in which Electronic Jazz never arrived, in which the Era of the Rhythmachine *never happened*."[19] This book has reckoned with a similar counterfactual: Science fiction studies and media history alike conceptualize radio drama as a significant site of productive and interpretive activity while acting as if race does not matter. I have argued, to the contrary, that learning from Black writers working in speculative modes, especially by learning what has been done with their work through adaptation, can shift the way we use sound to study.

Throughout *Audiofuturism*, I have argued that radio drama builds upon the reliability of formats within the radio programming available to particular audiences, and I have demonstrated that performances within those formats make the interventions of literature available to the listening public. The operations of the market and the interpretive agency of readers afford literature the tendency to accrue genre conventions and to represent subject formations existing in society.[20] These cultural processes help define the phenomena known as Afrofuturism or Black speculative fiction in textual forms. Perhaps when they are read aloud, Black speculative texts "regain" something from the repertoire of oral traditions that influences their authors' choices, consciously and unconsciously, something otherwise "lost" in print. If radio drama consisted solely of reading aloud over the airwaves, then we might be able to explain the relationship of science fiction radio plays to Black speculative texts through audiobooks, podcasts, or other media. Those forms have plenty to teach us, as well. But dramatization is more than reading aloud. Dramatic works for audio are not identical to their precursor texts because they are designed to enlist the senses, especially the spatial and embodied situations of listening, in ways that reading does not. The integral role of sound in African American literature shows how writing can both preserve and transform knowledge that is otherwise communicated through music and oral traditions. Accordingly, this study has emphasized how adaptation can showcase the innovations of Black speculative texts in distinctly sonic fashion. Just as science fiction radio plays define themselves by using sound to excite the interests of the science fiction reading public, interventions into radio drama from the Black fantastic imagination invoke a reading/listening public habituated to the sensorium of African American literature.

Margo Crawford likens the idea of African American literature to "a collective nervous system" in *What Is African American Literature?*[21] She employs this extended metaphor to frame the Black book in this tradition as an interface for the affect experienced by "the flesh" imagined as the Black body, writing:

"The body of black literature is produced by the tension of the flesh that has been named the 'black body.'"[22] My objective in citing Crawford here is to highlight her intuition that any effort to map the interior dimensions of Black life by first delineating the boundary between African American literature and American literature is facile. The boundary is not an edge; it's a surface. She advises, "The idea of African American literature remains a generative surface, a frame that remains a frame, not a threshold into an understanding of interiority that is the antithesis of surface."[23] Crawford's analysis follows Gérard Genette by treating paratexts as thresholds to be understood in conjunction with the texts they border on, rather than epiphenomenal boundaries to be crossed in pursuit of understanding.

If literature itself is a surface made of writing, fashioned into a threshold, situated between one mode of understanding and another, it is not "just" a threshold. If paratexts augment the knowledge we derive from the texts associated with them, they are worth understanding on their own terms. In the case of radio drama, adaptations are paratexts in that generative sense: They are encounters with literature that present themselves at the surface of another art form. Black speculative texts themselves comprise a threshold between the conventions of science fiction defined by a predominantly white publishing industry and academy, on one side, and the Black fantastic imagination, on the other. Radio adaptations of Black speculative texts comprise yet another sonic interface between the traditions the texts invoke and the futures they portend.

Every stage in the process of adaptation redefines the value held in place by a text, but the poetics of the respective forms it may assume—literature, performance, electroacoustic manipulation, broadcasting—accentuate differences within its identity. Through adaptation, we can recognize that the identity of cultural production is not stable across different modalities and valuations. Identity *is* the undulating surface that affords seemingly discrete acts (in language, in sound) the capacity to appear continuous. The radio plays assessed in this book do not offer derivative or reductive versions of Black utopia, speculation, and the supernatural. They are generative contributions to Black and American culture.

Acknowledgments

I was in a position to perform the labor of writing this book thanks to individuals, institutions, policies, and investments that sustain the enterprise of academic research and the working conditions in higher education that make it practical. I worked at Drexel University when I started this book, and I finished it at the University of California, Riverside. More people ought to be employed in jobs like those I've held, and everyone deserves the quality of life my job affords. I have enjoyed doing this work while sharing my life with Jeb Butler and our dog, the late Benjamin Banneker, and I am grateful for their love.

The Wolf Humanities Center (the erstwhile Penn Humanities Forum) welcomed me as a regional fellow at an early moment in my research process. Jim English was an affirming influence on my work at Penn. I benefited from a Career Development Award at Drexel that allowed me to confer with Alex Weheliye for guidance about the project's early stages. That development also introduced me to Jennifer Lynn Stoever: a foundational thinker in Sound Studies. My life changed significantly when I obtained a fellowship at the Radcliffe Institute for Advanced Study at Harvard. I was able to spend a year in community with luminous colleagues: Evie Shockley, Tanisha Ford, Ja'Tovia Gary, Robin Bernstein, Kaitlyn Greenidge, Sky Hopinka, and EJ Hill. When I was at Harvard, I also befriended Chanda Prescod-Weinstein, Kinitra Brooks, Stacey Robinson, and Barrington Edwards. I made my first research trip to the Huntington Library in Pasadena during that year to access the Octavia E. Butler Papers, and I would subsequently return on a short-term fellowship. My sincere thanks to the Butler estate.

The Eaton Collection of Science Fiction and Fantasy at UC Riverside has been an indispensable resource in my career. I joined the faculty at UC

Riverside after collaborating with scholars and artists who have leveraged its distinctive place in science fiction studies several times over the years. Since then, I have had opportunities to access support from the Center for Ideas and Society and the University of California Humanities Research Initiative to further my work and that of the graduate students I have been privileged to mentor. A Mellon Sawyer Seminar I co-directed at UC Riverside, Unarchiving Blackness, connected me with new colleagues, including the Butler scholars Ayana Jamieson and Alyssa Collins. A workshop administered at UC Davis titled "Faculty of California United in Scholarship" (FOCUS) provided time and aid to work on my manuscript. I did a great deal of writing in 2024 during a summer residency at the National Humanities Center and the University of Tulsa Second Book Institute. Constructive feedback on my applications for National Endowment for the Humanities fellowships enhanced my efforts.

Readers and fellow writers have been great company, especially after the onset of the COVID-19 pandemic, which isolated us from our neighbors. Thank you to Robin, Brian Herrera, and Patrick McKelvey, for bringing us together online, and thank you Thomas O'Donnell and Narine Yegiyan for making time for our writing, too. I can also thank Shanté Smalls and Reynaldo Anderson for applying their expertise to reading this manuscript.

I thank Patricia Cumper, MBE, FRSA, FRSL, for the scripts to her superb radio adaptation of Toni Morrison's *Beloved*. The British Library and the BBC provided me with access to recordings in spite of technical difficulties. The Schomburg Center for Research in Black Culture, New York Public Library, and numerous libraries in the University of California system made access to items I needed possible. Old-time radio enthusiasts and generations of science fiction fans have preserved aspects of American culture for almost a century, and I have them to thank for making my improbable research agenda practical.

I am grateful to newer colleagues for thinking in their company since I moved to California: Jalondra Davis, Armando Garcia, John Jennings, Phoenix Alexander, Courtney Baker, Vorris Nunley, Tananarive Due, Debbie Duarte, Brandy Lewis, and Jasmine Strickland. I found out that Alex Smith and Rasheedah Phillips were building Black futures when I lived in Philadelphia, and I am grateful for any chance to work with them. I can thank every bookstore, library, conference, reader, reviewer, editor, and student who has responded to my writing for motivating me to keep doing it, including Richard Morrison. Mentors and friends who have known me for many years influenced this book through their affirming presence. Jennifer Doyle, Karen Tongson, Kyla Wazana

Tompkins, Sherryl Vint, Tavia Nyong'o, Robert Reid-Pharr, and Duchess Harris are some of their names. Some of my day ones—Dennis Tyler, Astrid Kane, Alisha Gaines, Regina Bradley, Josh Chambers-Letson, Roy Perez, Uri Mc-Millan, and Stephanie Hsu—have witnessed this book grow with me. I hope to celebrate with all of you in the future.

Notes

Introduction. Jim Crow and the Golden Age

1. Henry Sampson, *Swingin' on the Ether Waves: A Chronological History of African Americans in Radio and Television Programming, 1925–1955* (Scarecrow, 2005), 1:4.

2. Eric Rothenbuhler and Tom McCourt, "Radio Redefines Itself, 1947–1962," in *Radio Reader: Essays in the Cultural History of Radio*, ed. Michelle Hilmes and Jason Loviglio (Routledge, 2002), 369–71.

3. Christopher Sterling and John Kitross, *Stay Tuned: A History of American Broadcasting* (Taylor and Francis, 2001), 214.

4. Tim DeForest, *Radio by the Book: Adaptations of Literature and Fiction on the Airwaves* (McFarland, 2008).

5. Mary Helen Washington, "'Disturbing the Peace: What Happens to American Studies If You Put African American Studies at the Center?': Presidential Address to the American Studies Association, October 29, 1997," *American Quarterly* 50, no. 1 (1998): 1–23.

6. Langston Hughes, "Curtain Time," in *Collected Works of Langston Hughes, vol. 9: Essays on Art, Race, Politics, and World Affairs*, ed. Christopher De Santis (University of Missouri Press, 2002), 305.

7. Hughes, qtd. in Arnold Rampersad, *The Life of Langston Hughes, vol. 2: 1941–1967, I Dream A World* (Oxford University Press), 75.

8. William Barlow, *Voice Over: The Making of Black Radio* (Temple University Press, 1999); Barbara Savage, *Broadcasting Freedom: Radio, War, and the Politics of Race, 1938–1948* (University of North Carolina Press, 1999).

9. John Hope Franklin, "The Two Worlds of Race: A Historical View," *Daedalus* 140, no. 1 (2011): 28–43.

10. Brian Aldiss, *Trillion-Year Spree: The History of Science Fiction* (Gollancz, 1986); M. Keith Booker, *Science Fiction Handbook* (Wiley-Blackwell, 2009); Mark Bould and Sherryl Vint, *The Routledge Concise History of Science Fiction* (Routledge, 2011); Adam Roberts, *The History of Science Fiction* (Palgrave MacMillan, 2016); James Gunn, *Alternate Worlds: The Illustrated History of Science Fiction* (McFarland, 2018); Lester Del Rey, *The World of Science Fiction: History of a Subculture, 1926–1976* (Routledge, 2021); Mark Bould, Andrew Butler, and Sherryl Vint, eds., *The New Routledge Handbook to Science Fiction* (Routledge, 2024).

11. Donna-lyn Washington cites Janice Radway's discussion of Wright, from *A Feeling for Books*, her study of the club, in order to draw inferences about Yerby's readership and the impact of his selection as a romance writer of choice for readers. Donna-lyn Washington, "Frank Yerby and His Readers," in *Rediscovering Frank Yerby: Critical Essays*, ed. Matthew Teutsch (University of Mississippi Press, 2020), 57–58.

12. Gerry Canavan and Benjamin Robertson, "Guilty Pleasures: Late Capitalism and Mere Genre," *Extrapolation* 58, nos. 2–3 (2017): 123–28.

13. John Plotz, "Samuel Delany on Capitalism, Racism, and Science Fiction," *Public Books*, August 6, 2019, http://publicbooks.org/samuel-delany-on-capitalism-racism-and-science-fiction.

14. See, for example, Kenneth Warren, *Black and White Strangers: Race and American Literary Realism* (University of Chicago Press, 1993); Gene Andrew Jarrett, *Deans and Truants: Race and Realism in African American Literature* (University of Pennsylvania Press, 2007); Kara Keeling, *The Witch's Flight: The Cinematic, the Black Femme, and the Image of Common Sense* (Duke University Press, 2007); Michael Gillespie, *Film Blackness: American Cinema and the Idea of Black Film* (Duke University Press, 2016); Darieck Scott, *Keeping It Unreal: Black Queer Fantasy and Superhero Comics* (New York University Press, 2022).

15. Henriette Gunkel and kara lynch, eds., *We Travel the Space Ways: Black Imagination, Fragments, and Diffractions* (transcript Verlag, 2019).

16. Isiah Lavender III, *Afrofuturism Rising: The Literary Prehistory of a Movement* (Ohio State University Press, 2019), 196.

17. Simone Murray, *The Adaptation Industry: The Cultural Economy of Contemporary Literary Adaptation* (Routledge, 2011), 7–8; Johannes Fehrle, "Introduction: Adaptation in a Convergence Environment," in Johannes Fehrle and Werner Schäfke-Zell, *Adaptation in the Age of Media Convergence* (Amsterdam University Press, 2019), 8.

18. Gérard Genette, "Introduction to the Paratext," trans. Marie Maclean, *New Literary History* 22, no. 2 (1991): 263–64.

19. Georg Stanitzek, "Texts and Paratexts in Media," *Critical Inquiry* 32, no. 1 (2005): 27–42; Neil Randall, "Source as Paratext: Videogame Adaptations and the Question of Fidelity," in *Emerging Genres in New Media Environments*, ed. Carolyn Miller and Ashley Kelly (Palgrave Macmillan, 2017), 171–73.

20. Fehrle, "Introduction," 8.

21. Murray, *The Adaptation Industry*, 6.

22. Murray, *The Adaptation Industry*, 20.

23. John Rieder, *Science Fiction and the Mass Cultural Genre System* (Wesleyan University Press, 2017), 161.

24. Rieder, *Science Fiction and the Mass Cultural Genre System*, 1–2.

25. Rieder, *Science Fiction and the Mass Cultural Genre System*, 35.

26. Rieder, *Science Fiction and the Mass Cultural Genre System*, 169.

27. Rieder, *Science Fiction and the Mass Cultural Genre System*, 2.

28. Jennifer Lynn Stoever, *The Sonic Color Line: Race and the Cultural Politics of Listening* (New York University Press, 2016), 4.

29. Stoever, *The Sonic Color Line*, 4.

30. Fred Moten, *In the Break: The Aesthetics of the Black Radical Tradition* (New York University Press, 2003), 1; Julie Beth Napolin, *The Fact of Resonance: Modernist Acoustics and Narrative Form* (Fordham University Press, 2020), 213.

31. Stefanie Alisch and Carla J. Maier, "The Sound of Afrofuturism," in *We Travel The Spaceways*, 134.

32. Erik Steinskog, *Afrofuturism and Black Sound Studies* (Palgrave Macmillan, 2018), 15.

33. Steinskog, *Afrofuturism and Black Sound Studies*, 16.

34. Steinskog, *Afrofuturism and Black Sound Studies*, 9.

35. Steinskog, *Afrofuturism and Black Sound Studies*, 24.

36. Karen Hellekson, "Radio and Podcasts," in *New Routledge Handbook to Science Fiction*, 163.

37. Hellekson, "Radio and Podcasts," 162–63.

38. Susan Douglas, *Listening In: Radio and the American Imagination* (University of Minnesota Press, 2004); Tom McEnaney, *Acoustic Properties: Radio, Narrative, and the New Neighborhood of the Americas* (Northwestern University Press, 2017).

39. Hellekson, "Radio and Podcasts," 164.

40. Gustavus Stadler, "On Whiteness and Sound Studies," *Sounding Out!*, July 6, 2015, http://soundstudiesblog.com/2015/07/06/on-whiteness-and-sound-studies.

41. Marie Thompson, "Whiteness and the Ontological Turn in Sound Studies," *Parallax* 23, no. 3 (2017): 4.

42. Thompson, "Whiteness and the Ontological Turn in Sound Studies," 11.

43. Thinking that conflates Blackness with loudness threatens to limit our ability to appreciate foundational contributions to sound studies. For example, in the first issue of the journal *Sound Studies*, one critic writes: "We should not be surprised that Moten's examples—Lincoln, Roach, Ayler, Brown—again draw upon extreme levels of loudness that push beyond linguistic meaning." Following Quashie, I would modify this analysis to say that while we might consider sound integral to the epistemology Moten is instructing, we should not take loudness, as one of the properties of sound, for granted. When should we be surprised, if not in response to textual strategies aimed at producing shock or simulating violence? Michael Heller, "Between Silence and Pain: Loudness and the Affective Encounter," *Sound Studies* 1, no. 1 (2015): 54.

44. Kevin Quashie, *The Sovereignty of Quiet: Beyond Resistance in Black Culture* (Rutgers University Press, 2012), 3.

45. Béla Balazs, "Radio Drama," trans. Russell Stockman, *October* 116 (2006): 47–48.

46. Shawn Vancour, "Arnheim on Radio: *materialtheorie* and Beyond," in *Arnheim for Film and Media Studies*, ed. Scott Higgins (Routledge, 2010), 178.

47. Vancour, "Arnheim on Radio," 178–79.

48. Milton Kaplan, "The Radio Play as an Introduction to Drama," *The English Journal* 29, no. 1 (1950): 23.

49. Kaplan, "The Radio Play as an Introduction to Drama," 26.

1. Race, Reverie, and Utopia: *New World A-Coming*

1. *Henry Sampson, Swingin' on the Ether Waves: A Chronological History of African Americans in Radio and Television Programming* (Scarecrow, 2005), 2:1233–37.

2. W. E. B. Du Bois, "Criteria of Negro Art," in *Crisis: A Record of the Darker Races, vol.* 32–33: 1926–1925 (Negro Universities Press, 1969), 296, http://babel.hathitrust.org/cgi/pt?id=uc1.32106010761010&seq=7.

3. Robin Kelley, *Freedom Dreams: The Black Radical Imagination* (Beacon, 2002); Michael Denning, *The Cultural Front: The Laboring of American Culture in the Twentieth Century* (Verso, 2010).

4. Jennifer Wilks, *Race, Gender, and Comparative Black Modernism: Suzanne Lacascade, Marita Bonner, Suzanne Césaire, and Dorothy West* (Louisiana State University Press, 2008); Carole Boyce Davies, *Left of Karl Marx: The Political Life of Black Communist Claudia Jones* (Duke University Press, 2007).

5. José Esteban Muñoz, *Disidentifications: Queers of Color and the Performance of Politics* (University of Minnesota Press, 1999).

6. Joanna Neuman, "The Famous Forgotten," *American Legacy* 15, no. 3 (2009): 64.

7. Mark Huddle, *Roi Ottley's World War II: The Lost Diary of an African American Journalist* (University of Kansas Press, 2011), 6.

8. Huddle, *Roi Ottley's World War II*, 13.

9. Huddle, *Roi Ottley's World War II*, 18–19.

10. "Ottley Wins Author's Award," *Philadelphia Tribune*, July 10, 1943, 20.

11. Huddle, Roi *Ottley's World War II*, 18.

12. Edward Perry, "Squelch Snipers at Ottley Book," *Amsterdam News*, September 4, 1943.

13. Ben Burns, "Ottley's New World," *Chicago Defender*, August 14, 1943, 15; J. A. Rogers, "Rogers Says: Roi Ottley's New Book Is Best Report on Racial Situation in America Today," *Pittsburgh Courier*, August 28, 1943, 7; "Roi Ottley to Make 18 Months' World Tour," [Norfolk] *New Journal and Guide*, September 25, 1943, B13.

14. Hamilton Butler, "Negro Conditions and Aspirations Drawn by Harlem Newspaper Man," *Detroit Free Press*, September 5, 1943, Part 4, 6; Howard Taylor,

"The History of Harlem and Its Implications," *Philadelphia Inquirer*, August 15, 1943, 10; Rackham Holt, "A Tenth of a Nation: New World A-Coming by Roi Ottley," *New York Times*, August 15, 1943, BR3.

15. Roi Ottley, "Coronet Bookette: New World A-Coming," *Coronet*, December 1943, 177–93. Hereafter *NWAC*.

16. "Winners," Anisfield-Wolf Book Awards, http://anisfield-wolf.org/winners.

17. Jayne Beilke, "The Changing Emphasis of the Rosenwald Fellowship Program, 1928–1948," *Journal of Negro Education* 66, no. 1 (1997): 12.

18. Ethel Williams, "A Tribute to the Negro War Correspondent," *Negro History Bulletin* 8, no. 5 (1945): 112.

19. Ottley, *NWAC*, 268.

20. Ottley, *NWAC*, 287.

21. The poet MacLeish, author of the radio classics *The Fall of the City and Air Raid*, was a central figure in homefront propaganda. See Grover Smith, *Archibald MacLeish*, Pamphlets on American Writers 99 (Minnesota Archive Editions, 1969).

22. Ottley, *NWAC*, 285.

23. Ottley, *NWAC*, 280.

24. Ottley, *NWAC*, 277.

25. Ottley, *NWAC*, 287.

26. Christopher Daly, "When the 99% Had a Paper," *Columbia Journalism Review*, http://archives.cjr.org/essay/when_the_99_had_a_paper.php.

27. "Roi Ottley, 50, Dies; Author of Four Books; Wrote for the Tribune Since 1953," *Chicago Tribune*, October 2, 1960, A14.

28. Rogers, *Pittsburgh Courier*; Burns, *Chicago Defender*.

29. Butler, *Detroit Free Press*.

30. Coronet, back cover, n.p.

31. "One Thing and Another," *New York Times*, May 10, 1942, X10.

32. L.B., "*The Young Go First*: Drama of Theater of Action Presented at the Park," *New York Herald Tribune*, May 29, 1935, 14; "Four Major Networks to Carry Truman's Address Tomorrow," New York Herald Tribune, January 5, 1947, C9; "Four Broadcasts on Civil Rights," *New York Herald Tribune*, February 22, 1948, C8.

33. Sampson, *Swingin' on the Ether Waves*, 1:4.

34. William Robson, "Open Letter on Race Hatred," in *Radio Drama in Action: Twenty-Five Plays of a Changing World*, ed. Eric Barnouw (Rinehart, 1945), 62–77.

35. Mitchell Grayson, Roi Ottley, Canada Lee, and Muriel Smith, "New World A-Coming," *New World A-Coming*, March 5, 1944.

36. "Says We Must Change Slogan to 'Win The Peace,'" *Amsterdam News*, February 17, 1945.

37. Mitchell Grayson, Roi Ottley, and Canada Lee, "Order on Fair Employment Practices," *New World A-Coming*, November 5, 1944.

38. "Muriel Burrell Smith Dies; Created 'Carmen Jones' Role," *Washington Post*, September 16, 1985, D6.

39. Ottley, *NWAC*, 299–300.

40. Ottley, *NWAC*, 300.

41. Harvey Gaul, "'The Taming of the Shrew' Done in Mufti at 'Y' Playhouse," *Pittsburgh Post-Gazette*, March 26, 1934, 5.

42. Cal Kuhl, "'Public Service' Radio Plays: Radio Drama in Action," *Hollywood Quarterly* 1, no. 3 (1946): 341.

43. Mitchell Grayson, Roi Ottley, Canada Lee, and Georgette Harvey, "The Mammy Legend," *New World A-Coming*, June 18, 1944.

44. Countee Cullen, "For a Lady I Know," in *My Soul's High Song*, ed. Gerald Early (Doubleday, 1991), 111.

45. "New World Show Paints True Picture of Race," *Pittsburgh Courier*, April 1, 1944, 13.

46. Horace Cayton, "Selling the Race," *Pittsburgh Courier*, January 23, 1943, 13.

47. Grayson, Ottley, Lee, and Harvey, "The Mammy Legend."

48. Cheryl Black, "Harvey, Georgette Mickey," in *African American National Biography* (Oxford African American Studies Center), May 31, 2013, http://oxfordaasc.com.

49. Ottley, "The Negro Domestic," in *Radio Drama in Action: Twenty-Five Plays of a Changing World*, ed. Eric Barnouw (Rinehart, 1945), 358–59.

50. Ottley, "The Negro Domestic," 361–62.

51. Ottley, "The Negro Domestic," 363–64.

52. Ottley, "The Negro Domestic," 364–65.

53. Ottley, "The Negro Domestic," 366–67.

54. Ottley, "The Negro Domestic," 368.

55. Langston Hughes, "White Folks Do the Funniest Things," *Negro Digest*, February 1944, 31–36.

56. Morris Janowitz, "European Beliefs Regarding the United States," *American Journal of Sociology* 56, no. 1 (1950): 118–19.

57. Hughes, "White Folks Do the Funniest Things," 31–32.

58. Hughes, "White Folks Do the Funniest Things," 34.

59. Elijah Wald, *Josh White: Society Blues* (Taylor & Francis, 2013), 52–53.

60. Wald, *Josh White*, 89.

61. Josh White, "Jim Crow Train," in *Josh White*, vol. 4: 1940–1941, Document Records (Alexander Street, 1995), http://search.alexanderstreet.com/view/work/282818.

62. Wald, *Josh White*, 107.

63. Josh White, "The House I Live In," in *Josh White*, vol. 6: 1944–1945, Document Records (Alexander Street, 1998), http://search.alexanderstreet.com/view/work/286642.

64. Jonathan Shandell, *The American Negro Theatre and the Long Civil Rights Era* (University of Iowa Press, 2018), 74.

65. See, for example, Denning, *The Cultural Front*; Cedric Robinson, *Black Marxism: The Making of the Black Radical Tradition*, 3rd ed. (University of North Carolina Press, 2021).

66. Eben Miller, "In Moran Weston's Harlem," in *Born Along the Color Line: The 1933 Armenia Conference and the Rise of a National Civil Rights Movement* (Oxford, 2012), 256.

67. "Negro in New World Symposium Topic," *Amsterdam News*, January 22, 1944, 2.

68. Hardwick Moseley to Negro Freedom Rally, May 29, 1944, "New World A-Coming," 1944, MS African America, Communists, and the National Negro Congress, 1933–1947, Box 81, Folder 11, New York Public Library, Archives Unbound, Gale.

69. "Rally Pageant Attacks Bias, Segregation," *New York Amsterdam News*, July 1, 1944, 5A.

70. Owen Dodson, "New World A-Coming: An Original Pageant of Hope," Black Drama, (Alexander Street), 4, http://search.alexanderstreet.com/view/work/bibliographic_entity%7Cbibliographic_details%7C3607114.

71. Owen Dodson, "Dorie Miller," "New World A-Coming," 1944, MS African America, Communists, and the National Negro Congress, 1933–1947, Box 81, Folder 11, New York Public Library, Archives Unbound, Gale.

72. "Duke's Carnegie Date December 11," *Baltimore Afro-American*, November 13, 1943, 8.

73. Edward Kennedy "Duke" Ellington, *Music Is My Mistress* (Da Capo, 1976), 181.

74. Owen Dodson, Lyrics for "There's a New World a Coming, by Owen Dodson," "New World A-Coming," 1944, MS African America, Communists, and the National Negro Congress, 1933–1947, Box 81, Folder 11, New York Public Library.

75. Ellington, *Music Is My Mistress*, 183.

76. "Books—Authors," *New York Times*, November 30, 1943, 25.

77. Dan Burley, "The Duke Back at Carnegie Hall for Concert, but Fans Are Mostly Letdown on His Program," *New York Amsterdam News*, December 18, 1943, 18.

78. Ellington, *Music Is My Mistress*, 342.

2. Silence Is Golden: Samuel Delany in *The Star-Pit*

1. John Clute, "DELANY & Grand Masters," *SFWA Bulletin* 48, no. 1 (2014): 32.

2. Samuel Delany, "Notes on *The Star-Pit*," PennSound: Center for Programs on Contemporary Writing, University of Pennsylvania, 2005, http://writing.upenn.edu/pennsound/x/text/Delany/notes_on_the_star_pit.html.

3. Samuel Delany, Daniel Landau, et al., "The Star Pit," Mind's Eye Theatre, hosted by Baird Searles, WBAI, Pacifica Radio Archives, 2013, http://pacificaradioarchives.org/recording/bb3818o2a.

4. Samuel Delany, *The Star-Pit, Worlds of Tomorrow* 4, no. 3 (1967): 7–57.

5. Samuel Delany and John Varley, *The Star-Pit* and *Tango Charlie and Foxtrot Romeo*, Tor Double Edition (Tor, 1989).

6. Delany, *The Star-Pit*, 16.

7. Delany, Landau, et al., "The Star Pit," Pacifica Radio Archives.

8. Lisa Freinkel, "Catachresis," in *Princeton Encyclopedia of Poetry and Poetics*, ed. Steven Cushman et al. (Princeton University Press, 2012), 210–11.

9. Elzbieta Chrzanowska-Kluczewska, "Catachresis—a Metaphor or a Figure in Its Own Right?," in *Beyond Cognitive Metaphor Theory: Perspectives on Literary Metaphor*, ed. Monika Fludernik (Taylor and Francis, 2011), 39.

10. Chrzanowska-Kluczewska, "Catachresis," 41.

11. Chrzanowska-Kluczewska, "Catachresis," 44.

12. Sian Hawthorne and Adriaan van Klinken, "Catachresis: Religion, Gender, and Postcoloniality," *Religion and Gender* 3, no. 2 (2013): 160.

13. Callie Gardner, "Queer, Wonderful Misunderstandings," in *Error, Ambiguity, and Creativity: A Multidisciplinary Reader*, ed. Sila Popat and Sarah Whatley (Palgrave, 2020), 107.

14. See Delany's own reflections on the writing in which he participates: Samuel Delany, *The Jewel-Hinged Jaw: Notes on the Language of Science Fiction* (Wesleyan University Press, 2009); Samuel Delany, "An American Literary History Interview: The Situation of American Writing Today," in *About Writing: 7 Essays, 4 Letters, 5 Interviews* (Wesleyan University Press, 2006), 271–97; Samuel Delany, "The Gestation of Genres: Literature, Fiction, Romance, Science Fiction, Fantasy," in *Occasional Views: More "About Writing" and Other Essays* (Wesleyan University Press, 2021), 51–60.

15. Tom Shippey, *Hard Reading: Learning from Science Fiction* (Liverpool University Press, 2016), 11.

16. James Berger, *The Disarticulate: Language, Disability, and the Narratives of Modernity* (New York University Press, 2014), 27.

17. Berger, *The Disarticulate*, 29.

18. See, for example, Samuel Delany, *Shorter Views: Queer Thoughts and the Politics of the Paraliterary* (Wesleyan University Press, 1999), which includes "Street Talk/Straight Talk," "On the Unspeakable," "The Politics of Paraliterary Criticism," and an interview with *Paradoxa*, "Inside and Outside the Canon."

19. Samuel Delany and Takayuki Tatsumi, "Some *Real* Mothers . . . : The *SF Eye* Interview," in *Silent Interviews: On Language, Race, Sex, Science Fiction, and Some Comics* (Wesleyan University Press, 1994), 165.

20. Delany and Tatsumi, "Some *Real* Mothers," 165–66.

21. Delany and Tatsumi, "Some *Real* Mothers," 165–66.

22. Samuel Delany, "Lines of Power," *Fantasy and Science Fiction* 34, no. 5 (1968): 4–46. Reprinted in Samuel Delany, *Driftglass* (Doubleday, 1971), 130–83.

23. Delany and Tatsumi, "Some *Real* Mothers," 166.

24. Chrzanowska-Kluczewska, "Catachresis," 53.

25. Chrzanowska-Kluczewska, "Catachresis," 48.

26. Neil Easterbrook, "State, Heterotopia: The Political Imagination in Heinlein, Le Guin, Delany," in *Political Science Fiction*, ed. Donald Hassler and Clyde Wilcox (University of South Carolina Press, 1997), 43–75; Robert Reid-Pharr, "Disseminating Heterotopia," *African American Review* 50, no. 4 (2017): 923–33; C. Riley Snorton, "An Ambiguous Heterotopia: On the Past of Black Studies' Future," *The Black Scholar* 44, no. 2 (2014): 29–36.

27. Delany, Landau, et al., "The Star Pit," Pacifica Radio Archives.
28. Delany, "Notes on *The Star-Pit*," 5.
29. Delany, *The Star-Pit*, 13.
30. Delany, *The Star-Pit*, 21.
31. Delany, *The Star-Pit*, 20–23.
32. Delany, *The Star-Pit*, 17.
33. Delany, Landau, et al., "The Star Pit," Pacifica Radio Archives.
34. Delany, "Notes on *The Star-Pit*," 5.
35. Delany, *The Star-Pit*, 17.
36. *Garner's Modern English Usage*, http://oxfordreference.com/display/10.1093/acref/9780190491482.001.0001/acref-9780190491482-e-6150.
37. Delany, *The Star-Pit*, 17.
38. Delany, Landau, et al., "The Star Pit," Pacifica Radio Archives.
39. Delany, *The Star-Pit*, 13.
40. Delany, *The Star-Pit*, 16.
41. The term "black" appeared on the US Census in 1970, where it was an option for self-identification, for the first time since 1920, when it was one of the options applied by enumerators. D'Vera Cohn, "Race and the Census: The 'Negro' Controversy," Pew Research Center, January 21, 2010, http://pewresearch.org/social-trends/2010/01/21/race-and-the-census-the-negro-controversy.
42. Delany, *The Star-Pit*, 21.
43. Delany, Landau, et al., "The Star Pit," Pacifica Radio Archives.
44. Delany, *The Star-Pit*, 29.
45. Delany, *The Star-Pit*, 23.
46. Delany, *The Star-Pit*, 24.
47. Delany, *The Star-Pit*, 22.
48. Jane Lin-fu, *Neonatal Narcotic Addiction* (US Department of Health Education and Welfare, 1967), http://hdl.handle.net/2027/umn.31951d03543079q; Theodore Rosenthal, Sherman Patrick, and Donald Krug, "Congenital Neonatal Narcotics Addiction: A Natural History," *American Journal of Public Health* 54, no. 8 (1964): 1252–62; Patricia Ferguson, Thomas Lennox, and Dan Letieri, eds., *Drugs and Pregnancy: The Effects of Nonmedical Use of Drugs on Pregnancy, Childbirth, and Neonates* (National Institute on Drug Abuse, 1974).
49. Delany, *The Star-Pit*, 22.
50. Delany, *The Star-Pit*, 24.
51. Delany, Landau, et al., "The Star Pit," Pacifica Radio Archives.
52. Delany, *The Star-Pit*, 35.
53. Delany, *The Star-Pit*, 38.
54. Delany, *The Star-Pit*, 39.
55. "Indian Peafowl," eBird, http://ebird.org/species/compea; Jeremy Montagu, "Oboe," in *The Oxford Companion to Music*, Oxford Reference, http://oxfordreference.com/view/10.1093/acref/9780199579037.001.0001/acref-9780199579037-e-4798.
56. Delany, *The Star-Pit*, 40.

57. Delany, "Notes on *The Star-Pit*," 6.
58. Delany, *The Star-Pit*, 55.
59. Delany, *The Star-Pit*, 21.
60. Delany, *The Star-Pit*, 32.
61. Delany, *The Star-Pit*, 33.
62. Delany, *The Star-Pit*, 47.
63. Delany, *The Star-Pit*, 48.
64. Delany, *The Star-Pit*, 49.
65. Delany, *The Star-Pit*, 49.
66. Delany, Landau, et al., "The Star Pit," Pacifica Radio Archives.
67. Delany, "Notes on *The Star-Pit*," 6.
68. Sami Schalk, *Bodyminds Reimagined: (Dis)ability, Race, and Gender in Black Women's Speculative Fiction* (Duke University Press, 2018), 25.
69. Tavia Nyong'o, "Back to the Garden: Queer Ecology in Samuel Delany's *Heavenly Breakfast*," *American Literary History* 24, no. 4 (2012): 755.
70. Nyong'o, "Back to the Garden," 751.
71. Seth McEvoy, *Samuel Delany* (Frederick Ungar, 1984), 92.
72. Samuel Delany, *The Journals of Samuel R. Delany, vol. 1: 1957–1969: In Search of Silence*, ed. Kenneth James (Wesleyan University Press, 2017), 480.

3. The Audible Epigraph in Octavia E. Butler's *Kindred*

1. Gerry Canavan, *Octavia E. Butler*, Modern Masters of Science Fiction (University of Illinois Press, 2016), 56.
2. Ramón Saldívar, "Historical Fantasy, Speculative Realism, and Postrace Aesthetics in Contemporary American Fiction," *American Literary History* 23, no. 3 (2011): 592.
3. Commonplace book, OEB 1128, Octavia E. Butler Papers, Henry E. Huntington Library, San Marino, California, Box 61.
4. Index card, OEB 1219, Box 62.
5. Notecard, Box 385, Ephemera, Folder 2, Maryland 1977.
6. Timothy Spaulding, *Re-forming the Past: History, the Fantastic, and the Postmodern Slave Narrative* (Ohio State University Press, 2005), 29.
7. Katherine McKittrick, "'I lost an arm on my last trip home': Black Geographies," in *Demonic Grounds: Black Women and the Cartographies of Struggle* (University of Minnesota Press, 2006), 34–69; Sami Schalk, "Metaphor and Materiality: Disability and Neo-Slave Narratives," in *Bodyminds Reimagined: (Dis)ability, Race, and Gender in Black Women's Speculative Fiction* (Duke University Press, 2020), 33–58.
8. Octavia Butler, *Kindred* (Beacon, 1979), 1.
9. Denise Ferreira da Silva focuses on this opening line in *Kindred* as a figure for value in the modern world that reflects the material significance of slavery, referring to Dana's final state as "the wounded captive body in the scene of subjugation." Denise Ferreira da Silva, *Unpayable Debt* (Sternberg, 2022), 15.

10. Karla Holloway, *Legal Fictions: Constituting Race, Composing Literature* (Duke University Press, 2014).

11. Butler, *Kindred*, 57.

12. Butler, *Kindred*, 108–9.

13. Octavia E. Butler to *Redbook*, November 28, 1977, OEB 4250, Box 214.

14. Octavia E. Butler to Victoria Rose, September 7, 1972, OEB 4260, Box 214.

15. Journal entry, August 18–20, 1977, OEB 1004, Box 57.

16. N. K. Jemisin, *How Long 'Til Black Future Month?* (Orbit, 2018).

17. Octavia E. Butler to Jeff Elliott, *Negro History Bulletin*, Questions and Answers: questionnaire, 1978, p. 2, OEB 2390, Box 127.

18. Journal entry, December 14, 1974, OEB 999, Box 57.

19. Butler, *Kindred*, 57.

20. Journal entry, April 19, 1986, OEB 3188, Box 174.

21. Merilee Heifetz, c/o Octavia E. Butler, to Nicholas Brandt, April 25, 1997, OEB Box 302, Folder 9.

22. Merilee Heifetz c/o Octavia E. Butler to Nicholas Brandt and Sigurjon Sighvatsson, May 16, 2000, Box 302, Folder 9.

23. Heifetz, c/o Butler, to Brandt, April 25, 1997.

24. Heifetz, c/o Butler, to Brandt, May 16, 2000.

25. USA Networks to Octavia E. Butler, c/o Writers' House, May 17, 2000, Box 303, Folder 24.

26. OEB 2390.

27. Brian Smith and Jacqueline Cuscuna, "Directors' Notes," SciFi.com: *Kindred*, http://web.archive.org/web/20060315053422/http://www.scifi.com/kindred/notes.html. Captured by Wayback Machine, Internet Archive, March 15, 2006.

28. Octavia E. Butler to Victoria Rose, April 22, 1976, OEB 8374.

29. Journal entry, August 2, 1976, Box 61, OEB 1188.

30. Journal entry, ca. July 1976, OEB 1188.

31. Tony Daniel, Kindred: screenplay: printout, 2001, p. 50, Box 191, OEB 3325.

32. Federal Writers' Project, *Slave Narrative Project*, vol. 1: *Alabama, Aarons–Young, 1936–1937*, 157–64, Manuscript/Mixed Material. Retrieved from the Library of Congress, http://loc.gov/item/mesn010.

33. Butler, *Kindred*, 79.

34. Butler, *Kindred*, 80.

35. Photocopy with author's manuscript notes, from Virginia Writers' Project, *The Negro in Virginia*, Arno Press, 1969, p. 44, Box 289, Folder 8.

36. Butler, *Kindred*, 98.

37. Notecard, with author's manuscript notes, *The Negro in Virginia*, 46.

38. Frederick Douglass, *Narrative of the Life of Frederick Douglass*, 41, Documenting the American South, Beginnings to 1920, University of North Carolina, http://docsouth.unc.edu/neh/douglass/douglass.html.

39. Butler, *Kindred*, 102.

40. Daniel, Kindred: screenplay: printout, 46.

41. Daniel, Kindred: screenplay: printout, 47.
42. Daniel, Kindred: screenplay: printout, 39.
43. Maureen Fennell Mazzaoui, "Linen Industry," in *Oxford Encyclopedia of Economic History*, 2005, http://oxfordreference.com/view/10.1093/acref/9780195105070.001.0001/acref-9780195105070-e-0445.
44. Daniel, Kindred: screenplay: printout, 40.
45. Daniel, Kindred: screenplay: printout, 11.
46. Daniel, Kindred: screenplay: printout, 49.
47. Daniel, Kindred: screenplay: printout, 56.
48. Butler, *Kindred*, 29.
49. Butler, *Kindred*, 119.
50. Butler, *Kindred*, 228.
51. Butler, *Kindred*, 259.
52. Daniel, Kindred: screenplay: printout, 120.
53. Daniel, Kindred: screenplay: printout, 7.
54. Daniel, Kindred: screenplay: printout, 80.
55. Daniel, Kindred: screenplay: printout, 80.
56. Daniel, Kindred: screenplay: printout, 89.
57. Jean Fagan Yellin, *Harriet Jacobs: A Life* (Basic Civitas, 2004), 26–27.
58. Butler, *Kindred*, 223–24.
59. Photocopy with author's manuscript notes, from Eric Lenneberg, *Biological Foundations of Language*, Wiley, 1967, pp. 61–65, Box 289, Folder 8.

4. Haunting and Futurity in the *Woman's Hour*: Toni Morrison's *Beloved*

1. Toni Morrison, "The Site of Memory," in *The Source of Self-Regard: Selected Essays, Speeches, and Meditations* (Knopf, 2019), 93.
2. Toni Morrison, "On *Beloved*," in *The Source of Self-Regard: Selected Essays, Speeches, and Meditations* (Knopf, 2019), 296.
3. Michelle Commander, *Afro-Atlantic Flight: Speculative Returns and the Black Fantastic* (Duke University Press, 2017), 6.
4. Avery Gordon, "Some Thoughts on Haunting and Futurity," *Borderlands* 10, no. 2 (2011): 5.
5. Gordon, "Some Thoughts on Haunting and Futurity," 3.
6. Avery Gordon, Katherine Hite, and Daniela Jara, "Haunting and Thinking from the Utopian Margins: Conversation with Avery Gordon," *Memory Studies* 13, no. 3 (2020): 344.
7. See, for example, Carter Mathes, *Imagine the Sound: Experimental African American Literature After Civil Rights* (University of Minnesota Press, 2015); James Steintrager and Rey Chow, eds., *Sound Objects* (Duke University Press, 2019); Elke Huwiler, "Storytelling by Sound: A Theoretical Frame for Radio Drama Analysis," *Radio Journal* 3, no. 1 (2005): 45–59.

8. Bartosz Lutostanski, "A Narratology of Radio Drama: Voice, Narrative, Space," in *Audionarratology: Interfaces of Sound and Narrative*, ed. Jarmila Mildorf and Till Kinzel (De Gruyter, 2016), 118.

9. BBC Programme Index, January 4, 2016, http://genome.ch.bbc.co.uk.

10. "Both Sides of the Microphone," *Radio Times*, October 4, 1946, 5.

11. *Radio Times*, October 4, 1946, 7.

12. Kate Murphy, "BBC *Woman's Hour*," in *The Routledge Companion to Radio and Podcast Studies*, ed. Mia Lindgren and Jason Loviglio (Routledge, 2022), 209.

13. Sally Feldman, "Twin Peaks: The Staying Power of BBC Radio 4 *Woman's Hour*," in *Women and Radio: Airing Differences*, ed. Caroline Mitchell (Routledge, 2000), 67.

14. "*Woman's Hour* Drama to Turn Airwaves Blue," *London Evening Standard*, February 17, 2016, 18.

15. Georgina Henry, "Big Sisters Watching You: How *Woman's Hour* Is Holding the Line," *Guardian*, September 2, 1991, 23.

16. Melinda Wittstock, "Men Open Hearts to *Woman's Hour*—BBC Radio 4," *The Times*, November 6, 1991.

17. Jeremy Howe, "A Name Change for Dramas on Radio 4," *The Radio 4 Blog*, January 31, 2012, http://bbc.co.uk/blogs/radio4/entries/4e2b804f-5be0-32fc-a05a-6cc434b3ecb3.

18. HighLites originated as an Afternoon Play, with its forty-five-minute pilot on February 10, 2012. BBC Programme Index, http://genome.ch.bbc.co.uk/schedules/service_bbc_radio_fourfm/2012-02-10; BBC PI, "HighLites," http://genome.ch.bbc.co.uk/b01bwdr3. BBC PI, February 20, 2012, http://genome.ch.bbc.co.uk/schedules/service_bbc_radio_fourfm/2012-02-20.

19. BBC PI, October 22, 1991, http://genome.ch.bbc.co.uk/50c411e3270a4807bac2b4ab518c7808.

20. Will Hodgkinson, "The Guide: Radio: Sound Bites," *Guardian*, March 13, 2004, 73.

21. BBC PI, August 2, 2004, http://genome.ch.bbc.co.uk/90e93854c65e44018e5bf2353b20750b; BBC PI, August 3, 2004, http://genome.ch.bbc.co.uk/6b82bf5975f84652af70616fc3a66fd8; BBC PI, August 4, 2004, http://genome.ch.bbc.co.uk/375ada66e4944ff08fd6ca3d5cca4c5d; BBC PI, August 5, 2004, http://genome.ch.bbc.co.uk/409eb97bd5e147129dca0ebd927ded04; BBC PI, August 6, 2004, http://genome.ch.bbc.co.uk/09c3f78c0c624a538d6e926ddc722b10.

22. BBC PI, August 2, 2004, http://genome.ch.bbc.co.uk/schedules/service_bbc_radio_fourfm/2004-08-02.

23. BBC PI, http://genome.ch.bbc.co.uk/search/0/20?order=first&filt=is_radio&q=Patricia+Cumper.

24. BBC PI, March 17, 1997, http://genome.ch.bbc.co.uk/schedules/service_bbc_radio_fourfm/1997-03-17.

25. Feldman, "Twin Peaks," 67.

26. *Woman's Hour*, BBC Radio 4, January 6, 2016.
27. Toni Morrison, *Beloved* (Vintage, 2004), 1.
28. BBC Radio 4—Maya Angelou's Autobiographies, http://bbc.co.uk/programmes/b0b7mg80.
29. "Toni Morrison's *Beloved*," Episode 1, 15 Minute Drama, BBC Radio 4 Extra, October 18, 2018.
30. Patricia Cumper, *Beloved*, Episode 2, Script, 2015, 10.
31. Episode 1, 7.
32. Episode 1, 8.
33. Episode 1, 11.
34. Episode 1, 12.
35. Episode 1, 14.
36. Episode 2, 1.
37. Episode 2, 2.
38. Episode 2, 3.
39. Episode 2, 4.
40. Morrison, *Beloved*, 38.
41. Episode 2, 5.
42. Episode 2, 7.
43. Episode 2, 8.
44. Morrison, *Beloved*, 43.
45. Episode 2, 10.
46. Episode 3, 1.
47. Episode 3, 2.
48. Episode 3, 4.
49. Episode 3, 6.
50. Episode 3, 6.
51. Episode 3, 16.
52. Episode 3, 12.
53. Episode 3, 9.
54. Episode 1, 6.
55. Lutostanski, "A Narratology of Radio Drama," 120.
56. Jennifer Stoever describes the listening ear as "a historical aggregate of normative American listening practices" and "a socially constructed ideological system producing but also regulating cultural ideas about sound." Stoever's emphasis on the material relations and encounters through which the listening ear takes shape serves a related theory of the sonic color line that associates racial identity with sounds in American life. Jennifer Stoever, *The Sonic Color Line: Race and the Cultural Politics of Listening* (New York University Press, 2016), 13.
57. Morrison's writing appears as a touchstone for the sonic dimensions of African American literature in criticism by Daphne Brooks, Madhu Dubey, Carter Mathes, Robert Stepto, Alexander Weheliye, and many others.
58. Morrison, "The Site of Memory," 100.

59. "Toni Morrison's *Beloved*," Episode 3, October 10, 2018.
60. Episode 4, 3.
61. Episode 4, 6.
62. Episode 4, 6.
63. Episode 5, 4.
64. Episode 5, 5.
65. Episode 5, 8.
66. Episode 5, 9.
67. Episode 5, 10.
68. Episode 5, 11.
69. "Toni Morrison's *Beloved*," Episode 5, October 12, 2018.
70. Episode 5, 11.
71. Claudine Raynaud, "*Beloved* or the Shifting Shapes of Memory," in *The Cambridge Companion to Toni Morrison*, ed. Justine Tally (Cambridge University Press, 2007), 44.
72. Raynaud, "*Beloved* or the Shifting Shapes of Memory," 49.
73. Morrison, *Beloved*, 206–7.
74. "Toni Morrison's *Beloved*," Episode 8, October 17, 2018.
75. Episode 8, 5.
76. Morrison, *Beloved*, 5.
77. Morrison, *Beloved*, 62.
78. Episode 3, 10.
79. Morrison, *Beloved*, 62.
80. Peter Capuano, "Truth in Timbre: Morrison's Extension of Slave Narrative Song in *Beloved*," *African American Review* 37, no. 1 (2003): 96.
81. Episode 8, 7.
82. Episode 8, 12.
83. Episode 8, 13.
84. Episode 2, 6.
85. Episode 7, 10.
86. Episode 8, 1.
87. Episode 9, 3.
88. Episode 9, 8.
89. Episode 9, 12.
90. Episode 7, 1.
91. Episode 7, 8.
92. Episode 5.
93. Episode 9, 11.
94. Episode 9, 13.
95. Morrison, *Beloved*, 297.
96. Episode 9, 14.
97. Episode 9, 15.
98. Episode 9, 15.

99. Jonquil Bailey, "Breaking the Back of Words: Sound and Subversion in Toni Morrison's *Beloved*," *Palimpsest* 6, no. 1 (2017): 28–43; Capuano, "Truth in Timbre"; Nancy Jesser, "Violence, Home, and Community in Toni Morrison's *Beloved*," *African American Review* 33, no. 2 (1999): 325–45; Roxanne Reid, "The Restorative Power of Sound: A Case for Communal Catharsis in Toni Morrison's *Beloved*," *Journal of Feminist Studies in Religion* 23, no. 1 (2007): 55–71.

100. Episode 7, 6.

101. "Toni Morrison's *Beloved*," Episode 9, October 18, 2018.

102. Episode 7, 6.

103. Capuano, "Truth in Timbre," 96.

Conclusion. Generative Adaptations

1. Richard Hand, "Radio Adaptation," in *The Oxford Handbook of Adaptation Studies*, ed. Thomas Leitch (Oxford, 2017), 343.

2. Tim DeForest, *Radio by the Book: Adaptations of Literature and Fiction on the Airwaves* (McFarland, 2008), 199.

3. DeForest, *Radio by the Book*, 212.

4. DeForest, *Radio by the Book*, 213.

5. Susan Merrill Squier, ed., *Communities of the Air: Radio Century, Radio Culture* (Duke University Press, 2003); Josh Kun, *Audiotopia: Music, Race, and America* (University of California Press, 2005).

6. Debra Rae Cohen, Michael Coyle, and Jane Lewty, eds., *Broadcasting Modernism* (University Press of Florida, 2009), 4.

7. Duncan Bell, *Dreamworlds of Race: Empire and the Utopian Destiny of Anglo-America* (Princeton University Press, 2021), 5, 44, 203.

8. W. T. Stead, qtd. in Bell, *Dreamworlds of Race*, 21n65.

9. Aaron Worth, *Imperial Media: Colonial Networks and Information Technologies in the British Literary Imagination, 1857–1918* (Ohio State University Press, 2014), 11–12.

10. Bell, *Dreamworlds of Race*, 212.

11. Stuart Hall, "Whose Heritage? Un-settling 'The Heritage,' Re-imagining the Post-Nation," *Third Text* 13, no. 49 (1999): 4.

12. Hall, "Whose Heritage?," 8.

13. Samuel Delany, "The Mirror of Afrofuturism," *Extrapolation* 61, nos. 1–2 (2020): 183.

14. "SCIFI.COM® Casts Alfre Woodard to Star in an Audio-Drama Adaptation of the Landmark African-American Sci Fi Novel 'Kindred' for Black History Month; Lynn Whitfield to Co-Star in This Seeing Ear Theatre Special Presentation," *PR Newswire*, January 25, 2001, http://advance.lexis.com/api/document?collection=news&id=urn%3acontentItem%3a4272-N6J0-010D-R2B1-00000-00&context=1519360&identityprofileid=FDHWQZ56385.

15. The 2011 assessment of the BBC radio services engendered press coverage and public discussion in the United Kingdom with the perceived conflict between

breadth of appeal and quality as a characteristic theme. John Plunkett, "Radio 4 Told to Switch US Focus and Reach More Younger Listeners," *The Guardian*, February 8, 2011, http://theguardian.com/media/2011/feb/08/radio-4-us-focus; "BBC Trust Should Let Radio 4 Do What It Already Does Best," *The Times* (London), Letters to the Editor, Thursday, February 10, 2011, 29; Caroline Gammell, "BBC Standards 'Will Drop' to Get Ethnic Minorities on Air," *Daily Telegraph*, February 14, 2011, 10.

16. BBC Trust, "Service Review: BBC Radio 3, BBC Radio 4 & BBC Radio 7," February 2011, 57, retrieved via the Internet Archive, http://archive.org/web/20120303191208if_/http://www.bbc.co.uk/bbctrust/assets/files/pdf/regulatory_framework/service_licences/service_reviews/radio_347/radio_347_final.pdf.

17. "The presence or absence of a pronounced [r] in the syllable coda, a quality termed rhoticity, is an important feature in categorizing and describing dialects of English. . . . It is a very salient feature of English regional and social variation, being an indication of prestige or stigma as well as location. . . . The majority opinion is that non-rhoticity in America resulted from prestige imitation from across the Atlantic: close ties between the upper classes of Southern England and those of New England and the Southeast led to the adoption of non-rhotic pronunciations by upper-class Americans in those regions and to the diffusion of the features regionally." Nancy Elliott, "Rhoticity in the Accents of American Film Actors: A Sociolinguistic Study," *Voice and Speech Review* 1, no. 1 (2013): 103–4; see also Dan Nosowitz, "How a Fake British Accent Took Old Hollywood by Storm," *Atlas Obscura*, October 27, 2016, http://atlasobscura.com/articles/how-a-fake-british-accent-took-old-hollywood-by-storm.

18. Jessica Baker, "Sugar, Sound, Speed: 'Area Code 869' and Sonic Fiction," *Representations* 154, no. 1 (2021): 23–34; Lucía Beaumont, "2029: Una Pieza Sonora de Sonic Fiction en el Contexto Postpandemia en Lima, Perú," *Artilugio* 8 (2022): 183–91; Nettrice Gaskins, "Deep Sea Dwellers: Drexciya and the Sonic Third Space," *Shima* 10, no. 2 (2016): 68–80; Holger Schulze, *Sonic Fiction* (Bloomsbury, 2020); Jean-Christophe Sevin, "Marseille 1984. La radio, le sound system et la fiction sonore de l'aïoli," *Volume!* 19, no. 2 (2022): 55–73; Nicola Zolin, "Sonic Worlding," *Connessioni Remote* 8 (2024).

19. Kodwo Eshun, *More Brilliant Than the Sun: Adventures in Sonic Fiction* (Quartet Books, 1998), 00-002.

20. andré carrington, *Speculative Blackness: The Future of Race in Science Fiction* (Minnesota University Press, 2016).

21. Margo Natalie Crawford, "Introduction: The Affective Atmosphere of African American Literature," in *What Is African American Literature?* (Wiley, 2021), 19–20.

22. Crawford, "Introduction," 7.

23. Crawford, "Introduction," 9.

Bibliography

Primary Source Collections

BBC Programme Index. http://genome.ch.bbc.co.uk.

Octavia E. Butler Papers. Henry E. Huntington Library. San Marino, California.

J. Lloyd Eaton Collection of Science Fiction & Fantasy. University of California, Riverside.

Pacifica Radio Archives. http://pacificaradioarchives.org.

National Negro Congress et al. *African America, Communists, and the National Negro Congress, 1933–1947*. Gale, Cengage Learning, 2012.

Periodicals

Amsterdam News
Baltimore Afro-American
Chicago Defender
Chicago Tribune
Detroit Free Press
London Evening Standard
New Journal and Guide
New York Herald Tribune
New York Times
Philadelphia Tribune
Pittsburgh Courier
Pittsburgh Post-Gazette
Radio Times
The Guardian
The Times
Washington Post

Bibliography

Aldiss, Brian. *Trillion-Year Spree: The History of Science Fiction*. Gollancz, 1986.

Bailey, Jonquil. "Breaking the Back of Words: Sound and Subversion in Toni Morrison's *Beloved*." *Palimpsest* 6, no. 1 (2017): 28–43.

Baker, Jessica. "Sugar, Sound, Speed: 'Area Code 869' and Sonic Fiction." *Representations* 154, no. 1 (2021): 23–34.

Balazs, Béla. "Radio Drama." Trans. Russell Stockman. *October* 116 (2006): 47–48.

Barlow, William. *Voice Over: The Making of Black Radio*. Temple University Press, 1999.

Barnouw, Eric, ed. *Radio Drama in Action: Twenty-five Plays of a Changing World*. Rinehart, 1945.

BBC Trust. "Service Review: BBC Radio 3, BBC Radio 4 & BBC Radio 7." February 2011.

Beaumont, Lucía. "2029: Una Pieza Sonora de Sonic Fiction en el Contexto Postpandemia en Lima, Perú." *Artilugio* 8 (2022): 183–91.

Beilke, Jayne. "The Changing Emphasis of the Rosenwald Fellowship Program, 1928–1948." *Journal of Negro Education* 66, no. 1 (1997): 3–15.

Bell, Duncan. *Dreamworlds of Race: Empire and the Utopian Destiny of Anglo-America*. Princeton University Press, 2021.

Berger, James. *The Disarticulate: Language, Disability, and the Narratives of Modernity*. New York University Press, 2014.

Black, Cheryl. "Harvey, Georgette Mickey." In *African American National Biography*, Oxford African American Studies Center, May 31, 2013. http://oxfordaasc.com.

Booker, M. Keith. *Science Fiction Handbook*. Wiley-Blackwell, 2009.

Bould, Mark, Andrew Butler, and Sherryl Vint, eds. *The New Routledge Handbook to Science Fiction*. Routledge, 2024.

Bould, Mark, and Sherryl Vint. *The Routledge Concise History of Science Fiction*. Routledge, 2011.

Butler, Octavia E. *Kindred*. Beacon, 1979.

Canavan, Gerry. *Octavia E. Butler*. Modern Masters of Science Fiction. University of Illinois Press, 2016.

Canavan, Gerry, and Benjamin Robertson. "Guilty Pleasures: Late Capitalism and Mere Genre." *Extrapolation* 58, nos. 2–3 (2017): 123–28.

Capuano, Peter. "Truth in Timbre: Morrison's Extension of Slave Narrative Song in *Beloved*." *African American Review* 37, no. 1 (2003): 95–103.

carrington, andré. *Speculative Blackness: The Future of Race in Science Fiction*. University of Minnesota Press, 2016.

Clute, John. "Delany & Grand Masters." *SFWA Bulletin* 48, no. 1 (2014): 32–37.

Cohen, Debra Rae, Michael Coyle, and Jane Lewty, eds. *Broadcasting Modernism*. University Press of Florida, 2009.

Cohn, D'Vera. "Race and the Census: The 'Negro' Controversy." Pew Research Center, January 21, 2010. http://pewresearch.org/social-trends/2010/01/21/race-and-the-census-the-negro-controversy.

Commander, Michelle. *Afro-Atlantic Flight: Speculative Returns and the Black Fantastic*. Duke University Press, 2017.

Crawford, Margo. *What Is African American Literature?* Wiley, 2021.

Daly, Christopher. "When the 99% Had a Paper." *Columbia Journalism Review*. *http*://archives.cjr.org/essay/when_the_99_had_a_paper.php.

Davies, Carole Boyce. *Left of Karl Marx: The Political Life of Black Communist Claudia Jones*. Duke University Press, 2007.

DeForest, Tim. *Radio by the Book: Adaptations of Literature and Fiction on the Airwaves*. McFarland, 2008.

Delany, Samuel. *About Writing: 7 Essays, 4 Letters, 5 Interviews*. Wesleyan University Press, 2006.

———. *The Jewel-Hinged Jaw: Notes on the Language of Science Fiction*. Wesleyan University Press, 2009.

———. "Lines of Power." In *Driftglass*. Doubleday, 1971.

———. "Lines of Power." *Fantasy and Science Fiction* 34, no. 5 (1968): 4–46.

———. "The Mirror of Afrofuturism." *Extrapolation* 61, nos. 1–2 (2020): 173–84.

———. *Occasional Views: More "About Writing" and Other Essays*. Wesleyan University Press, 2021.

———. *Shorter Views: Queer Thoughts and the Politics of the Paraliterary*. Wesleyan University Press, 1999.

———. *Silent Interviews: On Language, Race, Sex, Science Fiction, and Some Comics*. Wesleyan University Press, 1994.

———. *The Star-Pit*. *Worlds of Tomorrow* 4, no. 3 (1967): 7–57.

Del Rey, Lester. *The World of Science Fiction: History of a Subculture, 1926–1976*. Routledge, 2021.

Denning, Michael. *The Cultural Front: The Laboring of American Culture in the Twentieth Century*. Verso, 2010.

Dodson, Owen. "New World A-Coming: An Original Pageant of Hope." 1944. Repr. Alexander Street, 2001.

Douglas, Susan. *Listening In: Radio and the American Imagination*. University of Minnesota Press, 2004.

Douglass, Frederick. *Narrative of the Life of Frederick Douglass*. Documenting the American South, Beginnings to 1920. University of North Carolina. http://docsouth.unc.edu/neh/douglass/douglass.html.

Du Bois, W. E. B. "Criteria of Negro Art." In *Crisis: A Record of the Darker Races, vol. 32–33: 1926–1927*, 290–97. Negro Universities Press, 1969. HathiTrust.

Early, Gerald, ed. *My Soul's High Song*. Doubleday, 1991.

Ellington, Edward Kennedy (Duke). *Music Is My Mistress*. Da Capo, 1976.

Elliott, Nancy. "Rhoticity in the Accents of American Film Actors: A Sociolinguistic Study." *Voice and Speech Review* 1, no. 1 (2013): 103–30.

Eshun, Kodwo. *More Brilliant Than the Sun: Adventures in Sonic Fiction*. Quartet Books, 1998.

Federal Writers' Project. *Slave Narrative Project. Vol. 1: Alabama, Aarons-Young*. 1936–1937. Library of Congress. http://loc.gov/item/mesn010.

Fehrle, Johannes, and Werner Schäfke-Zell. *Adaptation in the Age of Media Convergence*. Amsterdam University Press, 2019.

Ferguson, Patricia, Thomas Lennox, and Dan Letieri, eds. *Drugs and Pregnancy: The Effects of Nonmedical Use of Drugs on Pregnancy, Childbirth, and Neonates*. National Institute on Drug Abuse, 1974.

Ferreira da Silva, Denise. *Unpayable Debt*. Sternberg, 2022.

Fludernik, Monika, ed. *Beyond Cognitive Metaphor Theory: Perspectives on Literary Metaphor*. Taylor & Francis, 2011.

Franklin, John Hope. "The Two Worlds of Race: A Historical View." *Daedalus* 140, no. 1 (2011): 28–43.

Freinkel, Lisa. "Catachresis." In *Princeton Encyclopedia of Poetry and Poetics*, ed. Steven Cushman, 209–11. Princeton University Press, 2012.

Gaskins, Nettrice. "Deep Sea Dwellers: Drexciya and the Sonic Third Space." *Shima* 10, no. 2 (2016): 68–80.

Genette, Gérard. "Introduction to the Paratext." Trans. Marie Maclean. *New Literary History* 22, no. 2 (1991): 261–72.

Gillespie, Michael. *Film Blackness: American Cinema and the Idea of Black Film*. Duke University Press, 2016.

Gordon, Avery. "Some Thoughts on Haunting and Futurity." *Borderlands* 10, no. 2 (2011): 1–21.

Gordon, Avery, Katherine Hite, and Daniela Jara. "Haunting and Thinking from the Utopian Margins: Conversation with Avery Gordon." *Memory Studies* 13, no. 3 (2020): 337–46.

Gunkel, Henriette, and kara lynch, eds. *We Travel the Space Ways: Black Imagination, Fragments, and Diffractions*. transcript Verlag, 2019.

Gunn, James. *Alternate Worlds: The Illustrated History of Science Fiction*. McFarland, 2018.

Hall, Stuart. "Whose Heritage? Un-settling 'The Heritage,' Re-imagining the Post-Nation." *Third Text* 13, no. 49 (1999): 3–13.

Hassler, Donald, and Clyde Wilcox, eds. *Political Science Fiction*. University of South Carolina Press, 1997.

Hawthorne, Sian, and Adriaan van Klinken. "Catachresis: Religion, Gender, and Postcoloniality." *Religion and Gender* 3, no. 2 (2013): 159–67.

Heller, Michael. "Between Silence and Pain: Loudness and the Affective Encounter." *Sound Studies* 1, no. 1 (2015): 40–58.

Higgins, Scott, ed. *Arnheim for Film and Media Studies*. Routledge, 2010.

Hilmes, Michelle, and Jason Loviglio, eds. *Radio Reader: Essays in the Cultural History of Radio*. Routledge, 2002.

Holloway, Karla. *Legal Fictions: Constituting Race, Composing Literature*. Duke University Press, 2014.

Huddle, Mark. *Roi Ottley's World War II: The Lost Diary of an African American Journalist*. University Press of Kansas, 2011.

Hughes, Langston. *Collected Works of Langston Hughes: Essays on Art, Race, Politics, and World Affairs*. Vol. 9. Ed. Christopher De Santis. University of Missouri Press, 2002.

———. "White Folks Do the Funniest Things." *Negro Digest*, February 1944, 31–36.

Huwiler, Elke. "Storytelling by Sound: A Theoretical Frame for Radio Drama Analysis." *The Radio Journal* 3, no. 1 (2005): 45–59.

James, Kenneth, ed. *The Journals of Samuel R. Delany. Vol. 1: 1957–1969: In Search of Silence*. Wesleyan University Press, 2017.

Janowitz, Morris. "European Beliefs Regarding the United States." *American Journal of Sociology* 56, no. 1 (1950): 118–19.

Jarrett, Gene. *Deans and Truants: Race and Realism in African American Literature*. University of Pennsylvania Press, 2007.

Jemisin, N. K. *How Long 'Til Black Future Month?* Orbit, 2018.

Jesser, Nancy. "Violence, Home, and Community in Toni Morrison's *Beloved*." *African American Review* 33, no. 2 (1999): 325–45.

Kaplan, Milton. "The Radio Play as an Introduction to Drama." *The English Journal* 29, no. 1 (1950): 23–26.

Keeling, Kara. *The Witch's Flight: The Cinematic, The Black Femme, and the Image of Common Sense*. Duke University Press, 2007.

Kelley, Robin. *Freedom Dreams: The Black Radical Imagination*. Beacon, 2002.

Kuhl, Cal. "'Public Service' Radio Plays: *Radio Drama in Action*." *Hollywood Quarterly* 1, no. 3 (1946): 341–45.

Kun, Josh. *Audiotopia: Music, Race, and America*. University of California Press, 2005.

Lavender, Isiah. *Afrofuturism Rising: The Literary Prehistory of a Movement*. Ohio State University Press, 2019.

Leitch, Thomas, ed. *The Oxford Handbook of Adaptation Studies*. Oxford University Press, 2017.

Lindgren, Mia, and Jason Loviglio, eds. *The Routledge Companion to Radio and Podcast Studies*. Routledge, 2022.

Lin-fu, Jane. *Neonatal Narcotic Addiction*. US Department of Health Education and Welfare, 1967.

Mathes, Carter. *Imagine the Sound: Experimental African American Literature After Civil Rights*. University of Minnesota Press, 2015.

McEnaney, Tom. *Acoustic Properties: Radio, Narrative, and the New Neighborhood of the Americas*. Northwestern University Press, 2017.

McEvoy, Seth. *Samuel Delany.* Frederick Ungar, 1984.

McKittrick, Katherine. *Demonic Grounds: Black Women and the Cartographies of Struggle.* University of Minnesota Press, 2006.

Mildorf, Jarmila, and Till Kinzel, eds. *Audionarratology: Interfaces of Sound and Narrative.* De Gruyter, 2016.

Miller, Carolyn, and Ashley Kelly, eds. *Emerging Genres in New Media Environments.* Palgrave Macmillan, 2017.

Miller, Eben. *Born Along the Color Line: The 1933 Armenia Conference and the Rise of a National Civil Rights Movement.* Oxford University Press, 2012.

Mitchell, Caroline, ed. *Women and Radio: Airing Differences.* Routledge, 2000.

Morrison, Toni. *Beloved.* Vintage, 2004.

———. *The Source of Self-Regard: Selected Essays, Speeches, and Meditations.* Knopf, 2019.

Moten, Fred. *In the Break: The Aesthetics of the Black Radical Tradition.* University of Minnesota Press, 2003.

Muñoz, José Esteban. *Disidentifications: Queers of Color and the Performance of Politics.* University of Minnesota Press, 1999.

Murray, Simone. *The Adaptation Industry: The Cultural Economy of Contemporary Literary Adaptation.* Routledge, 2011.

Napolin, Julie. *The Fact of Resonance: Modernist Acoustics and Narrative Form.* Fordham University Press, 2020.

Neuman, Joanna. "The Famous Forgotten." *American Legacy* 15, no. 3 (2009): 62–70.

Nosowitz, Dan. "How a Fake British Accent Took Old Hollywood by Storm." *Atlas Obscura*, October 27 2016. http://atlasobscura.com/articles/how-a-fake-british-accent-took-old-hollywood-by-storm.

Nyong'o, Tavia. "Back to the Garden: Queer Ecology in Samuel Delany's *Heavenly Breakfast*." *American Literary History* 24, no. 4 (2012): 747–67.

Ottley, Roi. "Coronet Bookette: *New World A-Coming*." *Coronet*, December 1943, 177–93.

Plotz, John. "Samuel Delany on Capitalism, Racism, and Science Fiction." *Public Books*, August 6, 2019. http://publicbooks.org/samuel-delany-on-capitalism-racism-and-science-fiction.

Popat, Sila, and Sarah Whatley, eds. *Error, Ambiguity, and Creativity: A Multidisciplinary Reader.* Palgrave, 2020.

Quashie, Kevin. *The Sovereignty of Quiet: Beyond Resistance in Black Culture.* Rutgers University Press, 2012.

Rampersad, Arnold. *The Life of Langston Hughes. Vol. 2: 1941–1967, I Dream A World.* Oxford University Press, 1988.

Reid-Pharr, Robert. "Disseminating Heterotopia," *African American Review* 50, no. 4 (2017): 923–33.

Reid, Roxanne. "The Restorative Power of Sound: A Case for Communal Catharsis in Toni Morrison's *Beloved*." *Journal of Feminist Studies in Religion* 23, no. 1 (2007): 55–71.

Rieder, John. *Science Fiction and the Mass Cultural Genre System*. Wesleyan University Press, 2017.

Roberts, Adam. *The History of Science Fiction*. Palgrave Macmillan, 2016.

Robinson, Cedric. *Black Marxism: The Making of the Black Radical Tradition*. 3rd ed. University of North Carolina Press, 2021.

Rosenthal, Theodore, Sherman Patrick, and Donald Krug. "Congenital Neonatal Narcotics Addiction: A Natural History." *American Journal of Public Health* 54, no. 8 (1964): 1252–62.

Saldivar, Ramón. "Historical Fantasy, Speculative Realism, and Postrace Aesthetics in Contemporary American Fiction." *American Literary History* 23, no. 3 (2011): 574–99.

Sampson, Henry. *Swingin' on the Ether Waves: A Chronological History of African Americans in Radio and Television Programming*. Scarecrow, 2005.

Savage, Barbara. *Broadcasting Freedom: Radio, War, and the Politics of Race, 1938–1948*. University of North Carolina Press, 1999.

Schalk, Sami. *Bodyminds Reimagined: (Dis)ability, Race, and Gender in Black Women's Speculative Fiction*. Duke University Press, 2018.

Schulze, Holger. *Sonic Fiction*. Bloomsbury, 2020.

Scott, Darieck. *Keeping It Unreal: Black Queer Fantasy and Superhero Comics*. New York University Press, 2022.

Sevin, Jean-Christophe. "Marseille 1984. La radio, le sound system et la fiction sonore de l'aïoli." *Volume!* 19, no. 2 (2022): 55–73.

Shandell, Jonathan. *The American Negro Theatre and the Long Civil Rights Era*. University of Iowa Press, 2018.

Shippey, Tom. *Hard Reading: Learning from Science Fiction*. Liverpool University Press, 2016.

Smith, Grover. *Archibald MacLeish*. Pamphlets on American Writers 99. Minnesota Archive Editions, 1969.

Snorton, C. Riley. "An Ambiguous Heterotopia: On the Past of Black Studies' Future." *The Black Scholar* 44, no. 2 (2014): 29–36.

Spaulding, Timothy. *Re-forming the Past: History, the Fantastic, and the Postmodern Slave Narrative*. Ohio State University Press, 2005.

Squier, Susan, ed. *Communities of the Air: Radio Century, Radio Culture*. Duke University Press, 2003.

Stadler, Gustavus. "On Whiteness and Sound Studies." *Sounding Out!*, July 6, 2015. http://soundstudiesblog.com/2015/07/06/on-whiteness-and-sound-studies.

Stanitzek, Georg. "Texts and Paratexts in Media." *Critical Inquiry* 32, no. 1 (2005): 27–42.

Steinskog, Erik. *Afrofuturism and Black Sound Studies*. Palgrave Macmillan, 2018.

Steintrager, James, and Rey Chow, eds. *Sound Objects*. Duke University Press, 2019.

Sterling, Christopher, and John Kitross. *Stay Tuned: A History of American Broadcasting*. Taylor & Francis, 2001.

Stoever, Jennifer. *The Sonic Color Line: Race and the Cultural Politics of Listening*. New York University Press, 2016.
Tally, Justine, ed. *The Cambridge Companion to Toni Morrison*. Cambridge University Press, 2007.
Teutsch, Matthew, ed. *Rediscovering Frank Yerby: Critical Essays*. University Press of Mississippi, 2020.
Thompson, Marie. "Whiteness and the Ontological Turn in Sound Studies." *Parallax* 23, no. 3 (2017): 266–82.
Wald, Elijah. *Josh White: Society Blues*. Taylor & Francis, 2013.
Warren, Kenneth. *Black and White Strangers: Race and American Literary Realism*. University of Chicago Press, 1993.
Washington, Mary Helen. "'Disturbing the Peace: What Happens to American Studies If You Put African American Studies at the Center?': Presidential Address to the American Studies Association, October 29, 1997." *American Quarterly* 50, no. 1 (1998): 1–23.
Wilks, Jennifer. *Race, Gender, and Comparative Black Modernism: Suzanne Lacascade, Marita Bonner, Suzanne Césaire, and Dorothy West*. Louisiana State University Press, 2008.
Williams, Ethel. "A Tribute to the Negro War Correspondent." *Negro History Bulletin* 8, no. 5 (1945): 110–16, 118–19.
Worth, Aaron. *Imperial Media: Colonial Networks and Information Technologies in the British Literary Imagination, 1857–1918*. Ohio State University Press, 2014.
Yellin, Jean. *Harriet Jacobs: A Life*. Basic Civitas, 2004.
Zolin, Nicola. "Sonic Worlding." *Connessioni Remote* 8 (2024).

Index

Italicized page numbers refer to figures

andré m. carrington is a scholar of race, gender/sexuality, and genre in Black and American cultural production. He is an English professor at the University of California, Riverside, where he directs the program in Speculative Fictions and Cultures of Science. He is also the author of *Speculative Blackness: The Future of Race in Science Fiction* (2016) and editor of *The Black Fantastic: 20 Afrofuturist Stories* (2025).